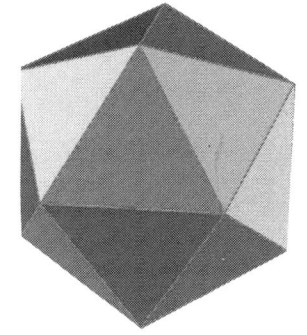

THE
MOST ADVANCED
Math ACT
WORKBOOK

Joseph Hammerman

Table of Contents

Chapter I

What This Book Does and Does Not Do

I found as a tutor that there was a lack of good materials for student looking for top score on standardized exams. Most books try to imitate real exams. There are books that were a little harder than real exams. However, when working with students going for good scores, I had to assign a large amount of problems and often just the last parts of several tests to get enough missed problems to go over in a lesson.

Most of the ACT and SAT books are very similar. They contain imitation exams, which are generally not as useful as real exams and they explain the basics of the material on the exam. What this book does is very different. It contains problems that are designed to be more challenging than real problems and more helpful in preparing the student to get a top score.

There were 3 books are really hard problems for the old pre-2016 SAT. I worked through all of those books and used them with students. However, to my knowledge no one has attempted to produce anything similar for the current version of the SAT or the ACT. Particularly for the math ACT, there are to my knowledge no competing advanced workbooks available.

This book concentrates on the hardest material on the exam. I also made problems similar to those on the exam, but made them harder in some ways. This is designed to make sure the student has the skills for similar problems and is prepared for any more difficult problems on future exams.

While this book does not try to imitate real exams in difficulty, it tries to keep the material as realistic as possible. Every problem is designed to test skills needed for the exam.

Obviously, this book is fairly long and it is fairly comprehensive. The math ACT includes a wider variety of topics than other standard exams. Almost every topics and type of problem that might be on the exam is included. The cover says "a must have", and this book should give you a major advantage if you are going for a top score.

My first book, published in September 2020 is the Ultimate Advanced Guide to the Math SAT 2 Subject Test. Unfortunately, as of this writing subject tests have been discontinued effective immediately. The subject test book had generally more difficult problems than this book, and emphasized more multiple solutions to the same problem, as was appropriate to the nature of that exam. This book includes a wider variety of topics, as almost anything in high school math excluding calculus can be on the ACT.

Not many high school students will be able to go through this book without missing many problems. However, this book is practical, and math competition coaches and high end math tutors and teachers will probably not find it challenging for themselves to work through, unlike the super challenging books for the old math SAT.

While the emphasis is strongly on what is likely to be on the test, this is book has value purely as a math book, containing fairly difficult problems covering most of high school math.

Although I would have preferred consistency, I changed the title of this book from the SAT 2 book to more accurately reflect its contents. There are lots of books called ultimate etc. I wanted to emphasize that this book is much more advanced than anything else available. It is also much more a workbook than a guide. The emphasis is on the challenging problems rather than explanation.

What this book does not do

The problems in this book are generally harder than real problems, so these problems should not be used to determine your projected score. These problems should also not be done timed. However, you should take some real or realistic practice tests timed.

While, this book can be used to make major improvements, and students have gotten perfect scores using my previous book and my tutoring, this book does not promise to help to improve to your score or to improve to any particular score.

This book is in the range that a student at just an above average level can learn from and may be better for some students at that level than other books. However, this book is not recommended for students with a current math ACT score of 23 or below. It concentrates on the most challenging material, and there are many books available that explain the basics.

The emphasis in this book is on the mathematics. Other books generally do a better job of imitating complicated word problems and problems with diagrams on the exam.

This book discusses techniques such of plugging in answers, making up numbers and graphing with your calculator, but the emphasis is not on test taking techniques.

The emphasis is also on challenging problems rather than on explanations. Some books have more emphasis on explanations.

Chapter II

Other Recommended Approaches

I recommend doing as many practice tests as possible. Real tests are best. When you are going for a top score, it is possible to do just the last 10, 20, or 30 questions from each test. My approach as a tutor has been to have students going for good scores just do problems 41-60 or 51-60 from a number of tests. That got us problems to go over.

There are many short videos on youtube covering all aspects of ACT and SAT preparation. Many of them are selling products and services, but the short videos may be better than what they are selling. Particularly, there are excellent videos on test taking techniques for all sections.

Chapter III

Least Common Multiple, Greatest Common Divisor and Prime Factorization

Least Common Multiple

1. What is the least common multiple of 100, 110, and 120?

    A. 3300

    B. 5500

    C. 6600

    D. 13200

    E. 2200

2. What is the least common multiple of the numbers 1, 2, 3, 4, 5, 6, 7, and 8?

    A. 420

    B. 840

    C. 1260

    D. 1680

    E. 3360

3. What is the least common multiple of $2^3 \cdot 3^2 \cdot 5$, $2 \cdot 3^3 \cdot 11$, and $5^2 \cdot 13 \cdot 17$?

    A. $2^3 \cdot 3^3 \cdot 5 \cdot 11 \cdot 13 \cdot 17$

    B. $2^4 \cdot 3^4 \cdot 5^2 \cdot 11 \cdot 13 \cdot 17$

    C. $2^3 \cdot 3^3 \cdot 5^2 \cdot 11 \cdot 13 \cdot 17$

    D. $2^5 \cdot 3^3 \cdot 5^2 \cdot 11 \cdot 13 \cdot 17$

    E. $2^4 \cdot 3^3 \cdot 5^2 \cdot 11 \cdot 13 \cdot 17$

4. What is the least common multiple of 360 and 432?

    A. 3240

    B. 8640

    C. 1080

    D. 2160

    E. 4320

Answer Key: 1C, 2B, 3C, 4D

Solutions

1. (C) $100 = 2^2 \cdot 5^2$, $110 = 2 \cdot 5 \cdot 11$ and $120 = 2^3 \cdot 3 \cdot 5 \Rightarrow 2^3 \cdot 3 \cdot 5^2 \cdot 11 = 6600$

2. (B) 2, 3, 2^2, 5, $2 \cdot 3$, 7, $2^3 \Rightarrow$ Taking every prime factor in either, $2^3 \cdot 3 \cdot 5 \cdot 7 = 840$

3. (C) You take every prime factor that is in any, taking the highest power in any.

4. (D) $2^3 \cdot 3^2 \cdot 5$ and $2^4 \cdot 3^3 \Rightarrow$ Taking every prime factor in either, $2^4 \cdot 3^3 \cdot 5 = 2160$

Greatest Common Divisor

1. For 12 and 21, what is the least common multiple divided by the greatest common divisor?

    A. 14

    B. 7

    C. 56

    D. 28

    E. 21

Solutions

1. (D) $12 = 2^2 \cdot 3$ and $21 = 3 \cdot 7 \Rightarrow$ GCD $= 3$ and LCM $= 2^2 \cdot 3 \cdot 7 = 84 \Rightarrow \dfrac{84}{3} = 28$

Prime Factorization

You can factor with a factoring tree. Any even number is divisible by 2 and any number ending in 5 or 0 is divisible by 5. If the sum of the digits is divisible by 3, the number is divisible by 3.

1. What is the prime factorization of 63000?

    A. $2^4 \cdot 3^2 \cdot 5^3 \cdot 7$

    B. $2^4 \cdot 3^2 \cdot 5^2 \cdot 7$

    C. $2^3 \cdot 3^2 \cdot 5^3 \cdot 7$

    D. $2^5 \cdot 3^2 \cdot 5^2 \cdot 7$

    E. $2^3 \cdot 3^2 \cdot 5^2 \cdot 7^2$

2. What is the prime factorization of 3564?

    A. $2^2 \cdot 3^4 \cdot 11$

    B. $2^3 \cdot 3^4 \cdot 11$

    C. $2^2 \cdot 3^2 \cdot 11^2$

    D. $2^4 \cdot 3^3 \cdot 11$

    E. $2^2 \cdot 3^3 \cdot 11$

Answer Key: 1C, 2A

Solutions

1. (C) $63 \cdot 1000 = 3^2 \cdot 7 \cdot 2^3 \cdot 5^3 = 2^3 \cdot 3^2 \cdot 5^3 \cdot 7$

2. (A) $2 \cdot 1782 = 2^2 \cdot 891 = 2^2 \cdot 3^2 \cdot 99 = 2^2 \cdot 3^4 \cdot 11$

Chapter IV

Fractions

Questions may be asked in ways that require adding fractions as in elementary school and make it hard to use a calculator.

1. What is the numerator of $\frac{1}{5} + \frac{1}{6} + \frac{1}{2}$ in simplest form?

    A. 5

    B. 11

    C. 4

    D. 19

    E. 13

2. What is $\frac{1}{2} \cdot \frac{1}{3} + \frac{1}{4} \cdot \frac{1}{5}$?

    A. $\frac{7}{30}$

    B. $\frac{13}{60}$

    C. $\frac{1}{5}$

    D. $\frac{1}{4}$

    E. $\frac{11}{60}$

3. $2\frac{1}{5}$ is what fraction of $3\frac{1}{3}$?

    A. $\dfrac{33}{50}$

    B. $\dfrac{31}{50}$

    C. $\dfrac{16}{15}$

    D. $\dfrac{27}{50}$

    E. $\dfrac{29}{50}$

4. What is $\dfrac{3! + 4!}{5! + 6!}$?

    A. $\dfrac{1}{28}$

    B. $\dfrac{1}{12}$

    C. $\dfrac{1}{30}$

    D. $\dfrac{1}{24}$

    E. $\dfrac{1}{14}$

Answer Key: 1E, 2B, 3A, 4A

Solutions

1. (E) $\dfrac{6}{30} + \dfrac{5}{30} + \dfrac{15}{30} = \dfrac{26}{30} = \dfrac{13}{15}$

2. (B) $\dfrac{1}{6} + \dfrac{1}{20} = \dfrac{10}{60} + \dfrac{3}{60} = \dfrac{13}{60}$

3. (A) $\dfrac{\frac{11}{5}}{\frac{10}{3}} = \dfrac{11 \cdot 3}{5 \cdot 10} = \dfrac{33}{50}$

4. (A) $\dfrac{6 + 24}{120 + 720} = \dfrac{30}{840} = \dfrac{1}{28}$

Chapter V

Units of Measure

1. If room is 3×5 yards, what is its area in square inches?

    A. 184500

    B. 16740

    C. 19440

    D. 19620

    E. 18540

2. How many cubic inches in one cubic mile (1 mile = 5280 feet)?

    A. 5.5×10^{12}

    B. 2.5×10^{14}

    C. 5.5×10^{14}

    D. 3.5×10^{14}

    E. 5.5×10^{13}

3. At $186,000 \, \dfrac{miles}{second}$, how many miles does a beam of light travel in a week?

    A. 1.7×10^{11}

    B. 3.4×10^{10}

    C. 1.12×10^{10}

    D. 1.12×10^{11}

    E. 1.7×10^{10}

4. If you need 450 square feet of carpet, how much will you have to pay at $28 per square yard?

    A. $12600

    B. $2800

    C. $1400

    D. $2100

    E. $1700

5. Bob ran 9 400-meter laps in 15 minutes. What was his average speed in kilometers per hour?

    A. 15.0

    B. 12.0

    C. 13.6

    D. 14.4

    E. 12.6

6. If you are traveling at $30 \frac{meters}{second}$, how many $\frac{kilometers}{hour}$ are you going?

    A. 100

    B. 108

    C. 104

    D. 112

    E. 96

7. If the distance from the sun to Neptune is 2.78 billion miles and light travels at 186,000 miles per second. How long in hours and minutes would it take a beam of light to travel from the sun to Neptune?

    A. 4 hours and 34 minutes

    B. 4 hours and 9 minutes

    C. 4 hours and 36 minutes

    D. 4 hours and 2 minutes

    E. 4 hours and 23 minutes

8. What is the minimum number of 3 by 4 inch tiles needed to cover a 10 by 20 yard room?

    A. 28,800

    B. 10,800

    C. 16,200

    D. 5,400

    E. 21,600

9. If there are 7.2×10^{14} nitrogen molecules in $2 \times 2 \times 3$ meter tank, how many nitrogen molecules are there per cubic centimeter?

    A. 8×10^7

    B. 7×10^7

    C. 6×10^7

    D. 5×10^7

    E. 9×10^7

Answer Key: 1C, 2B, 3D, 4C, 5D, 6B, 7B, 8E, 9C

Solutions

1. (C) $3 \cdot 5 \cdot (12 \cdot 3)^2 = 19440$

2. (B) $(12 \cdot 5280)^3$

3. (D) $186,000 \cdot 60 \cdot 60 \cdot 24 \cdot 7 = 1.12 \times 10^{11}$

4. (C) 450 square feet $= \dfrac{450}{3 \cdot 3} = 50$ square yards $\Rightarrow 50 \cdot 28 = 1400$

5. (D) $\dfrac{3.6 \ kilometers}{.25 \ hours} = 14.4 \ \dfrac{km}{h}$

6. (B) $30 \cdot \dfrac{3600}{1000} = 108$

7. (B) $\dfrac{2.78 \cdot 10^9}{1.86 \cdot 10^5} = 14946$ seconds $\Rightarrow \dfrac{14946}{60} = 249.1 \approx 4$ hours and 9 minutes.

8. (E) $\dfrac{10 \cdot 20 \cdot 36^2}{3 \cdot 4} = 21,600$ or each square yard needs $\dfrac{36}{3} \cdot \dfrac{36}{4} = 108$ tiles.
   $\Rightarrow 10 \cdot 20 = 200$ square yards $\Rightarrow 200 \cdot 108 = 21,600$ tiles.

9. (C) $12 \cdot (10^2)^3 = 1.2 \times 10^7$ cubic centimeters $\Rightarrow \dfrac{7.2 \times 10^{14}}{1.2 \times 10^7} = 6 \times 10^7$ molecules per cubic centimeter.

Chapter VI

Maps

1. If $\frac{1}{2}$ inch on a map is 30 miles. How far apart are towns that are $2\frac{3}{8}$ inches apart on the map?

   A. 135 miles

   B. 137.5 miles

   C. 142.5 miles

   D. 130 miles

   E. 132.5 miles

2. $\frac{1}{4}$ inch on the map is 75 miles. How far apart on the map in inches are two towns that are 400 miles apart?

   A. $1\frac{1}{4}$

   B. $1\frac{1}{2}$

   C. $\frac{2}{3}$

   D. $2\frac{1}{3}$

   E. $1\frac{1}{3}$

Answer Key: 1C, 2E

Solutions

1. (C) 1 inch = 60 miles, so $60 \cdot \dfrac{19}{8} = \dfrac{285}{2}$

2. (E) $\dfrac{x}{400} = \dfrac{\frac{1}{4}}{75} \Rightarrow x = 400 \cdot \dfrac{\frac{1}{4}}{75} = \dfrac{100}{75} = 1\,\dfrac{1}{3}$ inches or 1 inch is $4 \cdot 75 = 300$ miles
   $\Rightarrow \dfrac{400}{300} = 1\,\dfrac{1}{3}$ inches.

Chapter VII

Averages

What do you need on test?

The basic question is if you have an average of 77 on 4 tests, what do you need on the 5th to average 80 for all 5.

$$\frac{77 \cdot 4 + x}{5} = 80 \Rightarrow 308 + x = 400 \Rightarrow x = 92$$

There could be difficult problems like this involving variable expressions on the exam, and those are covered in the problems.

1. Your average on 5 equally weighted tests in 87. If you drop the lowest score of 75, what will the average of the remaining tests be?

    A. 90

    B. 89

    C. 93

    D. 92

    E. 91

2. You have a 76 average in a class going into the final, and that final is 40% of the grade. What do you need to score of the final to get 80 in the class?

    A. 87

    B. 86

    C. 85

    D. 84

    E. 88

3. If the final was 40% of your grade, you had a 78 going into the final and got an 81 in the class, what was your grade on the final?

    A. 85

    B. 84.5

    C. 85.5

    D. 84

    E. 86

4. If you average a 77 on 5 equally weighted tests, what do you need to average on the last 2 of the 7 equally weighted tests to average 80 for the class?

    A. 86.5

    B. 88.5

    C. 87.5

    D. 87

    E. 88

5. You have an average of x on 3 equally weighted tests. What do you need to score on the 4th test to raise your average to $x + 5$?

    A. $x + 20$

    B. $x + 15$

    C. $x + 25$

    D. $x + 30$

    E. $x + 40$

6. If your average for 6 tests is a and after taking a 7th test, your average for all 7 is b, what did you score on the 7th test?

    A. $6b - 5a$

    B. $6b - 6a$

    C. $8b - 7a$

    D. $6b - 7a$

    E. $7b - 6a$

7. If the final counted for 30% of your grade and your grade going into the final was a and your grade for the class was b, what did you score on the final?

A. $\dfrac{9b - 7a}{3}$

B. $\dfrac{7b - 7a}{3}$

C. $\dfrac{10b - 7a}{3}$

D. $\dfrac{8b - 7a}{3}$

E. $\dfrac{6b - 7a}{3}$

Answer Key: 1A, 2B, 3C, 4C, 5A, 6E, 7C

Solutions

1. (A) $\dfrac{5 \cdot 87 - 75}{4} = x = \dfrac{435 - 75}{4} = \dfrac{360}{4} = 90$

2. (B) $76 \cdot .6 + .4x = 80 \Rightarrow 45.6 + .4x = 80 \Rightarrow .4x = 34.4 \Rightarrow x = 86$

3. (C) $78 \cdot .6 + .4x = 81 \Rightarrow 46.8 + .4x = 81 \Rightarrow .4x = 34.2 \Rightarrow x = \dfrac{34.2}{.4} = 85.5$

4. (C) $\dfrac{77 \cdot 5 + 2x}{7} = 80 \Rightarrow 385 + 2x = 560 \Rightarrow 2x = 175 \Rightarrow x = 87.5$

5. (A) $\dfrac{3x + y}{4} = x + 5 \Rightarrow 3x + y = 4x + 20 \Rightarrow y = x + 20$

6. (E) $\dfrac{6a + x}{7} = b \Rightarrow 6a + x = 7b \Rightarrow x = 7b - 6a$

7. (C) $.7a + .3x = b \Rightarrow .3x = b - .7a \Rightarrow x = \dfrac{10b - 7a}{3}$

Weighted Average

To find the weighted average, you multiply the values by their frequencies, add them up, and divide by the total number of elements. So if 5 people get a 7 on a test, 3 people got an 8 and 2 people got a 9, the average score would be:

$$\frac{5 \cdot 7 + 3 \cdot 8 + 2 \cdot 9}{5 + 3 + 2} = \frac{35 + 24 + 18}{10} = 7.7$$

1. The average score of 10 students was 88 and the average score of another 14 students was 80. What was the average of all 24 students?

   A. 83.8

   B. 83.3

   C. 83.5

   D. 83.0

   E. 84.3

2. 2 customers gave a rating of 1, 5 customers a rating of 2, 11 customers a rating of 3 and 22 customers a rating of 4, what was the mean rating?

   A. 3.2

   B. 3.5

   C. 3.1

   D. 3.4

   E. 3.3

3. If 12 students averaged 90 on a test and the average for the whole class of 20 students was 80, what was the average of the other 8 students?

   A. 65

   B. 66

   C. 69

   D. 68

   E. 67

4. Scores on a test are as follows score:

Score	Frequency
10	3
9	8
8	10
7	4
6	3
5	1
4	1

What is the mean score on the test?

A. 7.8

B. 7.9

C. 8.0

D. 8.1

E. 8.2

5. If x students average a and y students averaged b, what is an expression for the average for all $x + y$ students?

A. $\dfrac{a + b}{x + y}$

B. $\dfrac{ax + by}{2x + 2y}$

C. $\dfrac{ax + by}{2xy}$

D. $\dfrac{ax + by}{x + y}$

E. $\dfrac{ax + by}{xy}$

Solutions

1. (B) $\dfrac{10 \cdot 88 + 14 \cdot 80}{10 + 14} = \dfrac{880 + 1120}{24} = \dfrac{2000}{24} = \dfrac{250}{3} = 83.3$

2. (E) $\dfrac{2 \cdot 1 + 5 \cdot 2 + 11 \cdot 3 + 22 \cdot 4}{40} = \dfrac{2 + 10 + 33 + 88}{40} = \dfrac{133}{40} = 3.33$

3. (A) $\dfrac{12 \cdot 90 + 8x}{20} = 80 \Rightarrow 1080 + 8x = 1600 \Rightarrow 8x = 520 \Rightarrow x = 65$

4. (B) $\dfrac{10 \cdot 3 + 9 \cdot 8 + 8 \cdot 10 + 7 \cdot 4 + 6 \cdot 3 + 5 \cdot 1 + 4 \cdot 1}{30} = \dfrac{237}{30} = 7.9$

5. (D) Taking total scores over number of students, $\dfrac{ax + by}{x + y}$

Finding Average

Apply the average formula, which means add up all the elements and divide by the number of elements. What is the average of the squares of the first 4 positive integers?

$$\frac{1+4+9+16}{4} = \frac{30}{4} = \frac{15}{2}$$

1. What rational number is halfway between $\frac{3}{7}$ and $\frac{4}{5}$?

    A. $\frac{22}{35}$

    B. $\frac{2}{3}$

    C. $\frac{43}{70}$

    D. $\frac{41}{70}$

    E. $\frac{4}{7}$

2. What fraction is the average of $\frac{1}{4}$, $\frac{1}{3}$ and $\frac{1}{2}$?

    A. $\frac{13}{36}$

    B. $\frac{10}{27}$

    C. $\frac{2}{5}$

    D. $\frac{25}{72}$

    E. $\frac{7}{24}$

Solutions

1. (C) $\dfrac{\frac{3}{7} + \frac{4}{5}}{2} = \dfrac{\frac{15+28}{35}}{2} = \dfrac{43}{70}$

    You could also add the decimal representations with a calculator and compare with the decimal representations of the answer choices.

2. (A) $\dfrac{\frac{4}{12} + \frac{3}{12} + \frac{6}{12}}{3} = \dfrac{\frac{13}{12}}{3} = \dfrac{13}{36}$

Median

The median is the middle element. If there are an even number of elements, the median is the average of the two middle elements. To make the median given a frequency distribution, add up the elements from either direction. The value of the section where the middle element appears is the median.

1. 2 customers gave a rating of 1, 5 customers a rating of 2, 11 customers a rating of 3 and 22 customers a rating of 4, what was the median rating?

   A. 4.5
   B. 3
   C. 3.8
   D. 3.5
   E. 4

2. What is the product of the mean and median of the first 7 prime numbers?

   A. 65
   B. 63
   C. 58
   D. 60
   E. 56

3. What is the difference between the mean and median of the set of numbers $\{1, 2, 3, 5, 8, 13, 21, 34\}$?

   A. 3.8
   B. 4.2
   C. 4.0
   D. 4.6
   E. 4.4

4. What is the difference between the mean and median of $\{1, 4, 9, 16\}$?

   A. 1
   B. .3
   C. 1.2
   D. .5
   E. 0

5. Scores on a test are as follows score:

Score	Frequency
10	3
9	8
8	10
7	4
6	3
5	1
4	1

What is the median score on the test?

    A. 6.5

    B. 7

    C. 8

    D. 7.5

    E. 8.5

Answer Key: 1E, 2C, 3E, 4A, 5C

Solutions

1. (E) There were 40 ratings. So the median is the average of the 20th and 21th rating in order, which occurs in 4.

2. (C) 2, 3, 5, 7, 11, 13, 17

   The median is the middle element, 7. The mean is $\dfrac{sum}{number\ of\ elements} = \dfrac{58}{7}$

   $\Rightarrow$ The product is $7 \cdot \dfrac{58}{7} = 58$

3. (E) median $= \dfrac{5+8}{2} = 6.5$ and mean $= \dfrac{87}{8} = 10.875 \Rightarrow 10.875 - 6.5 = 4.375$

4. (A) mean $= \dfrac{1+4+9+16}{2} = \dfrac{15}{2}$ and median $= \dfrac{4+9}{2} = \dfrac{13}{2} \Rightarrow \dfrac{15}{2} - \dfrac{13}{2} = 1$

5. (C) There are 30 elements, so the median is between the 15th and 16th element. That is contained in 8, so 8

Chapter VIII

Percentages

To find percentage of something, you just take $0.01 \times$ the percentage $\times$ what you are taking the percentage of. For example 8% of $\$1,500$ is $0.08 \times 1,500 = \$120$.

1. What is 0.052% of 8×10^6?

    A. $4,160$

    B. $4,000$

    C. $3,400$

    D. $4,200$

    E. $4,080$

2. What is 0.2% of 93×10^6?

    A. $86,500$

    B. $86,000$

    C. $106,000$

    D. $180,600$

    E. $186,000$

3. What is $\frac{2}{11}\%$ of $\frac{3}{4}$?

    A. $\dfrac{3}{1,100}$

    B. $\dfrac{3}{2,200}$

    C. $\dfrac{3}{4,400}$

    D. $\dfrac{7}{3,300}$

    E. $\dfrac{11}{3,300}$

4. What is 5% of 0.14% of 9.3×10^7?

    A. $6,110$

    B. $6,210$

    C. $6,310$

    D. $6,410$

    E. $6,510$

5. What is $a\%$ of b?

    A. $\dfrac{a \times b}{100}$

    B. $\dfrac{a \times b}{50}$

    C. $100 \times a \times b$

    D. $a \times b$

    E. $\dfrac{a}{100b}$

Solutions

1. (A) $0.00052 \times 8,000,000 = 4,160$

2. (E) $0.002 \times 93,000,000 = 186,000$

3. (B) $\dfrac{2}{11} \times \dfrac{1}{100} \times \dfrac{3}{4} = \dfrac{3}{2,200}$

4. (E) $9.3 \times 10^7 \times .0014 \times .05 \approx 6,510$

5. (A) $\dfrac{a}{100} \times b = \dfrac{a \times b}{100}$

Compound Percentages

1. You bought a car and its value went down 25% the first year and 10% each year after that. After 4 years, what is its value as a percentage of its original value to the nearest integer?

    A. 50

    B. 51

    C. 55

    D. 52

    E. 53

2. A number is increased by 80% and the resulting number is decreased by 80%. What percent is the new number of the original number?

    A. 40

    B. 42

    C. 45

    D. 50

    E. 36

3. A price is reduced by 20% of the existing price 3 times. What percent is the price after the 3 reductions of the original price?

    A. 40

    B. 60

    C. 55

    D. 57

    E. 51

4. The height of a cylinder is increased by 40%. By what percent must the radius increase for the volume to triple?

    A. 47%

    B. 46%

    C. 48%

    D. 49%

    E. 50%

5. If the radius of a cylinder is increased by 20% and its height is increased by 30%, by what percent is the volume increased by?

   A. 85%

   B. 88%

   C. 89%

   D. 90%

   E. 87%

6. The the side length of a cube is increased by 20%. What is the percent increase in its volume?

   A. 75

   B. 73

   C. 77

   D. 79

   E. 81

7. If the value of a business increases by 40% per year for 5 years, what is the percentage increase in its value over the 5 years?

   A. 200

   B. 538

   C. 338

   D. 40

   E. 438

8. Say a jacket is 10% off, then another 20% off, and finally 40% off. What percent less is the final price than the original price?

   A. 56%

   B. 58%

   C. 59%

   D. 57%

   E. 60%

Solutions

1. (C) $0.75 \times .9^3 = .547 \times 100(1 - .547) \approx 55$

2. (E) $1.8 \times .2 = .36$

3. (E) $0.8^3 = .512 \times 100 = 51.2\%$

4. (B) $1.4 \times x^2 = 3 \implies x = \sqrt{\dfrac{3}{1.4}} \approx 1.46$, so $(1.46 - 1) \times 100 = 46\%$

5. (E) $1.2 \times 1.3^2 \approx 1.87$

6. (B) $1.2^3 = 1.728 \implies (1.728 - 1) \times 100 = 72.8$

7. (E) $(1.4^5 - 1) \times 100 \approx 438$

8. (D) $0.9 \times .8 \times .6 \approx .43 \implies (1 - .43) \times 100 = 57\%$

What Percent?

If something increased from 124 to 128, to find the percent increase, you take $128 - 124$ and find the increase is 4. Then take $\dfrac{4}{124} \times 100 \approx 3.2\%$.

1. If sales increase from $\$1,100$ to $\$1,400$, what was the percentage increase?

    A. 22%

    B. 25%

    C. 28%

    D. 27%

    E. 30%

2. If water contains 47 parts per million of a toxin, what percent of the water is the toxin?

    A. 0.047%

    B. 0.0047%

    C. 0.47%

    D. 0.00047%

    E. 0.000047%

3. If a is 40% of b, what percent of a is b?

    A. 250%

    B. 200%

    C. 125%

    D. 80%

    E. 500%

4. $a \times 10^3$ is what percent of $b \times 10^4$?

    A. $\dfrac{10a}{b}$

    B. $\dfrac{a}{10b}$

    C. $\dfrac{100a}{b}$

    D. $\dfrac{1000a}{b}$

    E. $\dfrac{50a}{b}$

5. If the distance from the earth to the sun is 9.3×10^7 miles and the distance from Neptune to the sun is 2.8×10^9 miles, the distance from the earth to the sun is what percent of the distance from Neptune to the sun?

  A. 2.7%

  B. 2.8%

  C. 2.9%

  D. 3.1%

  E. 3.3%

6. a is what percent of b?

  A. $\dfrac{a \times 100}{b}$

  B. $\dfrac{a \times 10}{b}$

  C. $\dfrac{a \times 1000}{b}$

  D. $\dfrac{a \times 50}{b}$

  E. $\dfrac{a \times 200}{b}$

Solutions

1. (D) $\dfrac{1,400}{1,100} = 1.2727 \implies (1.27 - 1) \times 100 = 27\%$

2. (B) $\dfrac{47}{1,000,000} \times 100 = .0047\%$

3. (A) $a = .4b \implies b = 2.5a \implies 2.5 \times 100 = 250\%$

4. (A) $a \times 10^3 \times \dfrac{100}{b \times 10^4} = \dfrac{10a}{b}$

5. (E) $9.3 \times \dfrac{10^7}{2.8 \times 10^9} = .0332 \implies 3.3\%$

6. (A) Dividing and multiplying by 100 to convert to percent, $\dfrac{a \times 100}{b}$

Percent of What?

These problems are more difficult, and result in dividing by the percentage. Say 3% of the people in a country are 600,000 people. How many people in the country?

$$600,000 = .03x \implies \frac{600,000}{.03} = x \implies 20,000,000 = x$$

1. 17 is 13% of what?

    A. 132

    B. 133

    C. 131

    D. 134

    E. 135

2. A bicycle is selling for $250 at 30% off. What was the original price?

    A. $315

    B. $320

    C. $357

    D. $344

    E. $347

3. 11 is 5% of 4% of what?

    A. 4,400

    B. 6,600

    C. 5,500

    D. 6,050

    E. 4,950

4. Bob bought a bicycle for $440 after a 7% sales tax. What was the before tax price of the bicycle to the nearest dollar?

    A. $412

    B. $413

    C. $409

    D. $411

    E. $415

Answer Key: 1C, 2C, 3C, 4D

Solutions

1. (C) $17 = .13x \implies \dfrac{17}{.13} = x \implies 130.8 = x$

2. (C) $x \times .7 = 250 \implies x = \dfrac{250}{.7} \approx 357$

3. (C) $11 = .04 \times .05x \implies \dfrac{11}{.04 \times .05} = x \implies 5500 = x$

4. (D) $1.07x = 440 \implies x = \dfrac{440}{1.07} \approx 411$

Pie Chart

A pie chart is constructed using degrees between 0 and 360. So converting percentages to degrees, you multiply by 3.6, and divide by 3.6 to convert from pie chart degrees to percent.

1. A 15% share would be represented by a how many degree angle on a pie chart?

   A. 24

   B. 36

   C. 48

   D. 40

   E. 54

2. How many degrees would x% be represented as in a pie chart?

   A. $1.8°$

   B. $2.4°$

   C. $3.0°$

   D. $3.6°$

   E. $4.0°$

3. An x degree angle in a pie chart represents what percent of the total to the nearest hundredth percent?

   A. 0.28%

   B. 0.56%

   C. 0.32%

   D. 0.37%

   E. 0.41%

Answer Key: 1E, 2D, 3A

Solutions

1. (E) $\dfrac{15}{100} \times 360$

2. (D) $\dfrac{x}{100} \times 360$

3. (A) $\dfrac{x}{360} \times 100$

Chapter IX

Midpoint

A common low numbered problem is to just ask for the midpoint. That is not emphasized in this book, which concentrates on advanced material. The midpoint formula is $\left(\dfrac{x_1 + x_2}{2}, \dfrac{y_1 + y_2}{2}\right)$. Note it is a point, so there is both and x and y value. Also note that we are adding, since we are taking the average, unlike many formulas when you subtract to take the distance. To find the midpoint, just plug the x and y values into the formula. A less common problem is given one endpoint and the midpoint, find the other endpoint. There are various approaches, but the standard one is to plug the midpoint and one endpoint into the midpoint formula and solve for the other endpoint. Both types of problems are covered in the problems here.

1. $f(x) = x^2$, what is the midpoint between $(2, f(2))$ and $(6, f(6))$?

   A. $(4, 18)$

   B. $(4, 21)$

   C. $(4, 20)$

   D. $(5, 20)$

   E. $(5, 25)$

2. M is the midpoint between A and B. A is $(-11, -2)$ and M is $(1, -8)$. What is B?

   A. $(10, -14)$

   B. $(13, -14)$

   C. $(11, -14)$

   D. $(12, -14)$

   E. $(13, -15)$

Solutions

1. (C) $(2,4)$ and $(6,36)$. $\left(\dfrac{2+6}{2}, \dfrac{4+36}{2}\right) = (4,20)$

2. (B) $\dfrac{-11+x}{2} = 1 \implies \dfrac{-2+y}{2} = -8 \implies x - 11 = 2 \implies x = 13$
   $\implies y - 2 = -16 \implies y = -14$

Chapter X

Adding Rational Expressions

1. What is $\dfrac{x+3}{5} + \dfrac{x-2}{8}$?

   A. $\dfrac{14x+14}{40}$

   B. $\dfrac{15x+14}{40}$

   C. $\dfrac{13x+12}{40}$

   D. $\dfrac{13x+15}{40}$

   E. $\dfrac{13x+14}{40}$

2. What is the numerator in simplified form of $\dfrac{1}{x^2} + \dfrac{1}{x^2+5}$?

   A. $2x^2 + 6$

   B. $2x^2 + 4$

   C. $2x^2 + 3$

   D. $2x^2 + 5$

   E. $2x^2 + 2$

3. What is the numerator in simplified form of $\dfrac{2}{x^2-4} + \dfrac{3}{x^2+6x+8}$?

   A. $5x + 2$

   B. $3x + 2$

   C. $3x - 4$

   D. $5x + 4$

   E. $5x + 3$

Solutions

1. (E) $\dfrac{8 \times (x+3) + 5 \times (x-2)}{40} = \dfrac{8x + 24 + 5x - 10}{40} = \dfrac{13x + 14}{40}$

2. (D) $\dfrac{x^2 + 5 + x^2}{x^4 + 5x^2} = \dfrac{2x^2 + 5}{x^4 + 5x^2}$

3. (A) $\dfrac{2}{(x+2)(x-2)} + \dfrac{3}{(x+2)(x+4)} = \dfrac{2(x+4) + 3(x-2)}{(x+2)(x-2)(x+4)} = \dfrac{5x+2}{(x+2)(x-2)(x+4)}$

Chapter XI

Number Theory

Number theory is a significant part of this book, although a small part of the exam, because many of the trickiest problems on the exam are number theory ones. I have tried to cover everything, but it is impossible to predict what sort of number theory problem may appear.

Units Digit

These are fairly difficult problems. If you are asked to find the unit digit of 132^{87}, you treat it the same as 2^{87}. $2^2 = 4$, $2^3 = 8$, $2^4 = 6$ (taking just the units digit), and $2^5 = 2$. Since $2^5 = 2^1$ modulo 10, it repeats every 4. So we find out what 87 modulo 4 is. If you divide 87 by 4 by hand you get a remainder of 3. You can also take $\dfrac{87}{4}$ with you calculator and get 21.75. Then take $0.75 \times 4 = 3$. So $2^{87} = 2^3$, just looking at the units digit. So the answer is $2^3 = 8$.

1. What is the units digit of 38^{39}?

   A. 4

   B. 6

   C. 2

   D. 8

   E. 9

2. What is the unit digit of 53^{250}?

   A. 1

   B. 3

   C. 6

   D. 7

   E. 9

3. What is the units digit of $2^{37} \times 7^{59}$?

    A. 2

    B. 6

    C. 3

    D. 8

    E. 9

4. What is the units digit of the product of all the primes between 20 and 40?

    A. 1

    B. 3

    C. 5

    D. 9

    E. 7

Answer Key: 1C, 2E, 3B, 4D

Solutions

1. (C) $8^2 = 4 \mod 10 \implies 8^3 = 2 \mod 10 \implies 8^4 = 6 \mod 10 \implies 8^5 = 8 \mod 10$, so it repeats every 4.
   $39 = 3 \mod 4$, so $38^{39} = 38^3 \mod 10 = 2 \mod 10$

2. (E) $3^1 = 3 \implies 3^2 = 9 \implies 3^3 = 7 \implies 3^4 = 1$, looking only at the units digit, so it repeats every 4.
   $250 \mod 4 = 2$ so $3^{250} = 3^2 \mod 2$
   Therefore $3^2 = 9$

3. (B) $2^2 = 4 \mod 10 \implies 2^3 = 8 \mod 10 \implies 2^4 = 6 \mod 10 \implies 2^5 = 2 \mod 10$, so it repeats every 4.
   $7^2 = 9 \mod 10 \implies 7^3 = 3 \mod 10 \implies 7^4 = 1 \mod 10 \implies 7^5 = 7 \mod 10$, so it also repeats every 4.
   $37 \mod 4 = 1$, so $2^1 = 2 \implies 59 \mod 4 = 3$, so $7^3 = 3$
   $2 \times 3 = 6$

4. (D) $23 \times 29 \times 31 \times 37 \implies 3 \times 9 \times 1 \times 7 = 7 \times 7 = 9$

Digit in Decimal Representation

If you are asked for the 100th digit after the decimal in $\frac{1}{7}$, take $\frac{1}{7}$ with your calculator and get 0.142857 repeating. So it repeats every 6. Take $\frac{100}{6}$ and you get a remainder of 4. You can either divide by hand as in elementary school or divide with a calculator and multiply the decimal part 0.666666 by 6. You may be able to get a remainder from a calculator. So we take the 4th digit to the right of the decimal, which is 8.

1. What is the 88th digit to the right of the decimal in the expansion of $\frac{241}{999}$?

    A. 1

    B. 3

    C. 4

    D. 5

    E. 2

2. What is the 125th digit after the decimal in the decimal representation of $\frac{6}{7}$?

    A. 4

    B. 2

    C. 6

    D. 7

    E. 8

3. What is the product of the 100th and the 200th digits in the decimal representation of $\frac{4}{7}$?

    A. 8

    B. 16

    C. 35

    D. 28

    E. 40

Solutions

1. (E) $\dfrac{241}{999} = .241$ repeating.

   $88 \mod 3 = 1$, so we take the first digit, 2.

2. (A) $\dfrac{6}{7} = .\overline{857142}$ repeating.

   You can determine that with your calculator.

   $125 \mod 6 = 5$

   The 5th digit is a 4, so 4.

3. (D) $\dfrac{4}{7}$ is 0.571428 repeating. It repeats every 6.

   $100 \mod 6 = 4 \implies 200 \mod 6 = 2$

   The 4th digit is 4 and the 2nd digit is 7 $\implies 4 \times 7 = 28$

Other Number Theory

1. If x is an integer, the sum of $2x$ and $3x$ is always divisible by what?

    A. 2

    B. 5

    C. 3

    D. 6

    E. 10

2. What are all the digits that a perfect square cannot end in?

    A. $(2, 3, 7)$

    B. $(2, 3, 8)$

    C. $(2, 7, 8)$

    D. $(2, 3, 7, 8)$

    E. $(3, 7, 8)$

3. How many two digit numbers have a units digit that is twice the tens digit?

    A. 2

    B. 3

    C. 5

    D. 4

    E. 6

4. How many prime numbers are there between 100 and 130?

    A. 5

    B. 7

    C. 6

    D. 8

    E. 9

5. What fraction of the numbers from 10-99 have at least one digit that is a 3?

    A. $\dfrac{1}{7}$

    B. $\dfrac{1}{5}$

    C. $\dfrac{5}{7}$

    D. $\dfrac{7}{5}$

    E. $\dfrac{9}{5}$

6. What fraction of the numbers from 100-999 have at least one digit that is a 7?

    A. $\dfrac{25}{7}$

    B. $\dfrac{7}{5}$

    C. $\dfrac{7}{25}$

    D. $\dfrac{5}{7}$

    E. $\dfrac{17}{25}$

7. Which of the following could be the last two digits of a perfect square?

    A. 12

    B. 18

    C. 84

    D. 32

    E. 54

8. Which of the following could be the last two digits of a perfect square?

    A. 15

    B. 19

    C. 41

    D. 32

    E. 48

Solutions

1. (B) $2x + 3x = 5x$

2. (D) Just looking at the last digit, $1^2 = 1$, $2^2 = 4$, $3^2 = 9$, $4^2 = 6$, $5^2 = 5$, $6^2 = 6$, $7^2 = 9$, $8^2 = 4$, $9^2 = 1$, $0^2 = 0$, so a perfect square must end in 0, 1, 4, 5, 6, or 9.

3. (D) 12, 24, 36, and 48. There can be no more, because twice 5 or greater is not a digit. So 4.

4. (B) Take all the numbers in that range not divisible by 2, 3, or 5.
   If a number is divisible by 3, its digits add up to a multiple of 3.
   If it is divisible by 5, it ends in 5 or 0.
   101, 103, 107, 109, 113, 117, 119, 121, 127.
   119 is divisible by 7 and 121 is divisible by 11.
   We do not need to check 13 or higher primes, since $13^2 = 169 > 130$.
   So 101, 103, 107, 109, 113, 117, 127. 7 primes.

5. (B) $1 - \dfrac{8}{9} \times \dfrac{9}{10} = 1 - \dfrac{8}{10} = \dfrac{1}{5}$
   Or 13 23 30-39 43 53 63 73 83 93, $\dfrac{18}{90} = \dfrac{1}{5}$

6. (C) $1 - \dfrac{8}{9} \times \dfrac{9}{10} \times \dfrac{9}{10} = 1 - \dfrac{72}{100} = \dfrac{28}{100} = \dfrac{7}{25}$

7. (C) The last 2 digits of the first 25 perfect squares are as follows.
   After 25^2, they repeat counting down, that is $24^2 = 26^2$, $19^2 = 31^2$ etc., just looking at the last 2 digits. After 50^2 they repeat the first 50 perfect squares.
   There is probably some way to prove this with number theory.
   Anyway, you can work out the first 25 perfect squares if you encounter a problem like this. You can also eliminate choices ending in 2, 3, 7, and 8, which cannot be perfect squares.
   A problem like this did appear on the test, so it may appear again. 01 04 09 16 25 36 49 64 81 00 21 44 69 96 25 56 89 24 61 00 41 84 29 76 25

8. (C) Approach described above.

Chapter XII

Pythagorean Theorem

The Pythagorean Theorem is $a^2 + b^2 = c^2$, where a and b are the legs of a right triangle and c is the hypotenuse.

1. What is the exact value of the perimeter of an isosceles right triangle with legs $2\sqrt{10}$?

   A. $\sqrt{5} + \sqrt{10}$

   B. $2(\sqrt{5} + \sqrt{10})$

   C. $4(\sqrt{5} + \sqrt{10})$

   D. $4(2\sqrt{5} + \sqrt{10})$

   E. $3(\sqrt{5} + \sqrt{10})$

2. What is the perimeter of an isosceles right triangle with hypotenuse x?

   A. $(1 + \sqrt{2})x$

   B. $(2 + \sqrt{2})x$

   C. $(2 + 2\sqrt{2})x$

   D. $\sqrt{2}x$

   E. $2\sqrt{2}x$

3. The hypotenuse of a right triangle is 7 meters and one leg is 6 meters. What is the other leg to the nearest centimeter?

   A. 383

   B. 401

   C. 432

   D. 361

   E. 461

4. A right triangle has legs $5a$ and $8a$. What is the length of the hypotenuse?

    A. $\sqrt{39}a$

    B. $\sqrt{73}a$

    C. $\sqrt{85}a$

    D. $\sqrt{83}a$

    E. $\sqrt{89}a$

5. A right triangle has sides 2 and 3. What could be the other side?

    A. $\sqrt{5}$

    B. $\sqrt{5}$ or $\sqrt{13}$

    C. $\sqrt{13}$

    D. $\sqrt{5}$ or $\sqrt{11}$

    E. $\sqrt{5}$ or $\sqrt{14}$

6. A rhombus has perimeter of 30 and one diagonal is 10. What is the other diagonal?

    A. $\sqrt{5}$

    B. $10\sqrt{5}$

    C. $10\sqrt{2}$

    D. $8\sqrt{3}$

    E. $5\sqrt{5}$

Answer Key: 1C, 2A, 3D, 4E, 5B, 6E

Solutions

1. (C) Hypotenuse $= 2\sqrt{10} \times \sqrt{2} = 4\sqrt{5}$, so Perimeter $= 4(\sqrt{5} + \sqrt{10})$

2. (A) The legs $= \dfrac{x}{\sqrt{2}}$. The perimeter is $x + 2 \times \dfrac{x}{\sqrt{2}} = x + \sqrt{2}x$

3. (D) $x^2 + 6^2 = 7^2 \implies x = \sqrt{13} = 3.61 \implies 3.61 \times 100 = 361$

4. (E) $\sqrt{(5a)^2 + (8a)^2} = \sqrt{25a^2 + 64a^2} = \sqrt{89a^2} = \sqrt{89}a$

5. (B) $\sqrt{2^2 + 3^2} = \sqrt{13}$; $\sqrt{3^2 - 2^2} = \sqrt{5}$

6. (E) The sides are 7.5 and half the diagonal is 5.
   The diagonals of a rhombus are perpendicular and the diagonals bisect each other, so
   $5^2 + x^2 = \left(\dfrac{15}{2}\right)^2$
   $\implies 25 + x^2 = \dfrac{225}{4} \implies x^2 = \dfrac{125}{4} \implies x = 5\dfrac{\sqrt{5}}{2}$.
   The other diagonal is twice that, $5\sqrt{5}$

Chapter XIII

Scientific Notation

1. What is 362 million in scientific notation?

   A. 3.62×10^7

   B. 3.62×10^6

   C. 3.62×10^9

   D. 3.62×10^8

   E. 3.62×10^{10}

2. What is $3 \times 10^7 + 8 \times 10^5$ in scientific notation?

   A. 3.8×10^7

   B. 3.8×10^5

   C. 3.08×10^5

   D. 3.08×10^7

   E. 3.08×10^8

3. If a light year is 5.9×10^{12} miles, How many light years away to the nearest light year if that star that is 3.7×10^{15} miles away?

   A. 613

   B. 617

   C. 629

   D. 653

   E. 627

4. What value of x makes the following equation true: $2 \times 10^{11} \times 4.7 \times 10^{3x+5} = 93{,}000$?

    A. -2

    B. -3

    C. -5

    D. -6

    E. -4

5. What is $\sqrt{1.6 \times 10^{1301}}$?

    A. 4×10^{651}

    B. 4×10^{1300}

    C. 4×10^{649}

    D. 4×10^{1299}

    E. 4×10^{650}

6. If some water has 8 parts per million of a toxin, how many milliliters of the toxin will be in $20{,}000$ liters of the water?

    A. 160

    B. 16

    C. 1600

    D. 400

    E. 4000

7. What is $5 \times 10^{3000} \times 7 \times 10^{5000}$ in scientific notation?

    A. 3.5×10^{8001}

    B. 3.5×10^{8000}

    C. 3.5×10^{8002}

    D. 3.5×10^{7999}

    E. 3.5×10^{2000}

Solutions

1. (D) 3.62×10^8

2. (D) $3 \times 10^7 + .08 \times 10^7 = 3.08 \times 10^7$

3. (E) $\dfrac{3.7 \times 10^{15}}{5.9 \times 10^{12}} \approx 627$

4. (E) $11 + 3x + 5 = 4 \implies 3x = -12 \implies x = -4$

5. (E) $\sqrt{1.6 \times 10} = \sqrt{16} = 4 \implies \sqrt{10^{1300}} = 10^{650} \implies 4 \times 10^{650}$

6. (A) $\left(\dfrac{8}{1,000,000}\right) \times 20,000 = 0.16$
   $0.16 \times 1000 = 160$ milliliters.

7. (A) $7 \times 5 = 3.5 \times 10^1 \implies 10^{3000} \times 10^{5000} = 10^{8000} \implies 3.5 \times 10^1 \times 10^{8000} = 3.5 \times 10^{8001}$

Chapter XIV

First Degree Equations in One Variable

What number do you add to the numerator and denominator of $\frac{2}{7}$ to get $\frac{3}{4}$? $\frac{2+x}{7+x} = \frac{3}{4}$, cross multiplying, $4(2+x) = 3(7+x) \implies 8 + 4x = 21 + 3x \implies x = 13$

1. If $\frac{x}{3} + \frac{x}{5} = \frac{4}{7}$, then $x = ?$

    A. $\frac{14}{15}$

    B. $\frac{15}{14}$

    C. $\frac{12}{11}$

    D. 1

    E. $\frac{7}{6}$

2. If $\frac{1}{x} + \frac{1}{3x} = 5$, what is x?

    A. $\frac{2}{15}$

    B. $\frac{8}{25}$

    C. 10

    D. $\frac{4}{15}$

    E. $\frac{15}{8}$

3. If $\dfrac{2x}{5} + \dfrac{3x}{11} = \dfrac{3}{4}$, then what is x?

   A. $\dfrac{155}{148}$

   B. $\dfrac{165}{148}$

   C. $\dfrac{40}{37}$

   D. $\dfrac{41}{37}$

   E. $\dfrac{175}{148}$

4. What number can you add to the numerator and denominator of $\dfrac{1}{3}$ to get $\dfrac{3}{4}$?

   A. 4

   B. 6

   C. 7

   D. 5

   E. 8

5. What number can you add to the numerator and denominator of $\dfrac{a}{b}$ to get $\dfrac{3}{4}$?

   A. $3b - 2a$

   B. $3b + 4a$

   C. $3b - a$

   D. $3b - 4a$

   E. $b - a$

6. The sum of 4 consecutive integers is a. In terms of a, what is the sum of the larger 2 integers?

   A. $\dfrac{a}{2} + 3$

   B. $\dfrac{a}{2} + 4$

   C. $\dfrac{a}{3} + 3$

   D. $\dfrac{a}{3} + 5$

   E. $\dfrac{a}{2} + 2$

Solutions

1. (B) $\dfrac{(5+3)x}{15} = \dfrac{4}{7} \implies \dfrac{8x}{15} = \dfrac{4}{7} = x = \dfrac{4}{7} \times \dfrac{15}{8} = \dfrac{15}{14}$

2. (D) $\dfrac{3}{3x} + \dfrac{1}{3x} = 5 \implies \dfrac{4}{3x} = 5 \implies 15x = 4 \implies x = \dfrac{4}{15}$

3. (B) $\dfrac{22x + 15x}{55} = \dfrac{3}{4} \implies 148x = 165 \implies x = \dfrac{165}{148}$

4. (D) $\dfrac{1+x}{3+x} = \dfrac{3}{4} \implies (1+x) \times 4 = (3+x) \times 3 \implies 4 + 4x = 9 + 3x \implies x = 5$

5. (D) $\dfrac{a+x}{b+x} = \dfrac{3}{4} \implies 4a + 4x = 3b + 3x \implies x = 3b - 4a$

6. (E) $x + x + 1 + x + 2 + x + 3 = a \implies 4x + 6 = a \implies x = \dfrac{a}{4} - \dfrac{3}{2}$

   The sum of the larger 2 is $2x + 5 = 2\left(\dfrac{a}{4} - \dfrac{3}{2}\right) + 5 = \dfrac{a}{2} - 3 + 5 = \dfrac{a}{2} + 2$

Chapter XV

Lines

Slope

What is the slope?

The slope formula is $\dfrac{y_2 - y_1}{x_2 - x_1}$, the change in y divided by the change in x. If a linear equation is in slope-intercept form, that is solved for y, the coefficient in front of x is the slope.

1. What is the slope of the line through the origin and $\left(-\dfrac{5}{7}, -\dfrac{2}{3}\right)$?

    A. $\dfrac{15}{14}$

    B. $-\dfrac{15}{14}$

    C. $\dfrac{4}{5}$

    D. $-\dfrac{14}{15}$

    E. $\dfrac{14}{15}$

2. What is the slope of the line between $\left(\dfrac{2}{3}, \dfrac{3}{4}\right)$ and $\left(\dfrac{1}{2}, \dfrac{1}{3}\right)$?

    A. 2

    B. $\dfrac{8}{3}$

    C. $\dfrac{9}{4}$

    D. $\dfrac{13}{5}$

    E. $\dfrac{5}{2}$

3. If $f(x) = x^2 + 3x$, what is the slope of the line between $(-5, f(-5))$ and $(-2, f(-2))$?

   A. 4

   B. 2

   C. -2

   D. -5

   E. -4

4. What is the slope of $ax + by = c$?

   A. $\dfrac{a}{b}$

   B. $\dfrac{c-a}{b}$

   C. $-\dfrac{b}{a}$

   D. $\dfrac{b}{a}$

   E. $-\dfrac{a}{b}$

5. What is the slope of $\dfrac{3x}{5} + \dfrac{2y}{3} = 8$?

   A. $\dfrac{10}{9}$

   B. $-\dfrac{10}{9}$

   C. $\dfrac{9}{10}$

   D. $-\dfrac{9}{10}$

   E. -1

6. What is the slope of a line between (a, a^2) and (b, b^2)?

   A. $a - b$

   B. $a^2 + b$

   C. $a + 2b$

   D. $a + b$

   E. $a + 3b$

Answer Key: 1E, 2E, 3E, 4E, 5D, 6D

Solutions

1. (E) $\dfrac{-\dfrac{2}{3}}{-\dfrac{5}{7}} = \dfrac{2 \times 7}{3 \times 5} = \dfrac{14}{15}$

2. (E) $\dfrac{\dfrac{3}{4} - \dfrac{1}{3}}{\dfrac{2}{3} - \dfrac{1}{2}} = \dfrac{\dfrac{9}{12} - \dfrac{4}{12}}{\dfrac{4}{6} - \dfrac{3}{6}} = \dfrac{\dfrac{5}{12}}{\dfrac{1}{6}} = 5 \times \dfrac{6}{12} \times 1 = \dfrac{30}{12} = \dfrac{5}{2}$

3. (E) $(-5, 10)$ and $(-2, -2)$, so slope $= \dfrac{10 - (-2)}{-5 - (-2)} = \dfrac{12}{-3} = -4$

4. (E) $by = -ax + c \implies y = -\dfrac{ax}{b} + \dfrac{c}{b}$

5. (D) $\dfrac{2y}{3} = -\dfrac{3x}{5} + 8 \implies y = -\dfrac{9x}{10} + 12$

6. (D) $\dfrac{b^2 - a^2}{b - a} = \dfrac{(b+a)(b-a)}{b-a} = b + a$

Slope of Line Perpendicular

The slope of a perpendicular line is the negative reciprocal of the slope of the original line, therefore the product of the two slopes $= -1$. So a line perpendicular to a line with a slope of $\frac{3}{4}$ is $-\frac{4}{3}$.

1. What is the slope of a line perpendicular to $\dfrac{3y}{5} = \dfrac{2x}{7} + \dfrac{1}{3}$?

   A. $\dfrac{10}{21}$

   B. $-\dfrac{10}{21}$

   C. $\dfrac{21}{10}$

   D. $-\dfrac{21}{10}$

   E. $\dfrac{1}{2}$

2. What is the slope of a line perpendicular to $ax + by = c$?

   A. $-\dfrac{b}{a}$

   B. $\dfrac{b}{a}$

   C. $\dfrac{a}{b}$

   D. $-\dfrac{a}{b}$

   E. $\dfrac{c}{a}$

Solutions

1. (D) $y = \dfrac{10x}{21} + \dfrac{5}{9}$, so the slope is $\dfrac{10}{21}$. The negative reciprocal of that is $-\dfrac{21}{10}$

2. (B) $by = c - ax \implies y = \dfrac{c}{b} - \dfrac{ax}{b}$, so the slope of this line is $-\dfrac{a}{b}$. The slope of a line perpendicular is the negative reciprocal $\dfrac{b}{a}$

Other Slope

In these problems, you are given the slope and asked to solve for one or more coordinates of the points which determine the slope.

1. The slope of a line through $(1, a)$ and $(a, 2)$ is 5. What is a?

    A. $\dfrac{6}{7}$

    B. 1

    C. $\dfrac{7}{6}$

    D. $\dfrac{5}{4}$

    E. $\dfrac{9}{8}$

2. The slope of a line through (a, a) and $(4, 5)$ is -2, what is a?

    A. $\dfrac{13}{3}$

    B. $\dfrac{11}{3}$

    C. 4

    D. $\dfrac{14}{3}$

    E. $\dfrac{16}{3}$

Solutions

1. (C) $\dfrac{2-a}{a-1} = 5 \implies 2-a = 5a-5 \implies 7 = 6a \implies a = \dfrac{7}{6}$

2. (A) $\dfrac{a-5}{a-4} = -2 \implies a-5 = 8-2a \implies 3a = 13 \implies a = \dfrac{13}{3}$

Equations

You could be given 2 points and asked to find the equation of the line between them. First find the slope between them using $m = \dfrac{y_2 - y_1}{x_2 - x_1}$. Then find the equation of the line using $y - y_0 = m(x - x_0)$ or $y = mx + b$.

1. What is $\dfrac{3x}{5} + \dfrac{2y}{3} = 8$ in standard form?

    A. $9x + 10y = 130$

    B. $9x + 10y = 140$

    C. $9x + 10y = 150$

    D. $9x + 10y = 160$

    E. $9x + 10y = 120$

2. What is the equation in slope intercept form of a line with x-intercept 700 and slope $-\dfrac{3}{4}$?

    A. $y = -\dfrac{3x}{4} + 700$

    B. $y = -\dfrac{3x}{4} - 525$

    C. $y = -\dfrac{3x}{4} + 525$

    D. $y = -\dfrac{3x}{4} + \dfrac{2800}{3}$

    E. $y = -\dfrac{3x}{4} - 700$

3. What is the equation of the line between $(100, 300)$ and $(500, 3100)$?

    A. $y = 7x - 400$

    B. $y = 7x - 300$

    C. $y = 7x - 500$

    D. $y = 8x - 500$

    E. $y = 8x - 600$

4. What is the equation of a line through $\left(\frac{1}{3}, \frac{1}{2}\right)$ and $\left(\frac{1}{4}, \frac{1}{5}\right)$ in standard form?

    A. $36x + 10y = 10$

    B. $36x + 10y = 17$

    C. $36x + 10y = 19$

    D. $36x - 10y = 7$

    E. $36x - 10y = 17$

5. What is the x coordinate of the intersection point of the line between $(-4, -6)$ and $(5, -2)$ and the line between $(2, 4)$ and $(11, 4)$?

    A. $\dfrac{37}{2}$

    B. $\dfrac{77}{4}$

    C. $\dfrac{85}{4}$

    D. $\dfrac{73}{4}$

    E. $\dfrac{63}{4}$

6. What is the y coordinate of the intersection point of the line between $(3, -6)$ and $(-4, -2)$ and the line between $(5, 8)$ and $(3, 4)$?

    A. $-\dfrac{17}{5}$

    B. $-\dfrac{34}{9}$

    C. $-\dfrac{19}{5}$

    D. $-\dfrac{21}{5}$

    E. $-\dfrac{22}{5}$

Answer Key: 1E, 2C, 3A, 4D, 5A, 6B

Solutions

1. (E) Multiplying by 15, $9x + 10y = 120$

2. (C) $y - 0 = -\dfrac{3}{4}(x - 700) \implies y = -\dfrac{3x}{4} + 525$

3. (A) Slope $= \dfrac{3100 - 300}{500 - 100} = 7 \implies y - 300 = 7(x - 100) \implies y - 300 = 7x - 700$
   $\implies y = 7x - 400$

4. (D) Slope $= \dfrac{\dfrac{1}{2} - \dfrac{1}{5}}{\dfrac{1}{3} - \dfrac{1}{4}} = \dfrac{\dfrac{3}{10}}{\dfrac{1}{12}} = \dfrac{18}{5}$

   $y - \dfrac{1}{2} = \dfrac{18}{5}\left(x - \dfrac{1}{3}\right) \implies y - \dfrac{1}{2} = \dfrac{18x}{5} - \dfrac{6}{5} \implies y = \dfrac{18x}{5} - \dfrac{7}{10} \implies 10y = 36x - 7$

   $\implies 36x - 10y = 7$

5. (A) The first line has slope $\dfrac{-2 - (-6)}{5 - (-4)} = \dfrac{4}{9}$

   So the equation of the line is $y + 2 = \dfrac{4}{9}(x - 5) \implies y + 2 = \dfrac{4x}{9} - \dfrac{20}{9} \implies y = \dfrac{4x}{9} - \dfrac{38}{9}$

   The 2nd equation is $y = 4$

   So the intersection is $4 = \dfrac{4x}{9} * \dfrac{38}{9} \implies \dfrac{74}{9} = \dfrac{4x}{9} \implies x = \dfrac{37}{2}$

6. (B) The first line has slope $\dfrac{-2 - (-6)}{-4 - 3} = -\dfrac{4}{7}$

   So the equation of the line is $y + 6 = \left(-\dfrac{4}{7}\right)(x - 3) \implies y + 6 = -\dfrac{4x}{7} + \dfrac{12}{7} \implies y = -\dfrac{4x}{7} - \dfrac{30}{7}$

   The second line has slope $\dfrac{8 - 4}{5 - 3} = 2$

   So the equation of the line is $y - 4 = 2(x - 3) \implies y - 4 = 2x - 6 \implies y = 2x - 2$

   To find the intersection point, set the lines equal, $-\dfrac{4x}{7} - \dfrac{30}{7} = 2x - 2$

   $\implies -\dfrac{16}{7} = \dfrac{18x}{7} \implies x = -\dfrac{8}{9} \implies y = 2\left(-\dfrac{8}{9}\right) - 2 = -\dfrac{34}{9}$

   It is possible to sketch the lines from the points to get an estimate or graph the lines with a graphing calculator after you have the lines and find the intersection point.

Intercepts

If the equation is in slope-intercept form, the y-intercept is the constant term. For example if $y = 3x + 4$, the y-intercept is $(0, 4)$. To find the x-intercept, set $y = 0 \implies 0 = 3x + 4$ $\implies x = -\frac{4}{3} \implies \left(-\frac{4}{3}, 0\right)$

1. What is y coordinate of the y-intercept of a line with slope $\frac{5}{8}$ and x-intercept $(-12, 0)$?

    A. $-\dfrac{96}{5}$

    B. $\dfrac{15}{2}$

    C. $-\dfrac{17}{2}$

    D. $\dfrac{17}{2}$

    E. $-\dfrac{15}{2}$

2. If $f(x) = x^2$ and $g(x)$ is the line through $(2, f(2))$ and $(3, f(3))$, what is the y-coordinate of the y-intercept of $g(x)$?

    A. -3

    B. -6

    C. -4

    D. -5

    E. -7

3. If $y = x^2 - 6x + 8$, what is the equation of the line between the y-intercept and the smallest x-intercept?

    A. $y = -3x + 8$

    B. $y = -5x + 8$

    C. $y = -4x + 8$

    D. $y = -6x + 8$

    E. $y = -2x + 8$

4. What is the x intercept of $y = ax + b$?

    A. $-\dfrac{b}{a}$

    B. $\dfrac{b}{a}$

    C. ab

    D. $\dfrac{b^2}{a}$

    E. $\dfrac{a}{b}$

5. What is the y intercept of $ax + by = c$?

    A. $-\dfrac{c}{a}$

    B. $\dfrac{c}{a}$

    C. $\dfrac{c}{b}$

    D. $-\dfrac{c}{b}$

    E. $\dfrac{a}{c}$

6. What is the equation of a line with x intercept of 3 and slope of 10?

    A. $y = 3x - 30$

    B. $y = 10x - 30$

    C. $y = 3x - 10$

    D. $y = 10x - 10$

    E. $y = 10x - 3$

7. $f(x) = x^2$. What is the y intercept of the line between $(2, f(2))$ and $(10, f(10))$?

    A. -20

    B. 20

    C. 18

    D. -18

    E. -16

8. What is the equation of a line with x intercept $(a, 0)$ and y intercept $(0, b)$?

    A. $y = -\dfrac{bx}{a} + b$

    B. $y = \dfrac{bx}{a}$

    C. $y = bx + a$

    D. $y = -\dfrac{bx}{a}$

    E. $y = -\dfrac{bx}{a} + a$

9. If a line which has intercepts $(0, 5)$ and $(7, 0)$ is expressed in the form $ax + by = c$, where a, b, and c are integers, what is b?

    A. 35

    B. 5

    C. -5

    D. -7

    E. 7

Solutions

1. (B) $y - 0 = \dfrac{5}{8}(x + 12) = \dfrac{5x}{8} + 15/2 \implies \left(0, \dfrac{15}{2}\right)$

2. (B) $(2, 4)$ and $(3, 9)$

   Slope $= \dfrac{9 - 4}{3 - 2} = 5$

   $y - 4 = 5(x - 2) \implies y - 4 = 5x - 10 \implies y = 5x - 6$

3. (C) The solutions are 2 and 4, so $(2, 0)$ is the smallest x intercept. The y intercept is

   $(0, 8)$. So slope $= \dfrac{8 - 0}{0 - 2} = -4$

   So the equation of the line is $y = -4x + 8$

4. (A) $0 = ax + b \implies -b = ax \implies x = -\dfrac{b}{a}$

5. (C) $by = c - ax \implies y = \dfrac{c}{b} - \dfrac{ax}{b}$

6. (B) $y - 0 = 10(x - 3) = y = 10x - 30$

7. (A) $(2, 4)$ and $(10, 100)$, Slope $= \dfrac{100 - 4}{10 - 8} = 12$

   $y - 4 = 12(x - 2) \implies y - 4 = 12x - 24 \implies y = 12x - 20$

8. (A) Slope $= \dfrac{b - 0}{0 - a} = -\dfrac{b}{a}$, so $y = -\dfrac{bx}{a} + b$

9. (E) Slope $= \dfrac{5 - 0}{0 - 7} = -\dfrac{5}{7} \implies y = -\dfrac{5x}{7} + 5$ in slope intercept form.

   $7y = -5x + 35 \implies 5x + 7y = 35$

Perpendicular Bisector

Perpendicular bisector problems are rare on the exam. However, it is useful to be able to do them as they encompass many techniques in working with lines. To find the perpendicular bisector, first find the slope of the line, then find its negative reciprocal, which is the slope of a line perpendicular to the original line. Then fine the midpoint of the original line. Now find the equation of a line through the midpoint with a slope perpendicular to the original line. The procedure is used in the problems below.

1. If $f(x)$ is the perpendicular bisector line segment between $(0,4)$ an $(5,0)$, what is the x-intercept of $f(x)$?

   A. $\dfrac{3}{10}$

   B. $\dfrac{9}{10}$

   C. $\dfrac{7}{10}$

   D. $\dfrac{11}{10}$

   E. $\dfrac{13}{10}$

2. $f(x) = x^2$. What is the perpendicular bisector of the line between $(2, f(2))$ and $(10, f(10))$?

   A. $y = -\dfrac{x}{12} + \dfrac{97}{2}$

   B. $y = -\dfrac{x}{12} + \dfrac{99}{2}$

   C. $y = -\dfrac{x}{12} + \dfrac{101}{2}$

   D. $y = -\dfrac{x}{12} + \dfrac{109}{2}$

   E. $y = -\dfrac{x}{12} + \dfrac{105}{2}$

Solutions

1. (B) Slope $= -\frac{4}{5}$, midpoint $= \left(\frac{5}{2}, 2\right)$, slope of line perpendicular $= \frac{5}{4}$

   $y - 2 = \frac{5}{4}\left(x - \frac{5}{2}\right) \implies y - 2 = \frac{5x}{4} - \frac{25}{8} \implies y = \frac{5x}{4} - \frac{9}{8}$

   To find the x-intercept, set $y = 0$, so $0 = \frac{5x}{4} - \frac{9}{8} \implies \frac{9}{8} = \frac{5x}{4} \implies x = \frac{9}{10}$

2. (E) $(2, 4)$ and $(10, 100)$ slope is $\frac{100 - 4}{10 - 2} = \frac{96}{8} = 12$

   Slope of perpendicular bisector $= -\frac{1}{12}$

   Midpoint is $\left(\frac{2 + 10}{2}, \frac{4 + 100}{2}\right) = (6, 52) \implies y - 52 = -\frac{x}{12} + \frac{1}{2}$

   $\implies y = -\frac{x}{12} + \frac{105}{2}$

Chapter XVI

Rates

Rates Involving Travel

1. If you traveled 7 miles in 11 minutes, what is your average speed to the nearest mile per hour?

    A. 40

    B. 38

    C. 39

    D. 37

    E. 42

2. If a bird traveled 2 miles in 50 seconds, what was its average speed in mph?

    A. 288

    B. 136

    C. 108

    D. 72

    E. 144

3. If a train traveled 3000 kilometers in a 24 hour day, what was its average speed in meters/second?

    A. 33.7

    B. 33.1

    C. 34.7

    D. 32.7

    E. 34.3

4. If Bob ran 12 laps around a circular track with radius 200 meters in 37 minutes, what was his average speed in kilometers per hour?

    A. 22.5

    B. 24.5

    C. 25.5

    D. 21.5

    E. 23.5

5. Say you left at noon and traveled 250 miles and averaged 57 mph. What time would you arrive at your destination to the nearest minute?

    A. 4:23 PM

    B. 3:43 PM

    C. 4:13 PM

    D. 3:23 PM

    E. 4:03 PM

6. If a freight train left New York at 2 PM Tuesday and traveled 3000 miles to the west coast at an average speed of 48 mph, what day and time will it arrive at to the nearest 5 minutes?

    A. Friday at 5:30 AM

    B. Friday at 3:30 AM

    C. Friday at 2:30 AM

    D. Friday at 4:30 AM

    E. Friday at 1:30 AM

7. If a freight train left at 4:26 PM Monday and arrived at its destination 2300 miles away at 7:11 AM Wednesday, what was its average speed to the nearest mile per hour?

    A. 55

    B. 58

    C. 57

    D. 59

    E. 56

8. Bob averaged 30 mph going there and 60 mph going back. What was his average speed for the round trip?

    A. 44 mph

    B. 42 mph

    C. 40 mph

    D. 45 mph

    E. 43 mph

9. Steve average 60 mph for the first 120 miles and 80 mph for the 2nd 240 miles. What was his average speed in mph for the 360 miles trip?

    A. 71

    B. 73

    C. 70

    D. 75

    E. 72

Answer Key: 1B, 2E, 3C, 4B, 5A, 6D, 7D, 8C, 9E

Solutions

1. (B) $7 \cdot \dfrac{60}{11} = \dfrac{420}{11} \approx 38$

2. (E) $2 \cdot \dfrac{3600}{50} = 144$ mph

3. (C) $\dfrac{3000 \cdot 1000}{24 \cdot 3600} \approx 34.7$

4. (B) $200 \cdot 2\pi \cdot 12 = 15079.64$ meters $= 15.08$ kilometers $\Rightarrow 15.08 \cdot \dfrac{60}{37} = \dfrac{15.08 \cdot 60}{37} \approx 24.5$

5. (A) $\dfrac{250}{57} = 4.386 \Rightarrow .386 \cdot 60 \approx 23 \Rightarrow$ So 4:23

6. (D) $\dfrac{3000}{48} = \dfrac{125}{2} = 62.5$ hours, so 2 days, 14 hours, 30 minutes, Friday at 4:30 AM

7. (D) Hours $= 24 + 14 + \dfrac{3}{4} = \dfrac{155}{4} \Rightarrow$ mph $= \dfrac{2300}{\frac{155}{4}} \approx 59.4$ mph

8. (C) Say the trip was 120 miles. Then 4 hours going there and 2 hours going back. The total time is 6 hours and the total distance 120 miles, so the average speed is $\dfrac{240}{6} = 40$ mph

9. (E) 2 hours + 3 hours = 5 hours $\Rightarrow \dfrac{360 \text{ miles}}{5 \text{ hours}} = 72$ mph

Other Rates

1. A cylindrical pool with radius 20 meters and height of water 2 meters is filled at 2 cubic meters per second. To the nearest minute, how many minutes would it take for the pool to go from empty to full?

    A. 27

    B. 21

    C. 33

    D. 24

    E. 22

2. A point on a wheel with a radius of 100 meters travels 70 meters in 1 minute. How many degrees per second does the wheel rotate at?

    A. .5 degrees

    B. 1.1 degrees

    C. 1.4 degrees

    D. .7 degrees

    E. 1.3 degrees

3. A wheel with a radius of 100 meters rotates at 2 degrees per second. How many meters does a point on the wheel travel in 1 minute?

    A. $\dfrac{230\pi}{3}$

    B. $\dfrac{280\pi}{3}$

    C. $\dfrac{250\pi}{3}$

    D. $\dfrac{220\pi}{3}$

    E. $\dfrac{200\pi}{3}$

4. A pool is the area between two concentric circles and radii 5 and 8 feet and is 4 feet deep. A pump adds water to the pool at the rate of 7 cubic feet per minute. If the pool is empty at 1:20 PM and is filled at that rate, at what time to the nearest minute will the pool first be full?

    A. 2:45 PM

    B. 2:40 PM

    C. 2:25 PM

    D. 2:30 PM

    E. 2:35 PM

5. If a tire with radius 15 inches turns at 1000 revolutions per minute, what is the approximate speed of the vehicle in miles per hour (1 mile = 5,280 feet)?

    A. 84

    B. 82

    C. 89

    D. 104

    E. 97

Solutions

1. (B) Volume of pool $= 800\pi \Rightarrow \dfrac{800\pi}{2} = 400\pi \approx 1256 \Rightarrow \dfrac{1256}{60} \approx 21$ minutes

2. (D) $\dfrac{70}{100 \cdot 2\pi} = .1114$ of a circle per minute $\Rightarrow .1114 \cdot \dfrac{360}{60} = .668 \approx .7$ degrees

3. (E) $60 \cdot 2 = 120$ degrees per minute. Circumference $= 2\pi r = 200\pi \Rightarrow 200\pi \cdot \dfrac{120}{360} = \dfrac{200\pi}{3}$ meters.

4. (D) Volume of pool is $(8^2\pi - 5^2\pi) \cdot 4 = 156\pi \Rightarrow \dfrac{156\pi}{7} = 70.01 \Rightarrow$ So 70 minutes, so 2:30 PM

5. (C) Multiply by 2π to convert radius to circumference, multiply by 60 to convert to hours, and divide by 5280 to convert to miles $\Rightarrow \dfrac{1000 \cdot 2\pi \cdot 60 \cdot 15}{5280 \cdot 12} \approx 89.2$

Chapter XVII

Ratios

1. The ratio of a to b to 5:8 and b to c is 3:2. What is the ratio of a to c?

    A. 20:3

    B. 15:16

    C. 16:15

    D. 12:5

    E. 5:12

2. If a:$b = 3$:2 and b:$c = 4$:1, what is $\dfrac{a+b}{b+c}$?

    A. 3

    B. $\dfrac{5}{2}$

    C. 4

    D. 2

    E. $\dfrac{3}{2}$

3. Which ratio is equivalent to 8^5 to 16^3?

    A. 8:3

    B. 16:1

    C. 16:3

    D. 8:1

    E. 4:1

4. If $\dfrac{x + y}{2x + 5y} = a$, what is $\dfrac{y}{x}$?

    A. $\dfrac{1 - 2a}{5a - 1}$

    B. $\dfrac{5a - 2}{1 - 2a}$

    C. $\dfrac{5a - 4}{1 - 2a}$

    D. $\dfrac{5a - 1}{1 - 2a}$

    E. $\dfrac{5a - 3}{1 - 2a}$

5. If $\dfrac{3x + 5y}{5x + 2y} = \dfrac{4}{5}$, what is $\dfrac{y}{x}$?

    A. $\dfrac{-5}{11}$

    B. $\dfrac{5}{17}$

    C. $\dfrac{-1}{17}$

    D. $\dfrac{3}{11}$

    E. $\dfrac{-3}{17}$

6. What fraction of an 8-inch pizza contains the same amount of pizza as a slice of a 10-inch pizza cut into 8 equal slices, assuming all parts of all pizzas have the same thickness?

    A. $\dfrac{5}{16}$

    B. $\dfrac{7}{32}$

    C. $\dfrac{25}{128}$

    D. $\dfrac{1}{5}$

    E. $\dfrac{11}{64}$

7. The ratio of $a{:}b$ is 3:2. What is $\dfrac{2a+5b}{3a+b}$?

    A. $\dfrac{11}{16}$

    B. $\dfrac{20}{11}$

    C. $\dfrac{16}{11}$

    D. $\dfrac{21}{11}$

    E. $\dfrac{18}{11}$

8. The ratio of $a{:}b$ is 5:8 and the ratio of $b{:}c$ is 2:3. What is $\dfrac{3a+5b}{2b+3c}$?

    A. $\dfrac{18}{17}$

    B. $\dfrac{65}{52}$

    C. $\dfrac{57}{52}$

    D. $\dfrac{55}{52}$

    E. $\dfrac{49}{52}$

Answer Key: 1B, 2D, 3D, 4A, 5B, 6C, 7C, 8D

Solutions

1. (B) $\dfrac{a}{b} = \dfrac{5}{8}$ and $\dfrac{b}{c} = \dfrac{3}{2} \Rightarrow \dfrac{a}{c} = \dfrac{a}{b} \cdot \dfrac{b}{c} = \dfrac{5}{8} \cdot \dfrac{3}{2} = \dfrac{15}{16}$

2. (D) $\dfrac{a}{b} = \dfrac{3}{2} \Rightarrow a = \dfrac{3b}{2}$ and $\dfrac{b}{c} = \dfrac{4}{1} \Rightarrow c = \dfrac{b}{4}$

$\Rightarrow \dfrac{\frac{3b}{2} + b}{\frac{b}{4} + b} = \dfrac{\frac{5b}{2}}{\frac{5b}{4}} = 2$

3. (D) $\dfrac{\left(2^3\right)^5}{\left(2^4\right)^3} = \dfrac{2^{15}}{2^{12}} = 2^3 = 8$

4. (D) $x + y = 2ax + 5ay \Rightarrow x - 2ax = 5ay - y \Rightarrow (1 - 2a)x = (5a - 1)y \Rightarrow \dfrac{y}{x} = \dfrac{1 - 2a}{5a - 1}$

5. (B) $(3x + 5y) \cdot 5 = (5x + 2y) \cdot 4 \Rightarrow 15x + 25y = 20x + 8y \Rightarrow 17y = 5x \Rightarrow \dfrac{y}{x} = \dfrac{5}{17}$

6. (C) $\dfrac{100}{8} = 64x \Rightarrow x = \dfrac{100}{512} = \dfrac{25}{128}$

7. (C) $\dfrac{a}{b} = \dfrac{3}{2} \Rightarrow a = \dfrac{3b}{2} \Rightarrow \dfrac{2\left(\frac{3b}{2}\right) + 5b}{3\left(\frac{3b}{2}\right) + b} = \dfrac{8b}{\frac{11b}{2}} = \dfrac{16}{11}$

8. (D) $b = \dfrac{8a}{5}$ and $c = \dfrac{3b}{2} \Rightarrow$ So $c = \dfrac{3 \cdot \frac{8a}{5}}{2} = \dfrac{24a}{10} = \dfrac{12a}{5}$

Substituting to get everything in terms of a, $\dfrac{3a + 5b}{2b + 3c} = \dfrac{3a + 5 \cdot \frac{8a}{5}}{2 \cdot \frac{8a}{5} + 3 \cdot \frac{12a}{5}} = \dfrac{11a}{\frac{16a}{5} + \frac{36a}{5}} = \dfrac{11a}{\frac{52a}{5}}$

$\Rightarrow \dfrac{55a}{52a} = \dfrac{55}{52}$

Chapter XVIII

Absolute Value

This is another area emphasized in this guide, because extremely difficult absolute value problems may appear on the exam.

Solve Basic Equation

To solve $|2x - 3| = 5$, you split is into 2 problems $2x - 3 = 5$ and $2x - 3 = -5$ and solve both equations. $2x = 8$ or $2x = -2 \Rightarrow x = 4$ or $x = -1$.

1. What is $|11x + 4| = 21$?

   A. $\dfrac{17}{11}$ or $\dfrac{-25}{11}$

   B. $\dfrac{19}{11}$ or $\dfrac{-25}{11}$

   C. $\dfrac{19}{11}$

   D. $\dfrac{17}{11}$

   E. $\dfrac{-25}{11}$

2. What is the product of the solutions of $|x^2 - 9| = 4$?

   A. -36

   B. -65

   C. 65

   D. 9

   E. 36

Solutions

1. (A) $11x + 4 = 21$ or $11x + 4 = -21 \Rightarrow 11x = 17$ or $11x = -25 \Rightarrow \dfrac{17}{11}$ or $\dfrac{-25}{11}$

2. (C) $x^2 - 9 = 4$ or $x^2 - 9 = -4 \Rightarrow x^2 = 13$ or $x^2 = 5 \Rightarrow \sqrt{13}$ and $-\sqrt{13}$ or $\sqrt{5}$ and $-\sqrt{5}$

$\Rightarrow \sqrt{13} \cdot \sqrt{13} \cdot \sqrt{5} \cdot \sqrt{5} = 65$

Solve Basic Inequality

With absolute value inequalities, the solutions are ranges and you need to be careful when effectively dividing by a negative. Say you have $|4x - 5| \geq 7$, then you split it into two equations $4x - 5 \geq 7$ and $5 - 4x \geq 7 \Rightarrow 4x \geq 12$ and $-2 \geq 4x \Rightarrow x \geq 3$ or $\frac{-1}{2} \geq x$. In interval notation, the solution is $\left(-\infty, \frac{-1}{2}\right] \cup [3, \infty)$. You could also have done the second part of the problem $4x - 5 \leq -7$, switching the sign, $4x \leq -2 \Rightarrow x \leq \dfrac{-1}{2}$.

1. What is the solution of $|2x - 5| < 3$?

   A. $1 < x < 7$

   B. $1 \leq x \leq 4$

   C. $1 < x < 4$

   D. $x < 1$ or $x > 4$

   E. $0 < x < 5$

2. What is the solution set of $|2x - 7| > 5$?

   A. $(-\infty, 1)$

   B. $(-\infty, 1) \cup (6, \infty)$

   C. $(6, \infty)$

   D. $(-\infty, 1] \cup [6, \infty)$

   E. $(1, 6)$

3. What is the solution of $|x^2 - 3x - 7| > -2$?

   A. $(-\infty, \infty)$

   B. $\left(\dfrac{-7}{3}, \infty\right)$

   C. $(-\infty, -4) \cup \left(\dfrac{7}{3}, \infty\right)$

   D. $\left(\dfrac{7}{3}, \infty\right)$

   E. $\left(-\infty, \dfrac{-7}{3}\right)$

4. What is the solution of $|x - 5000| \leq 23$?

    A. $[4977, 5023]$
    B. $[0, 5023]$
    C. $[-23, 4977]$
    D. $[23, 4977]$
    E. $(4977, 5023)$

Solutions

1. (C) $2x - 5 < 3 \Rightarrow 2x < 8 \Rightarrow x < 4$ or $2x - 5 > -3 \Rightarrow 2x > 2 \Rightarrow x > 1$

2. (B) $2x - 7 > 5$ or $2x - 7 < -5 \Rightarrow 2x > 12 \Rightarrow x > 6$ or $2x < 2 \Rightarrow x < 1 \Rightarrow (-\infty, 1) \cup (6, \infty)$

3. (A) Any absolute value expression is greater than or equal to 0.

4. (A) $x - 5000 \leq 23$ or $x - 5000 \geq -23 \Rightarrow x \leq 5023$ or $x \geq 4977 \Rightarrow [4977, 5023]$

Other Equalities

1. What is the positive difference of the solutions of $|x + 11| = 35$?

    A. 60
    B. 70
    C. 140
    D. 50
    E. 35

2. What are the solutions of $(|x| - 7)^2 = 16$?

    A. $\{-11, 11\}$
    B. $\{-11, -3, 0, 3, 11\}$
    C. $\{-11, -3, 3, 11\}$
    D. $\{3, 11\}$
    E. $\{-3, 3\}$

3. What are all the solutions of $|x^2| + 4|x| - 21 = 0$?

    A. $\{3, -3\}$
    B. $\{-7, -3\}$
    C. $\{7, -7\}$
    D. $\{3, -3, 7, -7\}$
    E. $\{3, 7\}$

4. What are the solutions of $x^2 + 5|x| = 14$?

    A. $\{2\}$
    B. $\{-7, -2, 2, 7\}$
    C. $\{2, -2\}$
    D. $\{2, 7\}$
    E. $\{-2\}$

5. $|2x + 5| = a$. For what range of a is there no solution?

    A. $\left(-\infty, \dfrac{5}{2}\right)$
    B. $\left(\dfrac{-5}{2}, \dfrac{5}{2}\right)$
    C. $\left(-\infty, \dfrac{-5}{2}\right)$
    D. $(-\infty, 0]$
    E. $(-\infty, 0)$

106

6. If $|x| = x + 3$, what is x?

   A. $\dfrac{3}{2}$

   B. No solution

   C. $\left\{ \dfrac{-3}{2}, \dfrac{3}{2} \right\}$

   D. $\dfrac{-3}{2}$

   E. $\left\{ \dfrac{-3}{2}, 0 \right\}$

7. For what x does $|x + 2| = x + 5$?

   A. $\left\{ \dfrac{-7}{2}, \dfrac{7}{2} \right\}$

   B. $\left\{ \dfrac{-7}{2}, \dfrac{-3}{2} \right\}$

   C. $\dfrac{-7}{2}$

   D. $\left\{ \dfrac{-7}{2}, \dfrac{3}{2} \right\}$

   E. $\left\{ \dfrac{-7}{2}, \dfrac{1}{2} \right\}$

8. What are the solutions of $|x^2 - 5| = 2$?

   A. $\pm\sqrt{3}$

   B. $\pm\sqrt{7}$

   C. $\pm\sqrt{3}, \pm\sqrt{7}$

   D. 3 and 7

   E. $\pm\sqrt{3}, \pm\sqrt{2}$

9. What is the solution set of $|x - 5| = x - 5$?

   A. $x \geq 5$

   B. $x > 5$

   C. $x = 5$ or $x = -5$

   D. $x = 5$

   E. $x \geq 5$ or $x \leq -5$

Solutions

1. (B) $x + 11 = 35$ or $x + 11 = -35 \Rightarrow x = 24$ or $x = -46 \Rightarrow 24 - (-46) = 70$. It is possible to figure out the answer without working through the problem.

2. (C) $|x| - 7 = \pm 4 \Rightarrow |x| = 11$ or $|x| = 3 \Rightarrow -11, -3, 3, 11$

3. (A) $x^2 + 4x - 21 = 0 \Rightarrow x = 3$ or -7, and $x^2 - 4x - 21 = 0 \Rightarrow x = -3$ or 7

   Only 3 and -3 check.

4. (C) $x^2 + 5x - 14 = 0$ and $x^2 - 5x + 14 = 0 \Rightarrow$ Solutions are -7, -2, 2 and 7 $\Rightarrow$ But only 2 and -2 check.

5. (E) $a < 0 \Rightarrow$ Absolute value cannot be negative.

6. (D) $x = x + 3$ or $-x = x + 3 \Rightarrow 0 = 3$ or $-3 = 2x \Rightarrow \dfrac{-3}{2} = x$

7. (C) $x + 2 = x + 5$ or $-x - 2 = x + 5 \Rightarrow 2 = 5$ or $-7 = 2x \Rightarrow x = \dfrac{-7}{2}$

8. (C) $x^2 - 5 = 2 \Rightarrow x = \pm\sqrt{7}$ and $5 - x^2 = 2 \Rightarrow x = \pm\sqrt{3}$

9. (A) $x - 5 = x - 5$ for $x \geq 5$

Other Inequalities

1. What are the solutions of $|x - 3| \geq x$?

   A. $x \leq \dfrac{3}{2}$ or $x > 6$

   B. $x < \dfrac{3}{2}$

   C. $x \leq 0$

   D. $x \leq 3$

   E. $x \leq \dfrac{3}{2}$

2. How would you say in absolute value the temperature needs to be between 70 and 86 degrees Fahrenheit?

   A. $|T - 86| \leq 70$

   B. $|T - 78| \leq 16$

   C. $|T - 78| \leq 8$

   D. $|T - 86| \leq 16$

   E. $|T - 78| \leq 4$

3. How would you say in absolutely value that a part much have a radius of 12 cm plus or minus .02 cm?

   A. $|x - .02| \leq 12$

   B. $|x - 12| \leq .02$

   C. $|x - 12| \leq .04$

   D. $|x - 12| \leq .2$

   E. $|x - 12| \geq .02$

4. The temperatures in Fahrenheit recorded in Death Valley are given by $|T - 76| \leq 58$. What is the lowest temperature recorded in Death Valley?

   A. 14 degrees

   B. 18 degrees

   C. 16 degrees

   D. 20 degrees

   E. 12 degrees

5. Which is equivalent to $(|x| + 2)^2 < 25$?

    A. $-3 < x < 3$

    B. $x < 3$

    C. $-10 < x < 3$

    D. $0 < x < 3$

    E. $-5 < x < 3$

Answer Key: 1E, 2C, 3B, 4B, 5A

Solutions

1. (E) $x - 3 \geq x$ or $3 - x \geq x \Rightarrow -3 \geq 0$ or $3 \geq 2x \Rightarrow x \leq \dfrac{3}{2}$

2. (C) $\dfrac{70 + 86}{2} = 78$ and $\dfrac{86 - 70}{2} = 8$

3. (B) $|x - 12| \leq .02$

4. (B) $T - 76 \leq 58$ and $T - 76 \geq -58 \Rightarrow T \leq 134$ and $T \geq 18$

5. (A) $|x| + 2 < 5$ or $|x| + 2 < -5 \Rightarrow |x| < 3$ or $|x| < -7$

   $\Rightarrow$ The 2nd case does not work, so $x < 3$ and $x > -3 \Rightarrow -3 < x < 3$

Chapter XIX

Area Bounded By

1. What is the area of the region in the 1st quadrant bounded by $y = \dfrac{-5x}{4} + 6$ and the x and y axes?

   A. 15

   B. $\dfrac{31}{2}$

   C. $\dfrac{29}{2}$

   D. 14

   E. $\dfrac{72}{5}$

2. What is the area bounded by the x and y axes and the lines $y = \dfrac{x}{2} + 2$ and $x = 6$?

   A. 21

   B. 22

   C. 20

   D. 18

   E. 19

Solutions

1. (E) The y-intercept is (0,6). To find the x-intercept, $0 = \dfrac{-5x}{4} + 6 \Rightarrow \dfrac{5x}{4} = 6 \Rightarrow x = \dfrac{24}{5} \Rightarrow \left(\dfrac{24}{5}, 0\right)$

$$\Rightarrow \dfrac{bh}{2} = \dfrac{\frac{24}{5} \cdot 6}{2} = \dfrac{72}{5}$$

2. (A) y-intercept $y = \dfrac{0}{2} + 2 \Rightarrow y = 2 \Rightarrow (0,2)$. The lines intersect at $y = \dfrac{6}{2} + 2 = 5 \Rightarrow (6,5)$.

By the trapezoid area formula, $\left(\dfrac{5+2}{2}\right) \cdot 6 = 21$

Chapter XX

Radicals

Radical Equations

If $\sqrt{x+3} = 5 \Rightarrow$ You square both sides, $x + 3 = 25 \Rightarrow x = 22$. You are supposed to also check the solution in the original equation.

1. If $\sqrt{4 + \sqrt{x}} = 5$, then $x =$?

   A. 941

   B. 21

   C. 84

   D. 441

   E. 105

2. $\sqrt[5]{3x + 5} = 2$. What does $x =$?

   A. $\dfrac{37}{3}$

   B. 9

   C. 1

   D. $\dfrac{11}{3}$

   E. -1

3. $\sqrt{3x+2} + 5 = 11$. What is x?

    A. $\dfrac{35}{3}$

    B. $\dfrac{31}{3}$

    C. $\dfrac{32}{3}$

    D. 11

    E. $\dfrac{34}{3}$

4. $\sqrt{2}x = \sqrt{3}$. What does $x =$?

    A. $2\sqrt{3}$

    B. $\dfrac{\sqrt{6}}{4}$

    C. $\sqrt{6}$

    D. $\dfrac{\sqrt{6}}{2}$

    E. $2\sqrt{6}$

Solutions

1. (D) $4 + \sqrt{x} = 25 \Rightarrow \sqrt{x} = 21 \Rightarrow x = 441$

2. (B) $3x + 5 = 32 \Rightarrow 3x = 27 \Rightarrow x = 9$

3. (E) $\sqrt{3x + 2} = 6 \Rightarrow 3x + 2 = 36 \Rightarrow 3x = 34 \Rightarrow x = \dfrac{34}{3}$

4. (D) $x = \dfrac{\sqrt{3}}{\sqrt{2}} \Rightarrow x = \dfrac{\sqrt{6}}{2}$

Radical Expressions Squared or Multiplied

Just foil out the expressions and simplify.

1. What is $\left(4\sqrt{a} - 3\sqrt{b}\right)\left(4\sqrt{a} + 3\sqrt{b}\right)$?

   A. $256a - 81b$

   B. $4a - 9b$

   C. $16a - 9b$

   D. $64a - 9b$

   E. $16a + 9b$

2. What is $\left(\sqrt{a} + \sqrt{b}\right)^2$?

   A. $a + b^2 + 2\sqrt{ab}$

   B. $2a + 2b + 2\sqrt{ab}$

   C. $a + b + \sqrt{ab}$

   D. $a + 2\sqrt{ab}$

   E. $a + b + 2\sqrt{ab}$

3. What is $\left(2a + 3\sqrt{b}\right)\left(5a + 3\sqrt{b}\right)$?

   A. $10a^2 + 27a\sqrt{b} + 9b$

   B. $10a^2 + 18a\sqrt{b} + 9b$

   C. $10a^2 + 21a\sqrt{b} + 9b$

   D. $10a^2 + 20a\sqrt{b} + 9b$

   E. $10a^2 + 24a\sqrt{b} + 9b$

Solutions

1. (C) $16a - 9b$. These are conjugates. The irrational terms drop out when you foil them.

2. (E) $\left(\sqrt{a} + \sqrt{b}\right) \cdot \left(\sqrt{a} + \sqrt{b}\right) = a + b + 2\sqrt{ab}$

3. (C) Foiling, $10a^2 + 6a\sqrt{b} + 15a\sqrt{b} + 9b = 10a^2 + 21a\sqrt{b} + 9b$

Radical Expressions Added or Divided

First simplify the radical expression, taking out the real part. Then perform the operation.

1. What is $\dfrac{\sqrt{108}}{\sqrt{75}} =$?

    A. $\dfrac{6}{5}$

    B. $\dfrac{12}{5}$

    C. $\dfrac{\sqrt{6}}{2}$

    D. $\dfrac{9}{5}$

    E. $\dfrac{3}{5}$

2. What is $\dfrac{\sqrt{12}}{\sqrt{50}} =$?

    A. $\dfrac{\sqrt{3}}{5}$

    B. $\dfrac{\sqrt{6}}{25}$

    C. $\dfrac{2\sqrt{6}}{5}$

    D. $\dfrac{\sqrt{2}}{5}$

    E. $\dfrac{\sqrt{6}}{5}$

3. What is $\sqrt{8} + \sqrt{18}$?

    A. $4\sqrt{2}$

    B. $5\sqrt{2}$

    C. $6\sqrt{2}$

    D. $2\sqrt{2}$

    E. $2\sqrt{10}$

Solutions

1. (A) $\dfrac{6\sqrt{3}}{5\sqrt{3}} = \dfrac{6}{5}$

2. (E) $\dfrac{2\sqrt{3}}{5\sqrt{2}} \Rightarrow$ Multiplying by $\dfrac{\sqrt{2}}{\sqrt{2}} \Rightarrow = \dfrac{2\sqrt{6}}{10} = \dfrac{\sqrt{6}}{5}$

   Or, dividing the top and bottom in the original expression by $\sqrt{2} \Rightarrow \dfrac{\sqrt{6}}{\sqrt{25}} = \dfrac{\sqrt{6}}{5}$

3. (B) $2\sqrt{2} + 3\sqrt{2} = 5\sqrt{2}$

Fractional Exponents

You need to be able to convert back and forth between radical and fractional exponent form. You also should be able to to operation on exponential form, which follow the laws of logarithms.

1. The $\sqrt[3]{\sqrt[4]{x^5}} = x^a$. What is a?

   A. $\dfrac{12}{5}$

   B. $\dfrac{7}{12}$

   C. $\dfrac{12}{7}$

   D. $\dfrac{5}{12}$

   E. $\dfrac{11}{12}$

2. What is $\left(x^{\frac{7}{3}}\right)^{\frac{1}{2}}$ in radical form?

   A. $\sqrt[5]{x^7}$

   B. $\sqrt[3]{x^7}$

   C. $\sqrt[8]{x^7}$

   D. $\sqrt[6]{x^7}$

   E. $\sqrt[4]{x^7}$

3. Which is equivalent to $\sqrt[5]{x^3} \cdot \sqrt[3]{x^2}$?

   A. $x^{\frac{23}{15}}$

   B. $x^{\frac{17}{15}}$

   C. $x^{\frac{19}{15}}$

   D. $x^{\frac{13}{15}}$

   E. $x^{\frac{11}{15}}$

4. What is $a^{\frac{1}{3}}a^{\frac{1}{4}}$ in simplest radical form?

   A. $\sqrt[12]{a^7}$

   B. $\sqrt[24]{a^7}$

   C. $\sqrt[12]{a^5}$

   D. $\sqrt[8]{a^7}$

   E. $\sqrt[6]{a^7}$

Answer Key: 1D, 2D, 3C, 4A

Solutions

1. (D) $x^{5 \cdot \frac{1}{4} \cdot \frac{1}{3}} = x^{\frac{5}{12}}$

2. (D) $x^{\frac{7}{3} \cdot \frac{1}{2}} = x^{\frac{7}{6}} = \sqrt[6]{x^7}$

3. (C) $x^{\frac{3}{5}} \cdot x^{\frac{2}{3}} = x^{\frac{3}{5} + \frac{2}{3}} = x^{\frac{19}{15}}$

4. (A) $a^{\frac{1}{3} + \frac{1}{4}} = a^{\frac{4}{12} + \frac{3}{12}} = a^{\frac{7}{12}} = \sqrt[12]{a^7}$

Chapter XXI

Exponents

1. What is $\left(\dfrac{2a^4b^5}{3c^7} \right)^5$?

  A. $\dfrac{32a^{20}b^{25}}{81c^{30}}$

  B. $\dfrac{32a^{20}b^{25}}{81c^{35}}$

  C. $\dfrac{32a^{20}b^{25}}{243c^{25}}$

  D. $\dfrac{32a^{20}b^{25}}{243c^{40}}$

  E. $\dfrac{32a^{20}b^{25}}{243c^{35}}$

2. What is $\dfrac{\left(\dfrac{x^{11}}{x^3} \right)^2}{\dfrac{x^5}{x^2}}$?

  A. x^{10}

  B. x^{16}

  C. x^5

  D. x^{13}

  E. x^2

3. What is $\left(\dfrac{4}{3}\right)^{\frac{-5}{2}}$?

   A. $\dfrac{9\sqrt{3}}{4}$

   B. $\dfrac{9\sqrt{3}}{32}$

   C. $\dfrac{9\sqrt{3}}{8}$

   D. $\dfrac{9\sqrt{3}}{16}$

   E. $\dfrac{9\sqrt{3}}{64}$

4. What is $\dfrac{(3a^2b^5)^3}{(6a^4b^4)^2}$?

   A. $\dfrac{3b^8}{4a^2}$

   B. $\dfrac{3b^6}{4a^2}$

   C. $\dfrac{3b^7}{4a^2}$

   D. $\dfrac{3b^7}{a^2}$

   E. $\dfrac{3b^7}{8a^2}$

5. What is $\left(\left(x^2\right)^3\right)^{11}$?

   A. x^{15}

   B. x^{66}

   C. x^{55}

   D. x^{22}

   E. x^{132}

6. What is $(x^3)^5 \cdot (x^4)^6$?

   A. x^{41}

   B. x^{21}

   C. x^{360}

   D. x^{39}

   E. x^{51}

7. What is $\dfrac{\frac{x^{11}}{x^3}}{\frac{x^5}{x^2}}$?

   A. x^{13}

   B. x^{40}

   C. $x^{\frac{8}{3}}$

   D. x^5

   E. x^7

8. Which is equivalent to $\dfrac{(3x^2)^4}{x^{2^3}}$?

   A. $81x^2$

   B. $27x^2$

   C. $9x^2$

   D. $9x^4$

   E. $81x^6$

9. $(2x^3)^4 = ?$

  A. $8x^7$

  B. $4x^{12}$

  C. $16x^{12}$

  D. $2x^7$

  E. $32x^7$

10. What is $((2x^2)^3)^4$?

  A. $2048x^{12}$

  B. $4096x^{12}$

  C. $4096x^{24}$

  D. $512x^9$

  E. $4096x^9$

11. $(2a^{10} \cdot \sqrt{b})^4 = ?$

  A. $64a^{40}b^2$

  B. $16a^{40}b^2$

  C. $16a^{20}b^2$

  D. $8a^{40}b^2$

  E. $8a^{20}b^2$

12. What is $\dfrac{(3x^2)^4}{(2x^3)^2} = ?$

   A. $\dfrac{27x^2}{4}$

   B. $\dfrac{81x^2}{8}$

   C. $\dfrac{81x^5}{4}$

   D. $\dfrac{81x^{13}}{4}$

   E. $\dfrac{81x^2}{4}$

Solutions

1. (E) $\dfrac{2^5(a^4)^5(b^5)^5}{3^5(c^7)^5} = \dfrac{32a^{20}b^{25}}{243c^{35}}$

2. (D) $\dfrac{x^{8^2}}{x^3} = \dfrac{x^{16}}{x^3} = x^{13}$

3. (B) $\dfrac{\sqrt{3}^5}{\sqrt{4}^5}, \dfrac{9\sqrt{3}}{2^5} = \dfrac{9\sqrt{3}}{32}$

4. (C) $\dfrac{27a^6b^{15}}{36a^8b^8} = \dfrac{3b^7}{4a^2}$

5. (B) $x^{2\cdot3\cdot11} = x^{66}$, by the law of exponents.

6. (D) $x^{15} \cdot x^{24} = x^{39}$

7. (D) $\dfrac{x^8}{x^3} = x^5$

8. (A) $81\dfrac{x^8}{x^6} = 81x^2$

9. (C) $2^4(x^3)^4 = 16x^{12}$

10. (C) $(2x^2)^3 = 8x^6, (8x^6)^4 = 4096x^{24}$

11. (B) $16a^{40}b^2$

12. (E) $\dfrac{81x^8}{4x^6} = \dfrac{81x^2}{4}$

Chapter XXII

Expressions

1. If $a > 0$ and $b > 0$, what is $3 \cdot (a^0 + b^0)^4$?

   A. 96

   B. 64

   C. 48

   D. 54

   E. 192

2. What is $\dfrac{300x^7 + 108x^5}{12x^3}$?

   A. $25x^4 + 12x^2$

   B. $25x^4 + 6x^2$

   C. $25x^4 + 16x^2$

   D. $25x^4 + 9x^2$

   E. $25x^4 + 18x^2$

Answer Key: $1C, 2D$

Solutions

1. (C) Anything to the 0 power is 1, so $3 \cdot 2^4 = 48$

2. (D) $12x^5 \dfrac{25x^2 + 9}{12x^3} = 25x^4 + 9x^2$

Chapter XXIII

Range of Values for Variables

You need to figure out what maximizes or minimizes the expression and look at the end points of the inequalities.

1. $3 \leq x \leq 8$ and $10 \leq y \leq 20$. What is the largest value of $\dfrac{x+y}{y}$?

   A. $\dfrac{7}{5}$

   B. $\dfrac{8}{5}$

   C. $\dfrac{9}{5}$

   D. $\dfrac{11}{5}$

   E. $\dfrac{12}{5}$

2. If $3x + 5y = 20$ and $x \leq 4$, what is the range of values for y?

   A. $y \geq \dfrac{8}{5}$

   B. $y \geq \dfrac{9}{5}$

   C. $y \geq \dfrac{7}{5}$

   D. $y \geq \dfrac{6}{5}$

   E. $y \geq \dfrac{4}{5}$

Solutions

1. (C) $\dfrac{x+y}{y} = \dfrac{x}{y} + 1$, which is maximized when x is maximized and y is minimized. So
$$\frac{8+10}{10} = \frac{18}{10} = \frac{9}{5}$$

2. (A) $3 \cdot 4 + 5y = 20, y = \dfrac{8}{5}$

Chapter XXIV

Quadratic Equations

Solve Quadratic Equation

You can solve by factoring, the quadratic formula or completing the square. There are some problems that may ask for factored form and are easier using factoring. However, some equations cannot be factored, and it is surer to just apply a formula. You should memorize the quadratic formula $\dfrac{-b \pm \sqrt{b^2 - 4ac}}{2a}$. The formula is derived by completing the square. It is also helpful to know completing the square, which might be needed on some hard circle or conic section problem. Completing the square $x^2 - 4x + 2 = 0$, $x^2 - 4x + 4 = 2$, $(x-2)^2 = 2$, $x = 2 \pm \sqrt{2}$. Completing the square also works when there are irrational or complex solutions.

1. What is the solution set of $3x^2 - 5 = 0$?

A. $\left\{ \dfrac{\sqrt{15}}{3} \right\}$

B. $\left\{ \dfrac{-\sqrt{15}}{3} \right\}$

C. $\left\{ \dfrac{\sqrt{5}}{3}, \dfrac{-\sqrt{5}}{3} \right\}$

D. $\left\{ \dfrac{\sqrt{15}}{3}, \dfrac{-\sqrt{15}}{3} \right\}$

E. $\left\{ \dfrac{\sqrt{30}}{3}, \dfrac{-\sqrt{30}}{3} \right\}$

2. What are the two solutions of $5x^2 + x - 4 = 0$?

A. 1 and $\dfrac{4}{5}$

B. -1 and $\dfrac{4}{5}$

C. 1 and $\dfrac{-4}{5}$

D. $i + 2$ and $2 - i$

E. -2 and $\dfrac{4}{5}$

3. What are the solutions to $x^2 - 12x + 33 = 0$?

A. $12 \pm 2\sqrt{3}$

B. $6 \pm \sqrt{3}$

C. $3 \pm \sqrt{3}$

D. $9 \pm \sqrt{3}$

E. $3 \pm 2\sqrt{3}$

4. If $ax^2 + bx + c = 0$, what is x?

A. $\dfrac{b \pm \sqrt{b^2 - 4ac}}{2a}$

B. $\dfrac{-b \pm \sqrt{b^2 - 4ac}}{2}$

C. $\dfrac{-b \pm \sqrt{b^2 - 4ac}}{2a}$

D. $\dfrac{-b \pm \sqrt{b^2 - ac}}{2a}$

E. $\dfrac{-2b \pm \sqrt{b^2 - 4ac}}{2a}$

136

5. $x^2 + 4x + g = 0$. What are the solutions for x?

   A. $-2 \pm \sqrt{8 - g}$

   B. $-1 \pm \sqrt{4 - g}$

   C. $-2 \pm \sqrt{2 - g}$

   D. $-2 \pm \sqrt{4 - g}$

   E. $-4 \pm \sqrt{4 - g}$

Solutions

1. (D) $x^2 = \dfrac{5}{3}, x = \pm\dfrac{\sqrt{5}}{\sqrt{3}} = \pm\dfrac{\sqrt{15}}{3}$

2. (B) $5x^2 + 5x - 4x - 4 = 0$, $5x(x+1) - 4(x+1) = 0$, $(5x-4)(x+1) = 0$, -1 or $\dfrac{4}{5}$. You can also use the quadratic formula.

3. (B) $\dfrac{12 \pm \sqrt{144 - 132}}{2} = \dfrac{12 \pm 2\sqrt{3}}{2} = 6 \pm \sqrt{3}$. Or $x^2 - 12x + 36 = 3$, $(x-6)^2 = 3$, $x = 6 \pm \sqrt{3}$

4. (C) This is the quadratic formula. They won't ask it that way, but you need to know it. It can be derived by completing the square, but it is best to memorize it.

5. (D) $\dfrac{-4 \pm \sqrt{16 - 4g}}{2} = \dfrac{-4 \pm 2\sqrt{4 - g}}{2} = -2 \pm \sqrt{4 - g}$

Sum and Product of Quadratic Equation

It is helpful to know the formulas sum of solutions $= \dfrac{-b}{a}$, product of solutions $= \dfrac{c}{a}$. Both of these formulas can be derived from the quadratic formula. There derivations are in the solutions to problems, and it is recommended that you practice deriving the formulas. If you don't know the formula, you can just find the solution and take there sum or product.

1. What is the sum of the two solutions of $5x^2 + 4x + 11 = 0$?

    A. $\dfrac{-2}{5}$

    B. $\dfrac{2}{5}$

    C. $\dfrac{-4}{5}$

    D. $\dfrac{-8}{5}$

    E. $\dfrac{-16}{5}$

2. What is the product of the two solutions of $5x^2 + 4 + 11 = 0$?

    A. $\dfrac{11}{5}$

    B. $\dfrac{22}{5}$

    C. $\dfrac{-11}{5}$

    D. $\dfrac{-11}{10}$

    E. $\dfrac{11}{10}$

3. What is the sum of the solutions of the equation $3ux^2 + 4vx + 5 = 0$?

A. $\dfrac{-2v}{3u}$

B. $\dfrac{-4v}{3u}$

C. $\dfrac{-3u}{4v}$

D. $\dfrac{5}{3u}$

E. -4

4. If $2x^2 + 5x + 3 = 0$, what is the product of the sum of the solutions and the product of the solutions?

A. $\dfrac{15}{4}$

B. $\dfrac{3}{2}$

C. $\dfrac{-5}{2}$

D. $\dfrac{25}{4}$

E. $\dfrac{-15}{4}$

5. What is the product of the solutions of the equation $3ux^2 + 4vx + 5 = 0$?

A. $\dfrac{5}{3u}$

B. $\dfrac{3}{5u}$

C. $\dfrac{10}{3u}$

D. $\dfrac{5u}{6}$

E. $\dfrac{10u}{3}$

6. What is the sum of the solutions of $ax^2 + bx + c$?

    A. $\dfrac{-b}{2a}$

    B. $\dfrac{-b}{a}$

    C. $\dfrac{b}{a}$

    D. $\dfrac{b}{2a}$

    E. $\dfrac{c}{a}$

7. What is the product of the solutions of $ax^2 + bx + c$?

    A. $\dfrac{-c}{a}$

    B. $\dfrac{c}{2a}$

    C. $\dfrac{-b}{a}$

    D. $\dfrac{c}{a}$

    E. $\dfrac{-b}{2a}$

Solutions

1. (C) $\dfrac{-b}{a} = \dfrac{-4}{5}$, you can also solve the equation and add the solutions.

2. (A) $\dfrac{c}{a} = \dfrac{11}{5}$, you can also solve the equation and add the solutions.

3. (B) $\dfrac{-b}{a} = \dfrac{-4v}{3u}$. You can also use the quadratic formula, but that would be much longer

4. (E) $Sum = \dfrac{-b}{a} = \dfrac{-5}{2}, product = \dfrac{c}{a} = \dfrac{3}{2}$. Product of the two $= \dfrac{-5}{2} \cdot \dfrac{3}{2} = \dfrac{-15}{4}$

5. (A) Product of solutions $= \dfrac{c}{a}, \dfrac{5}{3u}$. You can also use the quadratic formula

6. (B) $\dfrac{-b+\sqrt{b^2-4ac}}{2a} + \dfrac{-b-\sqrt{b^2-4ac}}{2a} = \dfrac{-2b}{2a} = \dfrac{-b}{a}$

7. (D) $\dfrac{-b+\sqrt{b^2-4ac}}{2a} \cdot \dfrac{-b-\sqrt{b^2-4ac}}{2a}$, since these are conjugates,

$= \dfrac{b^2-(b^2-4ac)}{4a^2} = \dfrac{4ac}{4a^2} = \dfrac{c}{a}$

Quadratic Equation from Solutions

If the solutions of a quadratic equation are a and b, The equation is $(x-a)(x-b) = x^2 - (a+b)x + ab$. So if the solutions are -2 and 5, the equation is $(x+2)(x-5) = x^2 - 3x - 10$. If the solutions are $\frac{1}{2}$ and $\frac{1}{3}$, the equation is $(x - \frac{1}{2})(x - \frac{1}{3}) = x^2 - \frac{5x}{6} + \frac{1}{6} = 0$, since it is set to 0, we can multiply by 6 and clear the denominators, so $6x^2 - 5x + 1 = 0$. Irrational roots come in conjugate pairs, so if one root is $4 + \sqrt{3}$, the other is $4 - \sqrt{3}$, so $(x - 4 - \sqrt{3})(x - 4 + \sqrt{3}) = x^2 - 8x + 16 - 3 = x^2 - 8x + 13$. Finding the equation from complex roots works similarly and is covered elsewhere.

1. What quadratic equation with integer coefficients has $\frac{5}{8}$ as its only solution?

    A. $64x^2 + 80x + 25 = 0$

    B. $64x^2 - 80x + 25 = 0$

    C. $64x^2 + 84x + 25 = 0$

    D. $64x^2 - 84x + 25 = 0$

    E. $64x^2 - 72x + 25 = 0$

2. What is a quadratic equation with integer coefficients and solutions $\frac{3}{5}$ and $\frac{2}{3}$?

    A. $15x^2 - 21x + 6 = 0$

    B. $15x^2 - 23x + 6 = 0$

    C. $15x^2 - 19x + 6 = 0$

    D. $15x^2 - 17x + 6 = 0$

    E. $15x^2 - 25x + 6 = 0$

3. What quadratic equation has roots at 2 and 3 and $f(0) = 30$?

   A. $f(x) = x^2 - 5x + 30$

   B. $f(x) = x^2 - 5x + 6$

   C. $f(x) = 30x^2 - 25x + 30$

   D. $f(x) = 10x^2 - 25x + 30$

   E. $f(x) = 5x^2 - 25x + 30$

4. What quadratic equation has a root $5 + \sqrt{3}$?

   A. $x^2 - 10x + 22 = 0$

   B. $x^2 - 10x + 28 = 0$

   C. $x^2 - 10x + 19 = 0$

   D. $x^2 + 10x + 22 = 0$

   E. $x^2 - 10x + 34 = 0$

Answer Key: $1B, 2C, 3E, 4A$

Solutions

1. (B) $\left(x - \dfrac{5}{8}\right)^2 = 0, (8x - 5) \cdot (8x - 5) = 64x^2 - 80x + 25 = 0$

2. (C) $\left(x - \dfrac{3}{5}\right)\left(x - \dfrac{2}{3}\right) = 0, x^2 - \dfrac{3x}{5} - \dfrac{2x}{3} + \dfrac{2}{5} = 0, x^2 - \dfrac{19x}{15} + \dfrac{2}{5} = 0,$
   $15x^2 - 19x + 6 = 0$

3. (E) $(x - 2)(x - 3) = x^2 - 5x + 6, \dfrac{30}{6} = 5, 5 \cdot (x^2 - 5x + 6) = 5x^2 - 25x + 30$

4. (A) $(x - 5 - \sqrt{3})(x - 5 + \sqrt{3}) = x^2 - 10x + 25 - 3 = x^2 - 10x + 22 = 0$

Finding Quadratic Coefficient

You plug in the root and find the missing coefficient. For example if $x - 3$ is a solution to $5x^2 - 4x + k = 0$, what is k. Plug in 3, $5 \cdot 3^2 - 4 \cdot 3 + k = 0$, $45 - 12 + k = 0$, $k = -33$

1. $x^2 + bx + c = 0$ and the only possible value of x is 5. What is $b + c$?

   A. 10

   B. 12

   C. 15

   D. 20

   E. 25

2. $x^2 + 9x + c = 0$ has exactly one solution for what value of c?

   A. $\dfrac{9}{4}$

   B. $\dfrac{27}{4}$

   C. $\dfrac{81}{4}$

   D. 36

   E. 18

3. If $2x^2 + ux + 11 = 0$ has exactly one solution, what is u?

   A. $2\sqrt{22}$

   B. $-2\sqrt{22}$

   C. $\pm\sqrt{22}$

   D. $\sqrt{22}$

   E. $\pm 2\sqrt{22}$

4. If $ax^2 + bx + c = 0$ has exactly one solution, what is c in terms of a and b?

A. $\dfrac{b^2}{4a}$

B. $\dfrac{-b^2}{4a}$

C. $\dfrac{3b^2}{4a}$

D. $\dfrac{b^2}{8a}$

E. $\dfrac{b^2}{2a}$

5. If $x - 5$ is a factor is $3x^2 - 10x + k$, what is k?

A. -20

B. -25

C. -30

D. -15

E. 25

6. If $x^2 + hx + 10 = 0$ and 3 is a solution, what is h?

A. -6

B. $\dfrac{-17}{3}$

C. -5

D. $\dfrac{-19}{3}$

E. $\dfrac{-20}{3}$

Solutions

1. (C) $(x-5)(x-5) = x^2 - 10x + 25, -10 + 25 = 15$

2. (C) $b^2 - 4ac = 0, 81 = 4c, \dfrac{81}{4} = c$

3. (E) $b^2 - 4ac = 0, u^2 - 4 \cdot 2 \cdot 11 = 0, u^2 = 88, u = \pm\sqrt{88} = \pm 2\sqrt{22}$

4. (A) $b^2 = 4ac, c = \dfrac{b^2}{4a}$

5. (B) $3 \cdot 5^2 - 10 \cdot 5 + k = 0, 25 + k = 0, k = -25$

6. (D) $3^2 + h3 + 10 = 0, 3h = -19, h = \dfrac{-19}{3}$

Vertex

To find the vertex use the formula $x = \dfrac{-b}{2a}$, and then plug the x value is to get the y value. You can also use completing the square to get the equation into vertex form. For example, if $y = x^2 + 6x + 11$, using $\dfrac{-b}{2a}$, $x = \dfrac{-6}{2} = -3$. Plugging in -3, $(-3)^2 + 6(-3) + 11 = 2$, so $(-3, 2)$. Completing the square, $y = x^2 + 6x + 9 + 2 = (x+3)^2 + 2$, so $(-3, 2)$.

1. What is the vertex of $y = a(x - b)^2 + c$?

    A. $(b, -c)$

    B. (b, c)

    C. $(-b, c)$

    D. $\left(b, \dfrac{c}{b}\right)$

    E. $(b, c + b)$

2. What is the minimum value of $3x^2 - 2x + 5$?

    A. $\dfrac{8}{3}$

    B. $\dfrac{10}{3}$

    C. $\dfrac{11}{3}$

    D. $\dfrac{14}{3}$

    E. $\dfrac{16}{3}$

Solutions

1. (B) This equation is in vertex form.

2. (D) $\dfrac{-b}{2a} = \dfrac{-(-2)}{2 \cdot 3} = \dfrac{1}{3}$. Plugging in $x = \dfrac{1}{3}$, $3\left(\dfrac{1}{3}\right)^2 - 2 \cdot \dfrac{1}{3} + 5 = \dfrac{1}{3} - \dfrac{2}{3} + 5 = \dfrac{14}{3}$. This should be easier by graphing. You can also use completing the square, which would be more difficult than the vertex formula.

Factored Form

1. What is $2x^2 - x - 15$ in factored form?

    A. $(2x + 3)(x - 5)$

    B. $(x + 5)(2x - 3)$

    C. $(x - 5)(2x + 3)$

    D. $(2x - 5)(x + 3)$

    E. $(2x + 5)(x - 3)$

2. What is $10x^2 + 19x + 6$ in factored form?

    A. $(2x + 3)(5x + 2)$

    B. $(2x + 2)(5x + 3)$

    C. $(2x + 1)(5x + 6)$

    D. $(2x + 1)(5x + 6)$

    E. $(2x - 3)(5x - 2)$

Solutions

1. (E) We need two numbers that multiple to $2 \cdot (-15) = -30$ and add to -1, so 5 and -6. $2x^2 - 6x + 5x - 15$, $2x(x-3) + 5(x-3)$, so $(2x+5)(x-3)$.

2. (A) $4 \cdot 15 = 6 \cdot 10$ and $4 + 15 = 19$. So
$10x^2 + 4x + 15x + 6 = 2x(5x+2) + 3(5x+2) = (2x+3)(5x+2)$.
If you did not know how to do that, you could reverse engineer using the quadratic
formula $\dfrac{-19 \pm \sqrt{361 - 240}}{20} = \dfrac{-19 \pm 11}{20} = \dfrac{-3}{2}$ or $\dfrac{-2}{5}$,
$x = \dfrac{-3}{2}, x + \dfrac{3}{2} = 0, 2x + 3 = 0, x = \dfrac{-2}{5}, x + \dfrac{2}{5} = 0, 5x + 2 = 0$,
so $(2x+3)(5x+2)$. You could also multiply out the answer choices or make up numbers and plug them into the question and answers.

Chapter XXV

Inequalities

1. What is the range of x for which $x^2 > 4x$?

    A. $x > 0$ and $x < 4$

    B. $x \leq 0$ or $x > 4$

    C. $x < 0$ or $x > 4$

    D. $x \leq 0$ or $x \geq 4$

    E. $x > 4$

2. For what values is $x^2 + 3x \geq 10$?

    A. $(-\infty, -5] \cup [2, \infty)$

    B. $(-\infty, -5) \cup (2, \infty)$

    C. $[-5, 2]$

    D. $(-\infty, -5]$

    E. $[2, \infty)$

Answer Key: $1C, 2A$

Solutions

1. (C) $x^2 - 4x > 0, x(x-4) > 0$ critical points at 0 and 4, checking intervals, $x < 0$ or $x > 4$

2. (A) $x^2 + 3x - 10 \geq 0, (x+5)(x-2) \geq 0, (-\infty, -5] \cup [2, \infty)$

Chapter XXVI

Logic

You should know that the contrapositive has the same truth value as the original statement. To find the contrapositive, you switch the two parts and take the negative of both. So if all politicians are crooks, Bob is not a crook implies Bob is not a politician.

1. Which is logically equivalent to "All tables are flat"?

   A. "If it's not flat, it's a table"

   B. "If it's not a table, it's not flat"

   C. "If it's flat, it's a table"

   D. "If it's not flat, it isn't a table"

   E. "If it's a table, it might be flat"

Solutions

1. (D) The contrapositive is the same as the original, take the negation and converse, the negative and switch them.

Chapter XXVII

Angles

Angles of a Polygon

The sum of all the angles in a polygon is $180(n-2)$, where n is the number of sides. Therefore the angles in a regular polygon are $\dfrac{180(n-2)}{n}$.

1. What is the measure of each interior angle in a regular 20-sided polygon?

    A. $160°$

    B. $162°$

    C. $165°$

    D. $168°$

    E. $170°$

2. Two angles of a hexagon are each $150°$, what is the average value of the other 4 angles?

    A. $105°$

    B. $110°$

    C. $115°$

    D. $120°$

    E. $100°$

3. What is the measure of each interior angle of a regular octagon in radians?

A. $\dfrac{7\pi}{8}$

B. $\dfrac{2\pi}{3}$

C. $\dfrac{5\pi}{8}$

D. $\dfrac{3\pi}{4}$

E. $\dfrac{8\pi}{9}$

4. The measures of 7 interior angles of a regular octagon are all 120°. What is the measure of the 8th angle?

A. 120°

B. 180°

C. 240°

D. 270°

E. No such octagon

5. The measures of 7 interior angles of a regular octagon are all 100°. What is the measure of the 8th angle?

A. 140°

B. 160°

C. 270°

D. 300°

E. No such octagon

6. A regular polygon has angles 168°. How many sides does it have?

 A. 25

 B. 28

 C. 30

 D. 32

 E. 40

7. The interior angles of a pentagon are in the ratio of $3 : 4 : 5 : 6 : 7$. What is the measure of the smallest angle in degrees?

 A. 35°

 B. 40°

 C. 50°

 D. 55°

 E. 65°

Answer Key: $1B, 2A, 3D, 4C, 5E, 6C, 7E$

Solutions

1. (B) $\dfrac{180(n-2)}{n} = \dfrac{180 \cdot 18}{20} = 162$

2. (A) sum of angles $= 180(6-2) = 720$. $720 - 300 = 420, \dfrac{420}{4} = 105$

3. (D) $\dfrac{180(n-2)}{n} = 135, \; 135 \cdot \dfrac{\pi}{180} = \dfrac{3\pi}{4}$

4. (C) Sum of angles $= 180(n-2) = 1080, 120 \cdot 7 + x = 1080,$
   $840 + x = 1080, x = 240$

5. (E) Sum of angles $= 180(n-2) = 1080, 100 \cdot 7 + x = 1080, x = 380.$
   An angle of a polygon cannot be greater than 360

6. (C) $\dfrac{180(n-2)}{n} = 168, 180n - 360 = 168n, 12n = 360, n = 30.$

7. (E) sum of angles $= 180(5-2) = 540.$
   smallest angle $= 540 \cdot \dfrac{3}{3+4+5+6+7} = \dfrac{1620}{25} = \dfrac{324}{5} = 64.8°$

160

Clock angles

There are $\dfrac{360}{12} = 30$ degrees between each number on the clock. The hardest problem is how many degrees are the hands apart at a particular time. At $5:10$, the minute and is on 2 and the hour and is $\dfrac{1}{6}$ the way from 5 to 6. The angle between 2 and 5 is $3 \cdot 30 = 90°$. $\dfrac{1}{6} \cdot 30 = 5$. The answer is $90 + 5 = 95$ degrees.

1. How many degrees will the minute hand of a clock travel in 37 minutes?

    A. $212°$

    B. $217°$

    C. $222°$

    D. $242°$

    E. $252°$

2. How many degrees will the hour hand of the clock rotate between $5:45$ and $8:35$ in the same evening?

    A. $80°$

    B. $85°$

    C. $87°$

    D. $90°$

    E. $95°$

3. What is the angle formed by the hands of a clock at $3:30$?

    A. $72°$

    B. $82°$

    C. $77°$

    D. $75°$

    E. $80°$

4. If the minute hand of a clock has length $\dfrac{50}{\pi}$ cm, how far in cm does the tip of the minute hand travel between 1:50 and 6:10 the same afternoon?

    A. $66\ cm$

    B. $67\ cm$

    C. $68\ cm$

    D. $\dfrac{202}{3}\ cm$

    E. $\dfrac{200}{3}\ cm$

5. What is the angle formed by the hands of a clock at 3:40?

    A. $125°$

    B. $128°$

    C. $130°$

    D. $132°$

    E. $135°$

Solutions

1. (C) $\dfrac{37}{60} \cdot 360 = 222°$

2. (B) $2\dfrac{5}{6} \cdot 30 = \dfrac{17}{6} \cdot 30 = 85$

3. (D) The hour hand is half way between 3 and 4, and minute hand at 6, so $2 \cdot 30 + 15 = 75°$

4. (E) $3 + \dfrac{1}{3}$ revolutions. $2 \cdot \pi \cdot \dfrac{10}{\pi} \cdot \dfrac{10}{3} = \dfrac{200}{3} cm$

5. (C) hour hand $\dfrac{2}{3}$ of the way from 3 to 4, minute hand at 8, $4 \cdot 30 + 30 \cdot \dfrac{1}{3} = 130°$

Chapter XXVIII

Area and Volume

Volume and Surface Area 3D

Cubes

The volume of a cube $= s^3$, the long diagonal of a cube $= \sqrt{3}s$, and the surface are of a cube $= 6s^2$. All of these can be derived from the box formulas by setting $s = l = w = h$, or by basic principles.

1. The sides of a cube are 5 meters. What is its volume in cubic mm?

    A. $3.75 \cdot 10^{11}$

    B. $2.5 \cdot 10^{11}$

    C. $6.25 \cdot 10^{10}$

    D. $1.25 \cdot 10^{11}$

    E. $6.25 \cdot 10^{11}$

2. If the surface area of a cube is x, what is its volume?

    A. $\left(\dfrac{x}{6}\right)^{\frac{2}{3}}$

    B. $\left(\dfrac{x}{6}\right)^{\frac{3}{2}}$

    C. $\left(\dfrac{x}{6}\right)^{3}$

    D. $x^{\frac{3}{2}}$

    E. $x^{\frac{3}{4}}$

3. The volume of a cube is x. What is the surface area of the cube in terms of x?

    A. $2x^{\frac{2}{3}}$

    B. $3x^{\frac{2}{3}}$

    C. $6x^{\frac{3}{2}}$

    D. $6x^2$

    E. $6x^{\frac{2}{3}}$

4. The surface area of a cube is 100. What is its volume to the nearest integer?

    A. 68

    B. 70

    C. 73

    D. 75

    E. 80

5. The volume of a cube is x. What is longest diagonal of the cube in terms of x?

    A. $\sqrt{3} \cdot \sqrt{x}$

    B. $\sqrt[3]{x}$

    C. $\dfrac{\sqrt[3]{x}}{\sqrt{3}}$

    D. $\sqrt{3} \cdot \sqrt[3]{x}$

    E. $3\sqrt[3]{x}$

6. If the longest distance between two points on a cube is 5 meters, what is the volume of the cube to the nearest meter?

A. 24

B. 25

C. 26

D. 27

E. 28

Solutions

1. (D) $(5 \cdot 10^3)^3 = 125 \cdot 10^9 = 1.25 \cdot 10^{11}$

2. (B) $x = 6s^2, s = \sqrt{\dfrac{x}{6}}, V = s^3 = \left(\dfrac{x}{6}\right)^{\frac{3}{2}}$

3. (E) $x = s^3, \sqrt[3]{x} = s.$ Area $= 6s^2 = 6x^{\frac{2}{3}}$

4. (A) $6s^2 = 100s = \dfrac{10}{\sqrt{6}}, V = s^3 = \left(\dfrac{10}{\sqrt{6}}\right)^3 = \dfrac{100}{6\sqrt{6}} \approx 68$

5. (D) $s = \sqrt[3]{x}, d^2 = 3(\sqrt[3]{x})^2, d = \sqrt{3} \cdot \sqrt[3]{x}$

6. (A) sides $= \dfrac{5}{\sqrt{3}}, V = s^3 = \left(\dfrac{5}{\sqrt{3}}\right)^3 = \dfrac{125}{3\sqrt{3}} = \dfrac{125\sqrt{3}}{9} \approx 24.056$

Boxes

The formula for surface area of a box is $2(wl + wh + lh)$. The volume is $l \cdot w \cdot h$. The longest diagonal is $\sqrt{l^2 + w^2 + h^2}$

1. How many 3" $\times$ 4" $\times$ 6" little boxes can fit into a $2' \times 2' \times 5'$ big box?

    A. 240

    B. 360

    C. 420

    D. 480

    E. 540

2. How many cubic feet of mulch would you need to cover an area 20×30 yards to a depth of 2 inches?

    A. 600

    B. 800

    C. 900

    D. 1200

    E. 5400

3. A rectangular solid has a volume of 300 cubic centimeters. If the length and width are doubled and the height is multiplied by 5, what will the volume of the new solid be?

    A. 5400 cm^3

    B. 6000 cm^3

    C. 6200 cm^3

    D. 6400 cm^3

    E. 6600 cm^3

4. What is the surface area of a $2 \times 3 \times 5$ box?

    A. 52

    B. 60

    C. 62

    D. 72

    E. 84

5. The surface area of a $2 \times 3 \times z$ box is 80. What is z?

    A. 6.2

    B. 6.4

    C. 6.6

    D. 6.8

    E. 7.0

Solutions

1. (D) $4 \cdot 3 \cdot 2 = 24$ in each cubic feet, $2 \cdot 2 \cdot 5 = 20$ cubic feet. $24 \cdot 20 = 480$. There are various other methods.

2. (C) $60 \cdot 90 \cdot \dfrac{1}{6} = 900$ cubic feet

3. (B) $300 \cdot 2 \cdot 2 \cdot 5 = 6000$

4. (C) $2(lw + lh + wh) = 2(2 \cdot 3 + 2 \cdot 5 + 3 \cdot 5) = 62$

5. (D) $2(2 \cdot 3 + 3z + 2z) = 80, 12 + 10z = 80, 10z = 68, z = 6.8$

Spheres

The volume of a sphere is $\dfrac{4\pi r^3}{3}$ and the surface area is $4\pi r^2$. They will probably give you the formulas or you will just need to know volume is proportional to the cube etc.

1. A sphere has a volume of 10,000 cubic meters. What is its radius in meters?

    A. 13.4

    B. 13.7

    C. 14.4

    D. 17.2

    E. 23.3

2. Two spheres have radii $5a$ and $3a$. What is the ratio of the volume of the spheres?

    A. $\dfrac{25}{9}$

    B. $\dfrac{5}{1}$

    C. $\dfrac{125}{27}$

    D. $\dfrac{44}{9}$

    E. $\dfrac{4}{1}$

3. Two spheres have radii of 4 meters and 5 meters. What percent of the volume of the larger sphere is the volume of the smaller sphere?

    A. 51%

    B. 54%

    C. 57%

    D. 64%

    E. 80%

4. If Jupiter has a radius of $71,492$ kilometers, what is its volume in cubic kilometers?

    A. $2.5 \cdot 10^{15}$

    B. $1.5 \cdot 10^{15}$

    C. $3.5 \cdot 10^{15}$

    D. $4.5 \cdot 10^{15}$

    E. $7.5 \cdot 10^{15}$

5. The ratio of the surface areas of two spheres is $2 : 3$. What is the ratio of their volumes?

    A. $\dfrac{4}{9}$

    B. $\dfrac{8}{27}$

    C. $\dfrac{2}{3}$

    D. $\dfrac{\sqrt{2}}{\sqrt{3}}$

    E. $\dfrac{2\sqrt{2}}{3\sqrt{3}}$

Answer Key: $1A, 2C, 3A, 4B, 5E$

Solutions

1. (A) $10,000 = \dfrac{4\pi r^3}{3} = \dfrac{7,500}{\pi} = r^3, r = 13.37$

2. (C) $\dfrac{5^3}{3^3} = \dfrac{125}{27}$

3. (A) $\dfrac{4^3}{5^3} \cdot 100 = 51.2$

4. (B) $\dfrac{4\pi r^3}{3} = \dfrac{4\pi \cdot 71492^3}{3} \approx 1.5 \cdot 10^{15}$

5. (E) $2^{\frac{3}{2}} : 3^{\frac{3}{2}}$. You could use the formulas for surface area and volume, but this is easier.

174

Cylinders and Cones

The volume of a cylinder is $\pi r^2 h$ and the volume of a cone is $\dfrac{\pi r^2 h}{3}$. The surface area of a cylinder is $2\pi r^2 + 2\pi rh$. You should not need to know the surface area of a cone.

1. What is a formula for the radius of a cylinder in terms of its height and volume?

A. $\sqrt{\dfrac{V}{\pi h^2}}$

B. $\dfrac{V}{\pi h}$

C. $\sqrt{\dfrac{V}{\pi}}$

D. $\sqrt{\dfrac{V}{\pi h}}$

E. $\sqrt{\dfrac{V}{h}}$

2. The radius of a right circular cylinder is multiplied by a factor of 5 and the height divided by a factor of 2. What is the ratio of the volume old cylinder to the volume of the new one?

A. $\dfrac{2}{5}$

B. $\dfrac{2}{15}$

C. $\dfrac{2}{25}$

D. $\dfrac{5}{8}$

E. $\dfrac{1}{10}$

3. A cylindrical tank has radius 2 meters and height 3 meters. If it is filled with water an a cubic meter of water weighs $2,205$ pounds, how many pounds does the water in the tank weigh in hundreds of pounds?

    A. 415

    B. 831

    C. 1662

    D. 1245

    E. 622

4. If a cylinder has height 5 and volume 180π, what is its total surface area?

    A. 132π

    B. 124π

    C. 128π

    D. 136π

    E. 13π

5. The area between $y = 6 - 2x$ and the x an y axes is rotated about the y axis. What is the volume?

    A. 12π

    B. 20π

    C. 24π

    D. 15π

    E. 18π

Solutions

1. (D) $V = \pi r^2 h, \dfrac{V}{\pi h} = r^2, r = \sqrt{\dfrac{V}{\pi h}}$

2. (C) $\dfrac{5^2}{2} = \dfrac{25}{2}$

3. (B) $V = \pi r^2 h = \pi 2^2 \cdot 3 = 12\pi$ cubic meters. $12\pi \cdot 2205 = 83,127$ pounds

4. (A) $V = \pi r^2 h, 180\pi = \pi r^2 \cdot 5, 36 = r^2, r = 6$, surface area $=$ area base $+$ lateral surface area $= 2\pi r^2 + 2\pi r h = 2\pi 6^2 + 2\pi 6 \cdot 5 = 72\pi + 60\pi = 132\pi$

5. (E) y intercept is $(0,6)$, x intercept is $(3,0)$. This is a cone, $r = 3, h = 6$. Volume of a cone formula $= \dfrac{\pi r^2 h}{3} = \dfrac{\pi 3^2 \cdot 6}{3} = 18\pi$. You could also use rotation of solids in caluculus.

Rectangles

1. If a field has area 1000 square meters and its length is twice its width, what is its perimeter to the nearest meter?

    A. 128

    B. 130

    C. 132

    D. 134

    E. 136

2. The diagonal of a rectangle is 7 and one side is 6. What is the area of the rectangle?

    A. 18

    B. 27

    C. $6\sqrt{13}$

    D. $12\sqrt{13}$

    E. $\sqrt{13}$

3. One side of a rectangle as 3 inches longer than the other. If the diagonal is 10 inches, approximately how long is the shorter side?

    A. 5.6

    B. 5.3

    C. 5.2

    D. 5.5

    E. 5.4

Answer Key: $1D, 2C, 3E$

Solutions

1. (D) $w \cdot 2w = 1000, w^2 = 500, w = 10\sqrt{5}, l = 20\sqrt{5}$. Perimeter $= 2w + 2l = 60\sqrt{5} \approx 134$

2. (C) the other side $w = \sqrt{7^2 - 6^2} = \sqrt{13}$ by the Pythagorean Theorem. So the area$=$ $6\sqrt{13}$

3. (E) $x^2 + (x+3)^2 = 10^2, x^2 + x^2 + 6x + 9 = 100, 2x^2 + 6x - 91 = 0,$ $\dfrac{-6 \pm \sqrt{36 + 724}}{4}, \dfrac{-6 + \sqrt{760}}{4} \approx 5.4$

Area of Squares

1. What is the perimeter in meters of a square having an area of 76 square meters?

    A. $8\sqrt{19}$ m

    B. $19\sqrt{19}$ m

    C. $2\sqrt{19}$ m

    D. $4\sqrt{19}$ m

    E. 361 m

2. You have x feet of fencing. How many square feet of a square region could it enclose?

    A. $\dfrac{x^2}{4}$

    B. $\dfrac{x^2}{8}$

    C. $\dfrac{x^2}{12}$

    D. $\dfrac{x^2}{16}$

    E. $\dfrac{x^2}{32}$

3. One side of a square has endpoints $(3, 1)$ and $(1, 8)$. What is the area of the square?

    A. 49

    B. 53

    C. 55

    D. 57

    E. 64

Solutions

1. (A) $s = \sqrt{76} = 2\sqrt{19}, P = 4s = 8\sqrt{19}$

2. (D) Each side $= \dfrac{x}{4}$. Area $= \left(\dfrac{x}{4}\right)^2 = \dfrac{x^2}{16}$

3. (B) The side length of the square $= \sqrt{(8-1)^2 + (1-3)^2} = \sqrt{49+4} = \sqrt{53}$. So the area of the square $= \sqrt{53}^2 = 53$

Triangles

1. The ratio of the perimeters of two similar triangles is $2:5$. What is the ratio of their areas?

   A. $\dfrac{2}{5}$

   B. $\dfrac{4}{5}$

   C. $\dfrac{4}{25}$

   D. $\dfrac{4}{125}$

   E. $\dfrac{8}{125}$

2. One side of a triangle is 11 and another is 17. What is the range for possible values of the third side x?

   A. $6 \leq x \leq 28$

   B. $6 < x < 28$

   C. $6 < x$

   D. $\sqrt{67} < x < \sqrt{410}$

   E. $x < 34$

3. Two sides of a triangle are 2 and 3. For what range of the 3rd side x is the triangle acute?

   A. $\sqrt{5} < x < \sqrt{13}$

   B. $\sqrt{5} < x < \sqrt{15}$

   C. $\sqrt{5} < x < \sqrt{14}$

   D. $5 < x < 13$

   E. $1 < x < 5$

4. What is the area of an equilateral triangle with side a?

A. $\dfrac{\sqrt{3}a^2}{2}$

B. $\dfrac{3\sqrt{3}a^2}{4}$

C. $\dfrac{a^2}{2}$

D. $\dfrac{\sqrt{3}a^2}{4}$

E. $\dfrac{3\sqrt{3}a^2}{8}$

Answer Key: $1C, 2B, 3A, 4D$

Solutions

1. (C) $2^2 : 5^2 = 4 : 25$

2. (B) By the triangle inequality, and since the shortest distance between two points is a straight line, $17 - 11 < x < 17 + 11, 6 < x < 28$

3. (A) It has to be between the values for either possible right triangle. $\sqrt{3^2 - 2^2} = \sqrt{5}, \sqrt{3^2 + 2^2} = \sqrt{13}$

4. (D) Let h be the altitude. $h^2 + \left(\dfrac{a}{2}\right)^2 = a^2, h^2 = \dfrac{3a^2}{4}, h = \dfrac{\sqrt{3}a}{2}$.

   The area $= \dfrac{a \cdot \dfrac{\sqrt{3}a}{2}}{2} = \dfrac{\sqrt{3}a^2}{4}$

Area of Circles

Finding Area

The area of a circle is πr^2. Area of a section is $\pi r^2 \dfrac{\theta}{360}$.

1. A circle has circumference $10\sqrt{7}\pi$. What is its area?

   A. 500

   B. 550

   C. 150π

   D. 175π

   E. 200π

2. If a circle has circumference C, what is its area?

   A. $\dfrac{C^2}{4\pi}$

   B. $\dfrac{C^2}{2\pi}$

   C. $\dfrac{3C^2}{8\pi}$

   D. $\dfrac{C}{2\pi}$

   E. $\dfrac{C}{\pi}$

3. If r is the radius, what is the ratio of the area to the circumference of a circle?

   A. $\dfrac{r}{4}$

   B. $\dfrac{r}{2}$

   C. $\dfrac{r^2}{4}$

   D. r

   E. πr

4. 2 concentric circles have radii of 70 and 100 meters respectively. How many square meters is the area in the larger circle but not the smaller circle?

    A. 5000π

    B. 5200π

    C. 5100π

    D. 5300π

    E. 5400π

5. If the endpoints of the diameter of a circle are $(-2, -11)$ and $(4, 1)$, what is the area of the circle?

    A. 42π

    B. 45π

    C. 48π

    D. 44π

    E. 50π

6. The arc formed by a $40°$ angle is 6π. What is the area of the $40°$ section of the circle?

    A. 78π

    B. 84π

    C. 88π

    D. 81π

    E. 90π

Solutions

1. (D) $C = 2\pi r$, so $10\sqrt{7}\pi = 2\pi r, r = 5\sqrt{7}$. Area $= \pi r^2 = (5\sqrt{7})^2\pi = 175\pi$

2. (A) $C = 2\pi r, \dfrac{C}{2\pi} = r, A = \pi r^2 = \pi \left(\dfrac{C}{2\pi}\right)^2 = \pi\dfrac{C^2}{4\pi^2} = \dfrac{C^2}{4\pi}$

3. (B) $\dfrac{\pi r^2}{2\pi r} = \dfrac{r}{2}$

4. (C) $100^2\pi - 70^2\pi = 5100\pi$

5. (B) Distance between endpoints $= \sqrt{(4-(-2))^2 + (1-(-11))^2} = \sqrt{36+144} = \sqrt{180} = 6\sqrt{5}$. The radius is half of that, $3\sqrt{5}$. The area $\pi r^2 = \pi(3\sqrt{5})^2 = 45\pi$

6. (D) $6\pi = 2\pi r\dfrac{40}{360}, r = 27$, area of section $= \pi r^2\dfrac{40}{360} = 81\pi$.

Finding Radius or Circumference

The circumference of a circle is $2\pi r$. Arc length is $2\pi r \cdot \dfrac{\theta}{360}$.

1. If the area of a circle is 12π cm^2, what is its circumference in cm?

   A. $2\sqrt{3}\pi$

   B. $\sqrt{3}\pi$

   C. 6π

   D. 8π

   E. $4\sqrt{3}\pi$

2. The radius of a circle is 10 cm. What is the length to the nearest mm of a $5°$ arc?

   A. 9

   B. 10

   C. 11

   D. 12

   E. 13

3. If a circle with radius a is divided into b congruent arcs, what the length i of each arc?

   A. $\dfrac{4a\pi}{b}$

   B. $\dfrac{2a\pi}{b}$

   C. $\dfrac{6a\pi}{b}$

   D. $\dfrac{2a\pi}{3b}$

   E. $\dfrac{6a\pi}{5b}$

4. The area of a pie slice section of a circle is 20π and the section is formed by a $40°$ angle from the center. What is the radius of the circle?

A. $3\sqrt{10}$

B. $2\sqrt{5}$

C. $3\sqrt{5}$

D. $6\sqrt{5}$

E. $12\sqrt{5}$

Solutions

1. (E) $A = \pi r^2, 12\pi = \pi r^2, r^2 = 12, r = 2\sqrt{3}$
   $C = 2\pi r = 2\pi \cdot 2\sqrt{3} = 4\sqrt{3}\pi$ cm

2. (A) Arc length $= 2\pi r \dfrac{\theta}{360} = 2\pi \cdot 10 \cdot \dfrac{5}{360} = \dfrac{100\pi}{360} = \dfrac{5\pi}{18} = 0.873,$
   $0.873 \cdot 10 = 8.73$ mm

3. (B) Circumference $= 2\pi r = 2a\pi.$ Each arc $= \dfrac{2a\pi}{b}$

4. (D) Area of slice $= \pi r^2 \cdot \dfrac{\theta}{360}, 20\pi = \pi r^2 \dfrac{40}{360}, 180 = r^2, \sqrt{180} = r, 6 \cdot \sqrt{5} = r$

Area of Rhombus

The rhombus area formula is $\dfrac{d_1 \cdot d_2}{2}$, where d_1 and d_2 are the diagonals. This formula is easy to derive and also applies to squares.

1. A rhombus has diagonals 20 and 30. What is its perimeter?

    A. $20\sqrt{10}$

    B. $20\sqrt{11}$

    C. $20\sqrt{13}$

    D. $10\sqrt{23}$

    E. $40\sqrt{5}$

2. A rhombus has diagonals 20 and 30. What is its area?

    A. 240

    B. 280

    C. 300

    D. 320

    E. 330

Answer Key: $1C, 2C$

Solutions

1. (C) Half diagonals are 10 and 15. Each side of the rhombus $= \sqrt{10^2 + 15^2} = \sqrt{100 + 225} = \sqrt{325} = 5\sqrt{13}$. Perimeter $= 20\sqrt{13}$

2. (C) The rhombus area formula is $\dfrac{d_1 \cdot d_2}{2}$, $\dfrac{20 \cdot 30}{2} = 300$. You can also divide it into 4 triangles, $4 \cdot \dfrac{10 \cdot 15}{2} = 300$

Chapter XXIX

Inscribed Figures

2D

If a square is inscribed in a circle, the diameter of the circle = the diagonal of the square. If a right triangle is inscribed in a circle, the diameter of the circle = the hypotenuse of the triangle.

1.A square is inscribed in a circle. What is the ratio of the area of the square to the area of the circle?

    A. $9 : 4\pi$

    B. $4 : \pi^2$

    C. $2 : \pi$

    D. $10 : 3\pi$

    E. $5 : 6\pi$

2. A square is inscribed in a circle. What is the ratio of the perimeter of the square to the circumference of the circle?

    A. $2 : \pi$

    B. $3 : \pi$

    C. $5 : 2\pi$

    D. $2\sqrt{2} : \pi$

    E. $\sqrt{7} : \pi$

3. What is the largest circle that can be inscribed in $\dfrac{(x-4)^2}{9} + \dfrac{(y-2)^2}{25} = 1$?

A. $(x-4)^2 + (y-2)^2 = 9$

B. $(x-4)^2 + (y-2)^2 = 1$

C. $(x-4)^2 + (y-2)^2 = 25$

D. $(x-4)^2 + y^2 = 9$

E. $(x-4)^2 + y^2 = 1$

4. What is the area of the square inscribed in $(x-4)^2 + (y-2)^2 = 36$?

A. 75

B. 96

C. 72

D. 108

E. 80

5. A rectangle with sides 6 and 10 is inscribed in a circle. What is the area of the region inside the circle but outside of the rectangle?

A. $32\pi - 60$

B. $34\pi - 60$

C. $36\pi - 60$

D. $30\pi - 60$

E. $28\pi - 60$

6. A 3×7 *inch* rectangle is inscribed in a circle. What is the area of the circle?

    A. 15π

    B. 21π

    C. 18π

    D. $\dfrac{31\pi}{2}$

    E. $\dfrac{29\pi}{2}$

7. What is the area of a rhombus inscribed in $\dfrac{x^2}{4} + \dfrac{y^2}{9} = 1$?

    A. 10

    B. 11

    C. 12

    D. $8\sqrt{3}$

    E. $8\sqrt{2}$

8. A right triangle with legs 2 and 3 in inscribed in a circle. What is the area of the circle?

    A. 3π

    B. $\dfrac{15\pi}{4}$

    C. $\dfrac{11\pi}{4}$

    D. $\dfrac{13\pi}{4}$

    E. $\dfrac{25\pi}{8}$

Answer Key: $1C, 2D, 3A, 4C, 5B, 6E, 7C, 8D$

Solutions

1. (C) Say the circle has radius 1, then the diameter is 2, which is the diagonal of the square. The square's sides are $\sqrt{2}$, by the Pythagorean Theorem, $90 - 45 - 45$ triangle ratios or trigonometry. So the area of the square is $(\sqrt{2})^2 = 2$. The area or the circle is $\pi r^2 = \pi$. So the ratio is $2 : \pi$. You could use another number or x for the radius, but 1 makes it simplest.

2. (D) Let the radius of the circle be 1. Then the diagonal of the square is the diameter of the circle $= 2$. So the sides of the square are $\sqrt{2}$. The perimeter of the square is $4\sqrt{2}$ and the circumference of the circle is 2π. $4\sqrt{2} : 2\pi = 2\sqrt{2} : \pi$

3. (A) It should have the same center and diameter equal to the minor axis, so $(x - 4)^2 + (y - 2)^2 = 9$

4. (C) The radius is 6, so the diameter is 12. The area of the square is $\dfrac{d_1 \cdot d_2}{2} = \dfrac{12^2}{2} = 72$ by the rhombus formula. You can also determine that the sides are $\dfrac{12}{\sqrt{2}} = 6\sqrt{2}$ by the $90 - 45 - 45$ triangle ratios, the Pythagorean Theorem, or trigonometry. So the area of the square $= (6\sqrt{2})^2 = 72$.

5. (B) The diagonal of the rectangle is $\sqrt{6^2 + 10^2} = \sqrt{136} = 2\sqrt{34}$. The radius is $\sqrt{34}$, so the area of the circle $= \pi r^2 = 34\pi$. The area of the rectangle is $6 \cdot 10 = 60, 34\pi - 60$

6. (E) The diagonal $= \sqrt{3^2 + 7^2} = \sqrt{58}$. The radius of the circle is $\dfrac{\sqrt{58}}{2}$. The area of the circle is $\pi \left(\dfrac{\sqrt{58}}{2}\right)^2 = \dfrac{\pi 58}{4} = \dfrac{29\pi}{2}$

7. (C) The major axis is $\sqrt{9} \cdot 2 = 6$, minor axis is $\sqrt{4} \cdot 2 = 4$, so the diagonals are 4 and 6. area of a rhombus $= \dfrac{d_1 \cdot d_2}{2} = \dfrac{4 \cdot 6}{2} = 12$. You can also find the area of 4 right triangles with legs 2 and 3. $\dfrac{2 \cdot 3}{2} = 3$. $3 \cdot 4 = 12$ for all 4 triangles.

8. (D) Hypotenuse $= \sqrt{2^2 + 3^2} = \sqrt{13}$. The radius $= \dfrac{\sqrt{13}}{2}$. The area of the circle $= \pi r^2 = \left(\dfrac{\sqrt{13}}{2}\right)^2 \cdot \pi = \dfrac{13\pi}{4}$

3D

If a cube is inscribed in a sphere. The long diagonal of the cube = the diameter of the sphere. So the sides of a cube are $\dfrac{2r}{\sqrt{3}}$. The long diagonal of a cube is $\sqrt{3}\times$ side length, as is derived elsewhere.

1. A cube with side length 2 is inscribed in a sphere. What is the surface area of the sphere (surface area $= 4\pi r^2$)?

   A. 8π

   B. 10π

   C. 12π

   D. $\dfrac{32\pi}{3}$

   E. $\dfrac{25\pi}{2}$

2. A cube is inscribed in a sphere. What is the ratio of the volume of the sphere to the volume of the cube?

   A. $\pi : 2$

   B. $\sqrt{3}\pi : 2$

   C. $2\pi : 3$

   D. $\sqrt{3}\pi : 3$

   E. $9\pi : 8$

3. A cube is inscribed in a sphere. What is the ratio of the surface area of the sphere to the surface area of the cube?

   A. $\pi : 3$

   B. $2\pi : 5$

   C. $3\pi : 8$

   D. $4\pi : 9$

   E. $\pi : 2$

Solutions

1. (C) The long diagonal of the cube is $2\sqrt{3}$. That is the diameter of the sphere, so the radius of the sphere is $\sqrt{3}$. The surface area of the sphere is $4\pi r^2 = 4\pi(\sqrt{3})^2 = 4\pi \cdot 3 = 12\pi$

2. (B) Let the sides of the cube be 2, then the volume of the cube $= s^3 = 8$. The long diagonal of the cube is $2\sqrt{3}$, so the radius of the sphere is half that, $\sqrt{3}$. The volume of the sphere is $\dfrac{4\pi r^3}{3} = \dfrac{4\pi(\sqrt{3})^3}{3} = 4\pi\sqrt{3}$. The ratio is $4\pi\sqrt{3} : 8 = \sqrt{3}\pi : 2$

3. (E) Let the sides of the cube be 2, then the surface area of the cube $= 6s^2 = 24$. The long diagonal of the cube is $2\sqrt{3}$, so the radius of the sphere is half that, $\sqrt{3}$. The surface area of the sphere is $4\pi r^2 = 4\pi\sqrt{3}^2 = 12\pi. 12\pi : 24 = \pi : 2$

Chapter XXX

Taking Expressions to Powers

Squaring

Just multiply the monomials, foil them out, and combine like terms.

1. What is $(5x - 4y)^2$?

    A. $25x^2 + 16y^2$

    B. $25x^2 - 40 + 16y^2$

    C. $25x^2 - 20xy + 16y^2$

    D. $25x^2 - 40xy + 16y^2$

    E. $25x^2 - 80xy + 16y^2$

2. $\left(\dfrac{x}{3} + \dfrac{y}{5}\right)^2 = ?$

    A. $\dfrac{x^2}{3} + \dfrac{xy}{15} + \dfrac{y^2}{25}$

    B. $\dfrac{x^2}{9} + \dfrac{2xy}{15} + \dfrac{y^2}{25}$

    C. $\dfrac{x^2}{9} + \dfrac{xy}{6} + \dfrac{y^2}{25}$

    D. $\dfrac{x^2}{27} + \dfrac{2xy}{6} + \dfrac{y^2}{25}$

    E. $\dfrac{x^2}{9} + \dfrac{2xy}{6} + \dfrac{y^2}{75}$

3. What is the xy term of $\left(\dfrac{x}{3} + 4y\right)^2 = ?$

   A. $\dfrac{8xy}{3}$

   B. $\dfrac{10xy}{3}$

   C. $\dfrac{8xy}{5}$

   D. $8xy$

   E. $\dfrac{16xy}{3}$

4. What is $\left(2x + \dfrac{1}{2}\right)^2$?

   A. $4x^2 + 2x + 1$

   B. $4x^2 + 2x + \dfrac{1}{2}$

   C. $4x^2 + 2x + \dfrac{1}{4}$

   D. $4x^2 + 4x + \dfrac{1}{4}$

   E. $4x^2 + 4x + \dfrac{1}{2}$

Solutions

1. (D) Foiling, $25x^2 - 40xy + 16y^2$

2. (B) Foiling, $\dfrac{x^2}{9} + \dfrac{2xy}{15} + \dfrac{y^2}{25}$

3. (A) Foiling, $\dfrac{x^2}{9} + \dfrac{8xy}{3} + 16y^2$

4. (C) $(2x + \dfrac{1}{2}) \cdot (2x + \dfrac{1}{2}) = 4x^2 + x + x + \dfrac{1}{4} = 4x^2 + 2x + \dfrac{1}{4}$

Chapter XXXI

Equations and Values

1. If $a = b^2$, what is $ab =$ in terms of b?

   A. $8b^4$

   B. $2b^2$

   C. b^2

   D. b^3

   E. b^4

2. $3^{x+3} = a$. What does $3^x =$?

   A. $\dfrac{a}{27}$

   B. $\dfrac{a}{9}$

   C. $\dfrac{a}{81}$

   D. $\dfrac{a^2}{27}$

   E. $\dfrac{a^2}{9}$

3. $2^{x-1} = b$. What does $2^{x+4} =$?

   A. $16b$

   B. $8b$

   C. $32b$

   D. $16b^2$

   E. $8b^4$

4. $f(x) = x^5 + 5x^4$. What is $f(-2)$?

   A. 40

   B. 42

   C. 44

   D. 46

   E. 48

5. $(x - 2)^3 = 10$. What is x?

   A. 4.1

   B. 4.2

   C. 4.3

   D. 4.4

   E. 4.5

6. What is the y coordinate of the positive y intercept of $(x + 3)^2 + (y + 5)^2 = 36$?

   A. 0.2

   B. 0.4

   C. 0.6

   D. 0.9

   E. 1.2

7. $16^{x+3} = 8^{2-x}$. What is x?

   A. $\dfrac{-5}{7}$

   B. $\dfrac{-6}{7}$

   C. $\dfrac{-8}{7}$

   D. $\dfrac{-9}{7}$

   E. $\dfrac{-10}{7}$

8. What is $f(-4)$ when $f(x) = \dfrac{x^2 + 3x + 2}{x^2 - 2x - 15}$?

   A. $\dfrac{2}{3}$

   B. $\dfrac{8}{5}$

   C. $\dfrac{7}{5}$

   D. $\dfrac{6}{5}$

   E. $\dfrac{4}{5}$

Answer Key: $1D, 2A, 3C, 4E, 5B, 6A, 7B, 8A$

Solutions

1. (D) $b^2 \cdot b = b^3$

2. (A) $3^x \cdot 3^3 = a, 27 \cdot 3^x = a, 3^x = \dfrac{a}{27}$

3. (C) $2^{x+4} = 2^{x-1} \cdot 2^5 = 32b$

4. (E) $(-2)^5 + 5(-2)^4 = -32 + 80 = 48$

5. (B) $x - 2 = 10^{\frac{1}{3}} = 10^{\frac{1}{3}} + 2 \approx 4.2$

6. (A) $3^2 + (y+5)^2 = 36, (y+5)^2 = 27, y = -5 \pm \sqrt{27} \approx 0.2$

7. (B) $2^{4^{x+3}} = 2^{3^{2-x}}, 4x + 12 = 6 - 3x, 7x = -6, x = \dfrac{-6}{7}$. You can also do $(x+3)\ln 16 = (2 - x)\ln 8$, find the values of $\ln 8$ and $\ln 16$ and solve for x.

8. (A) $\dfrac{(-4)^2 + 3(-4) + 2}{(-4)^2 - 2(-4) - 15} = \dfrac{16 - 12 + 2}{16 + 8 - 15} = \dfrac{6}{9} = \dfrac{2}{3}$. It is also possible to graph it and find the y value at -4.

Chapter XXXII

Solve for Constant

In most of the problems I have seen, you need to just find the constant, not find other values of the equation.

1. If $(4, 1000)$ is on the graph of $y = ax^2$, what is a?

    A. 62.5

    B. 64

    C. 64.5

    D. 66

    E. 70.5

2. If $f(x) = x^2 - 3x + a$ goes through $(5, 7)$, what is $f(8)$?

    A. 33

    B. 34

    C. 35

    D. 36

    E. 37

3. $f(x) = \sqrt{5x + a}$ goes through $(2, 4)$. What is $f(5)$?

   A. $\sqrt{31}$

   B. $\sqrt{33}$

   C. $4\sqrt{2}$

   D. 5

   E. 6

4. If $f(x) = ax^2 - 2$ goes through $(3, 4)$, what is $f(5)$?

   A. 14

   B. 15

   C. $\dfrac{29}{2}$

   D. $\dfrac{44}{3}$

   E. $\dfrac{46}{3}$

5. If $f(x) = x^2 + ax + 2$ goes through $(5, 7)$, what is $f(8)$?

   A. 21

   B. 20

   C. 18

   D. 34

   E. 19

6. If $f(x) = (x - 2)^2 + a$ goes through $(5, 7)$, what is $f(8)$?

   A. 33

   B. 34

   C. 35

   D. 36

   E. 37

7. If $f(x) = \sqrt{x^3 + a}$ goes through $(3, 4)$ what is $f(5)$?

    A. 10

    B. $\sqrt{111}$

    C. $\sqrt{115}$

    D. $\sqrt{114}$

    E. 11

8. If $f(x) = ax^3 + 4$ passes through $(2, 7)$ what is $f(5)$?

    A. 47

    B. 48

    C. 49

    D. 50

    E. 51

9. If $\left(5, \dfrac{4}{7}\right)$ is on the graph of $f(x) = \dfrac{x}{x + a}$, what is $f(8)$?

    A. $\dfrac{3}{4}$

    B. $\dfrac{32}{47}$

    C. $\dfrac{9}{13}$

    D. $\dfrac{8}{11}$

    E. $\dfrac{4}{5}$

10. If $f(x) = ax^2 + 3x + 2$ goes through $(5, 7)$, what is $f(8)$?

A. 0.4

B. 10

C. 10.5

D. 11.5

E. 12.5

11. If $f(x) = ax^2 + 2ax + 2$ goes through $(5, 7)$, what is $f(8)$?

A. 11.4

B. 12.4

C. 13.4

D. 14.4

E. 15.4

Solutions

1. (A) $1000 = a4^2, a = \dfrac{1000}{16} = 62.5$

2. (E) $7 = 5^2 - 3 \cdot 5 + a, 7 = 25 - 15 + a, -3 = a, f(x) = x^2 - 3x - 3,$
   $f(8) = 8^2 - 3 \cdot 8 - 3 = 37$

3. (A) $4 = \sqrt{5 \cdot 2 + a}, 16 = 10 + a, a = 6, f(x) = \sqrt{5x + 6}, f(5) = \sqrt{31}$

4. (D) $4 = a3^2 - 2, 4 = 9a - 2, a = \dfrac{2}{3}, f(x) = \dfrac{2x^2}{3} - 2,$
   $f(5) = 2 \cdot \dfrac{5^2}{3} - 2 = \dfrac{50}{3} - \dfrac{6}{3} = \dfrac{44}{3}$

5. (D) $7 = 5^2 + 5a + 2, -20 = 5a, -4 = a, f(x) = x^2 - 4x + 2,$
   $f(8) = 64 - 32 + 2 = 34$

6. (B) $7 = (5 - 2)^2 + a, 7 = 3^2 + a, a = -2, f(x) = (x - 2)^2 - 2,$
   $f(8) = (8 - 2)^2 - 2 = 36 - 2 = 34$

7. (D) $4 = \sqrt{3^3 + a}, 16 = 27 + a, -11 = a, f(x) = \sqrt{x^3 - 11},$
   $f(5) = \sqrt{5^3 - 11} = \sqrt{114}$

8. (E) $7 = a2^3 + 4, 3 = 8a, a = \dfrac{3}{8}, f(x) = \dfrac{3x^3}{8} + 4,$
   $f(5) = \dfrac{3 \cdot 5^3}{8} + 4 = \dfrac{375}{8} + 4 = \dfrac{407}{8} = 50.875$

9. (B) $\dfrac{4}{7} = \dfrac{5}{5 + a}, (5 + a) \cdot 4 = 7 \cdot 5, 20 + 4a = 35, a = \dfrac{15}{4}.$
   $f(x) = \dfrac{x}{x + \dfrac{15}{4}}, f(8) = \dfrac{8}{8 + \dfrac{15}{4}} = \dfrac{8}{\dfrac{47}{4}} = \dfrac{32}{47}$

10. (A) $35a + 14 + 2 = 7, 35a = -9, a = \dfrac{-9}{35}, \dfrac{-9x^2}{35} + 3x + 2 = f(x),$
    $f(8) = \dfrac{-9(8^2)}{35} + 3 \cdot 8 + 2 = \dfrac{-576}{35} + 26 \approx 9.5$

11. (C) $25a + 10a + 2 = 7, 35a = 5, a = \dfrac{1}{7}, f(x) = \dfrac{x^2}{7} + \dfrac{2x}{7} + 2,$
    $f(8) = \dfrac{64}{7} + \dfrac{16}{7} + 2 = \dfrac{80}{7} + 2 = \dfrac{94}{7}$

Chapter XXXIII

Solve for Variable

First degree

You isolate the variable you are solving for. Sometimes you need to factor out the variable and divide by what is left.

1. If $F = 32 + \dfrac{9C}{5}$, what is C in terms of F?

    A. $\dfrac{5}{9}(F - 32)$

    B. $\dfrac{9}{5}(F - 32)$

    C. $\dfrac{5}{9}(F + 32)$

    D. $\dfrac{9}{5}(F + 32)$

    E. $\dfrac{5F}{9} - 32$

2. $A = (b_1 + b_2) \cdot \dfrac{h}{2}$. What is b_1 in terms of the other variables?

    A. $\dfrac{A}{h} - b_2$

    B. $\dfrac{2A}{h} - b_2$

    C. $2A - b_2$

    D. $\dfrac{2A}{h}$

    E. $\dfrac{2A}{h} + b_2$

3. $\dfrac{1}{x} + \dfrac{1}{a} = \dfrac{1}{b}$. What is x in terms of a and b?

    A. $\dfrac{ab}{a^2 - b^2}$

    B. $\dfrac{ab}{b - a}$

    C. $\dfrac{ab}{a - b + 1}$

    D. $\dfrac{ab}{a - b}$

    E. $\dfrac{ab}{a + b}$

4. If $\dfrac{x}{a} + \dfrac{x}{b} = c$, what is x in terms of a, b and c?

    A. $\dfrac{abc}{a + b}$

    B. $\dfrac{abc^2}{a + b}$

    C. $\dfrac{abc}{a - b}$

    D. $\dfrac{ab}{a - b}$

    E. $\dfrac{ab}{a + b}$

5. $ax + b = cx + d$. What is x?

    A. $\dfrac{d}{a + c}$

    B. $\dfrac{d}{a - c}$

    C. $\dfrac{d + b}{a - c}$

    D. $\dfrac{b}{a - c}$

    E. $\dfrac{d - b}{a - c}$

Answer Key: 1A, 2B, 3D, 4A, 5E

Solutions

1. (A) $F - 32 = \dfrac{9C}{5} \Rightarrow \dfrac{5}{9}(F - 32) = C$

2. (B) $\dfrac{2A}{h} = b_1 + b_2 \Rightarrow b_1 = \dfrac{2A}{h} - b_2$

3. (D) $\dfrac{1}{x} = \dfrac{1}{b} - \dfrac{1}{a} \Rightarrow \dfrac{1}{x} = \dfrac{a - b}{ab} \Rightarrow x = \dfrac{ab}{a - b}$

4. (A) $\dfrac{(a + b)x}{ab} = c \Rightarrow x = \dfrac{abc}{a + b}$

5. (E) $ax - cx = d - b \Rightarrow (a - c)x = d - b \Rightarrow x = \dfrac{d - b}{a - c}$

Not First Degree

1. If $2^{a+3} = 5b$, what is 2^a in terms of b?

    A. $\dfrac{5b}{8}$

    B. $\dfrac{5b}{2}$

    C. $\dfrac{3b}{8}$

    D. $\dfrac{5b}{4}$

    E. $\dfrac{5b}{16}$

2. What is an expression for r in $V = \dfrac{4\pi r^3}{3}$?

    A. $\sqrt[3]{\dfrac{3V}{5\pi}}$

    B. $\sqrt[3]{\dfrac{3V}{8\pi}}$

    C. $\sqrt[3]{\dfrac{5V}{4\pi}}$

    D. $\sqrt[3]{\dfrac{3V}{2\pi}}$

    E. $\sqrt[3]{\dfrac{3V}{4\pi}}$

3. If $\log_u (v \cdot w^3) = t$, what is w in terms of the other variables?

    A. $\dfrac{u^t}{v}$

    B. $\sqrt[3]{\dfrac{u^t}{v}}$

    C. $\sqrt[3]{\dfrac{u^t}{v^2}}$

    D. $\log_u \left(\dfrac{u^t}{v}\right)$

    E. $\sqrt[3]{\dfrac{u}{v}}$

4. Solve $A = P(1+r)^5$ for r.

A. $\dfrac{A}{P} - 1$

B. $\sqrt[5]{\dfrac{A}{P}} - 1$

C. $\sqrt[5]{\dfrac{A}{P}}$

D. $\sqrt[5]{AP} - 1$

E. $\sqrt[5]{\dfrac{A}{P} - 1}$

Answer Key: 1A, 2E, 3B, 4B

Solutions

1. (A) $2^a \cdot 2^3 = 5b \Rightarrow 2^a = \dfrac{5b}{8}$

2. (E) $\dfrac{3V}{4\pi} = r^3 \Rightarrow r = \sqrt[3]{\dfrac{3V}{4\pi}}$

3. (B) $v \cdot w^3 = u^t \Rightarrow w^3 = \dfrac{u^t}{v} \Rightarrow w = \sqrt[3]{\dfrac{u^t}{v}}$

4. (B) $\dfrac{A}{P} = (1+r)^5 \Rightarrow \sqrt[5]{\dfrac{A}{P}} = 1+r \Rightarrow r = \sqrt[5]{\dfrac{A}{P}} - 1$

Chapter XXXIV

Mixture

The basic mixture problem is you have 10 liters 10% acid. How much 90% acid would you have to add to make the mixture 25% acid. You take total acid over total liquid = the new percentage. So,

$$\frac{10 \cdot 0.1 + 0.9x}{10 + x} = 0.25 \Rightarrow 1 + 0.9x = 2.5 + 0.25x \Rightarrow 0.65x = 1.5 \approx 2.31$$

They may give easier mixture problems, which are covered in the excercizes.

1. 10 liters of 20% acid are mixed with 15 liters of pure acid. What percent acid is the resulting mixture?

   A. 74

   B. 68

   C. 76

   D. 72

   E. 70

2. A 120 liter solution that is 5% salt is mixed with 80 liter solution that is x% salt. The combined solution is 10% salt. What is the value of x?

   A. 22

   B. 16

   C. 18.75

   D. 17.5

   E. 20

3. The team has won 12 and lost 8. How many straight games does it need to win to increase its winning percentage to 80%?

    A. 24

    B. 20

    C. 21

    D. 18

    E. 22

4. How much of a is 80% salt solution would you need to add to 3 liters of 10% salt solution to make the mixture 30% salt?

    A. 1

    B. 2.4

    C. 1.8

    D. 1.5

    E. 1.2

Answer Key: 1B, 2D, 3B, 4E

Solutions

1. (B) $\dfrac{10 \cdot .2 + 15}{25} = \dfrac{17}{25} = 68\%$, taking total acid divided by total liquid.

2. (D) $\dfrac{120 \cdot .05 + 80x}{120 + 80} = .1 \Rightarrow 6 + 80x = 20 \Rightarrow 80x = 14 \Rightarrow x = \dfrac{7}{40}$

   As a percent, $\dfrac{7}{40} \cdot 100 = 17.5\%$

3. (B) $\dfrac{12 + x}{20 + x} = .8 \Rightarrow 12 + x = 16 + .8x \Rightarrow .2x = 4 \Rightarrow x = 20$

4. (E) $\dfrac{x \cdot .8 + 3 \cdot .1}{3 + x} = .3 \Rightarrow .8x + .3 = .9 + .3x \Rightarrow .5x = .6 \Rightarrow x = 1.2$

Chapter XXXV

Rationalizing Denominator

If you have an expression like $3 + \sqrt{2}$ in the denominator, you multiply top and bottom by the conjugate $3 - \sqrt{2}$ to eliminate irrational terms in the denominator. For example,

$$\frac{5 + 2\sqrt{3}}{4 + \sqrt{3}} = \frac{(5 + 2\sqrt{3})(4 - \sqrt{3})}{(4 + \sqrt{3})(4 - \sqrt{3})} = \frac{20 - 5\sqrt{3} + 8\sqrt{3} - 6}{16 - 3} = \frac{14 + 3\sqrt{3}}{13}$$

1. What is $\dfrac{\sqrt{5}}{\sqrt{7}}$ in simplest radical form?

   A. $\dfrac{\sqrt{7}}{35}$

   B. $\dfrac{\sqrt{14}}{7}$

   C. $\dfrac{\sqrt{35}}{7}$

   D. $\dfrac{\sqrt{105}}{7}$

   E. $\dfrac{\sqrt{35}}{35}$

2. What is $\dfrac{1}{\sqrt{3} - \sqrt{2}}$ without an irrational denominator?

   A. $\sqrt{3} + \sqrt{2}$

   B. $\dfrac{\sqrt{3} + \sqrt{2}}{6}$

   C. $\sqrt{3} - \sqrt{2}$

   D. $\dfrac{\sqrt{3} + \sqrt{2}}{2}$

   E. $\dfrac{\sqrt{3} + \sqrt{2}}{3}$

3. What is $\dfrac{3+\sqrt{5}}{4+\sqrt{5}}$?

    A. $\dfrac{7+\sqrt{5}}{12}$

    B. $\dfrac{7+\sqrt{5}}{10}$

    C. $\dfrac{7+\sqrt{5}}{11}$

    D. $\dfrac{7+\sqrt{5}}{13}$

    E. $\dfrac{7+\sqrt{5}}{9}$

4. What is $\dfrac{\sqrt{2}}{\sqrt{3}} + \dfrac{\sqrt{3}}{\sqrt{2}}$?

    A. $\dfrac{5\sqrt{6}}{6}$

    B. $\dfrac{5\sqrt{3}}{6}$

    C. $5\sqrt{6}$

    D. $\dfrac{5\sqrt{6}}{10}$

    E. $\dfrac{5\sqrt{6}}{2}$

5. What is $\dfrac{1}{\sqrt{2}} + \dfrac{1}{\sqrt{5}}$ with a single rational denominator?

    A. $\dfrac{5\sqrt{2}+2\sqrt{5}}{10}$

    B. $\dfrac{5\sqrt{2}+2\sqrt{5}}{20}$

    C. $\dfrac{\sqrt{2}+\sqrt{5}}{10}$

    D. $\dfrac{5\sqrt{2}+2\sqrt{5}}{5}$

    E. $\dfrac{5\sqrt{2}+\sqrt{5}}{20}$

Answer Key: 1C, 2A, 3C, 4A, 5A

Solutions

1. (C) $\dfrac{\sqrt{5} \cdot \sqrt{7}}{\sqrt{7} \cdot \sqrt{7}} = \dfrac{\sqrt{35}}{7}$

2. (A) $\dfrac{\sqrt{3} + \sqrt{2}}{(\sqrt{3} - \sqrt{2}) \cdot (\sqrt{3} + \sqrt{2})} = \sqrt{3} + \sqrt{2}$

3. (C) $\dfrac{(3 + \sqrt{5})(4 - \sqrt{5})}{(4 + \sqrt{5})(4 - \sqrt{5})} = \dfrac{7 + \sqrt{5}}{11}$

4. (A) $\dfrac{\sqrt{2} \cdot \sqrt{2} + \sqrt{3} \cdot \sqrt{3}}{\sqrt{6}} = \dfrac{5}{\sqrt{6}} = \dfrac{5\sqrt{6}}{6}$

5. (A) $\dfrac{\sqrt{5} + \sqrt{2}}{\sqrt{10}} = \dfrac{\sqrt{50} + \sqrt{20}}{10} = \dfrac{5\sqrt{2} + 2\sqrt{5}}{10}$ or $\dfrac{\sqrt{2}}{2} + \dfrac{\sqrt{5}}{5} = \dfrac{5\sqrt{2} + 2\sqrt{5}}{10} = \dfrac{5\sqrt{2} + 2\sqrt{5}}{10}$

Chapter XXXVI

Polynomials

Solve Polynomial Equation

You generally need to factor and then use the quadratic formula once you get it down to a quadratic. In some cases, one solution will be given and you will need to use long or synthetic division to reduce the equation and find the other solutions.

1. What are the solutions of $4x^5 = 30x^4$?

   A. $\left\{0, \dfrac{5}{4}\right\}$

   B. $\{0, 15\}$

   C. $\left\{0, \dfrac{15}{2}\right\}$

   D. $\left\{\dfrac{15}{2}\right\}$

   E. $\left\{0, \dfrac{15}{4}\right\}$

2. What are the solutions of $4x^3 = 25x$?

   A. $\left\{0, \dfrac{25}{4}\right\}$

   B. $\left\{0, \dfrac{5}{2}, \dfrac{-5}{2}\right\}$

   C. $\left\{0, \dfrac{5}{2}, 5\right\}$

   D. $\left\{0, \dfrac{5}{2}\right\}$

   E. $\left\{0, \dfrac{-5}{2}\right\}$

3. What are the solutions of $x^5 + 5x^4 + 4x^3 = 0$?

    A. $\{0, -2, -4\}$

    B. $\{-1, -4\}$

    C. $\{0, -4\}$

    D. $\{0, -3, -4\}$

    E. $\{0, -1, -4\}$

4. What is the largest solution of $x^4 + 5x^3 + 2x^2 = 0$?

    A. $\dfrac{5 + \sqrt{17}}{2}$

    B. $\dfrac{-5 - \sqrt{17}}{2}$

    C. $\dfrac{-5 + \sqrt{21}}{2}$

    D. $\dfrac{5 - \sqrt{17}}{2}$

    E. $\dfrac{-5 + \sqrt{17}}{2}$

5. What are the solutions of $x^5 + x^3 - 12x = 0$?

    A. $\{0, \sqrt{3}, -\sqrt{3}, 2, -2\}$

    B. $\{0, \sqrt{3}, -\sqrt{3}, 2i, -2i\}$

    C. $\{0, 3, -3, 2, -2\}$

    D. $\{0, \sqrt{2}, -\sqrt{2}, 3i, -3i\}$

    E. $\{0, 3, -3, 2i, -2i\}$

6. If 3 is a solution of $x^3 + 8x^2 - 29x - 12 = 0$, what are the other 2 solutions?

    A. $\dfrac{-11 \pm \sqrt{105}}{2}$

    B. $\dfrac{-11 \pm \sqrt{107}}{2}$

    C. $\dfrac{-11 \pm \sqrt{111}}{2}$

    D. $\dfrac{-11 \pm \sqrt{113}}{2}$

    E. $\dfrac{-11 \pm \sqrt{109}}{2}$

Solutions

1. (C) $4x^5 - 30x^4 = 0 \Rightarrow x^4(4x - 30) = 0 \Rightarrow x = 0$ or $x = \dfrac{15}{2}$

2. (B) $4x^3 - 25x = 0 \Rightarrow x(4x^2 - 25) = 0 \Rightarrow x(2x - 5)(2x + 5) = 0 \Rightarrow x = 0, \dfrac{5}{2}, \dfrac{-5}{2}$

3. (E) $x^3(x^2 + 5x + 4) = x^3(x + 4)(x + 1) = 0 \Rightarrow$ So $x = 0, -1, -4$

4. (E) $x^2(x^2 + 5x + 2) = 0 \Rightarrow \dfrac{-5 \pm \sqrt{25 - 8}}{2} \Rightarrow \dfrac{-5 \pm \sqrt{17}}{2}$

5. (B) $x(x^4 + x^2 - 12) = x(x^2 + 4)(x^2 - 3) = 0 \Rightarrow x = 0$ or $x^2 = -4$ or $x^2 = 3 \Rightarrow x = 0, \sqrt{3}, -\sqrt{3}, 2i, -2i$

6. (A)

$$
\begin{array}{r|rrrr}
3 & 1 & 8 & -29 & -12 \\
  &   & 3 & 33 & 12 \\
\hline
  & 1 & 11 & 4 & 0
\end{array}
$$

So $x^2 + 11x + 4 = 0 \Rightarrow x = \dfrac{-11 \pm \sqrt{121 - 16}}{2} = \dfrac{-11 \pm \sqrt{105}}{2}$

Factor Polynomial

You should know the difference of squares factorization formula,

$$a^2 - b^2 = (a + b)(a - b)$$

This may need to be applied twice. It is also useful for understanding irrational conjugates problems. It is helpful to know the cube factorization formulas, although the formula may be provided or the problem accomplished in other ways,

$$a^3 + b^3 = (a + b)(a^2 - ab + b^2)$$

$$a^3 - b^3 = (a - b)(a^2 + ab + b^2)$$

You can verify these formulas work by foiling out.

1. What is $x^4 - 16$ in fully factored form over reals?

    A. $(x^2 + 4)(x + 2)(x - 2)$

    B. $(x + 2)^2(x - 2)^2$

    C. $(x^2 + 4)(x^2 - 4)$

    D. $(x + 2i)(x - 2i)(x + 2)(x - 2)$

    E. $(x^2 + 1)(x + 4)(x - 4)$

2. What is a factorization of $8x^3 - 27$ over reals?

    A. $(2x + 3)(4x^2 - 6x + 9)$

    B. $(2x - 3)(4x^2 + 6x + 9)$

    C. $(2x - 3)(4x^2 - 6x + 9)$

    D. $(2x - 3)(4x^2 + 9)$

    E. $(2x + 3)(4x^2 + 9)$

Solutions

1. (A) $= (x^2 + 4)(x^2 - 4) = (x^2 + 4)(x + 2)(x - 2)$, using the difference of squares factorization formula twice.

2. (B) $a^3 - b^3 = (a - b)(a^2 + ab + b^2) \Rightarrow$ Substituting $a = 2x$ and $b = 3 \Rightarrow (2x - 3)(4x^2 + 6x + 9)$

Polynomial from Solutions

If a polynomial has solutions 2, 4, 11, 23 and 32, its equation is

$$(x - 2)(x - 4)(x - 11)(x - 23)(x - 32) = 0$$

1. What is a third degree equation with $x = 5$ as its only solution?

   A. $x^3 - 15x^2 + 90x - 125$

   B. $x^3 - 15x^2 + 75x - 125$

   C. $x^3 - 15x^2 + 80x - 125$

   D. $x^3 - 15x^2 + 70x - 125$

   E. $x^3 - 15x^2 + 100x - 125$

2. What polynomial equation in standard form has solutions -2, 1, and 5?

   A. $x^3 - 3x^2 - 8x + 10$

   B. $x^3 - 4x^2 - 5x + 10$

   C. $x^3 - 4x^2 - 8x + 10$

   D. $x^3 + 2x^2 - 8x + 10$

   E. $x^3 - 4x^2 - 7x + 10$

3. What the coefficient of x^3 in the 4th degree polynomial has solutions $2+\sqrt{5}$ and $3+\sqrt{5}$?

   A. 27

   B. -10

   C. 10

   D. 15

   E. -27

Solutions

1. (B) $(x-5)(x-5)(x-5) = (x^2 - 10x + 25)(x-5)$

   $\Rightarrow x^3 - 5x^2 - 10x^2 + 50x + 25x - 125 = x^3 - 15x^2 + 75x - 125.$

   Or using the binomial theorem,

   $_3C_0 x^3 + _3C_1 x^2(-5) + _3C_2 x(-5)^2 + _3C_3(-5)^3 = x^3 - 15x^2 + 75x - 125$

2. (E) $(x-5)(x+2)(x-1) = (x^2 - 3x - 10)(x-1)$

   $\Rightarrow x^3 - 3x^2 - 10x - x^2 + 3x + 10 = x^3 - 4x^2 - 7x + 10$

3. (B) $(x-2-\sqrt{5})(x-2+\sqrt{5})(x-3-\sqrt{5})(x-3+\sqrt{5}) = (x^2 - 4x - 1)(x^2 - 6x + 4)$

   $\Rightarrow x^4 - 6x^3 + 4x^2 - 4x^3 + 24x^2 - 16x - x^2 + 6x - 4 = x^4 - 10x^3 + 27x^2 - 10x - 4$

Find Polynomial Coefficients

It is likely that a problem on the test will ask for the constant term, but more difficult problems are included because they might occur and build relevant skills.

If $x + 5$ is a factor of $x^3 + 2x^2 + 3x + k$, what is k?

You plug in the root, -5,

$$(-5)^3 + 2 \cdot (-5)^2 + 3(-5) + k = 0 \Rightarrow -125 + 50 - 15 + k = 0 \Rightarrow k = 90$$

1. If $x + 2$ is a factor of $x^3 + 2x^2 + 3x + k$, what is k?

   A. 4

   B. 8

   C. 10

   D. -4

   E. 6

2. What is the value of v such that $x + 3$ is a factor of $x^3 + 3x^2 + vx - 12$?

   A. 4

   B. 2

   C. -4

   D. -2

   E. -1

3. What is the value of v such that $x - 2$ is a factor of $x^3 + vx^2 - 4x - 8$?

   A. 8

   B. 6

   C. 4

   D. 3

   E. 2

4. If -3 is a solution of $kx^3 + kx^2 + 2x - 5 = 0$, what is k?

   A. $\dfrac{-5}{9}$

   B. $\dfrac{11}{18}$

   C. $\dfrac{-13}{18}$

   D. $\dfrac{-11}{18}$

   E. $\dfrac{17}{18}$

Solutions

1. (E) $(-2)^3 + 2 \cdot (-2)^2 + 3 \cdot (-2) + k = 0 \Rightarrow -8 + 8 - 6 + k = 0 \Rightarrow k = 6$

2. (C) $(-3)^3 + 3 \cdot (-3)^2 - 3v - 12 = 0 \Rightarrow -27 + 27 - 3v - 12 = 0 \Rightarrow 3v = -12 \Rightarrow v = -4$

3. (E) $2^3 + v \cdot 2^2 - 4 \cdot 2 - 8 = 0 \Rightarrow 8 + 4v - 8 - 8 = 0 \Rightarrow v = 2$

4. (D) $k \cdot (-3)^3 + k \cdot (-3)^2 + 2 \cdot (-3) - 5 = 0 \Rightarrow -18k = 11 \Rightarrow k = \dfrac{-11}{18}$

Chapter XXXVII

Domain

There are certain things that cause restrictions on the domain. You cannot divide by 0, cannot take the square root of a negative number and cannot take the log of a negative number or 0.

1. What is the domain of $\dfrac{\sqrt{2-3x}}{\sqrt{x+4}}$?

   A. $\left(-4, \dfrac{-2}{3}\right)$

   B. $\left[-4, \dfrac{2}{3}\right]$

   C. $\left(-4, \dfrac{2}{3}\right]$

   D. $\left(-4, \dfrac{3}{2}\right)$

   E. $\left(-4, \dfrac{2}{3}\right)$

2. What is the domain of $y = \sqrt{25-x^2}$?

   A. $(-\infty, -5] \cup [5, \infty)$

   B. $(-\infty, -10] \cup [10, \infty)$

   C. $(-\infty, -25] \cup [25, \infty)$

   D. $(-5, 5)$

   E. $[-5, 5]$

3. What is NOT in the domain of $f(x) = \dfrac{1}{|2x+3|}$?

   A. $\left\{\dfrac{-3}{2}\right\}$

   B. $\left\{\dfrac{-3}{2}, \dfrac{3}{2}\right\}$

   C. $\left\{\dfrac{-3}{2}, \dfrac{1}{2}\right\}$

   D. $\left\{\dfrac{-3}{2}, 0, \dfrac{3}{2}\right\}$

   E. $\left\{\dfrac{3}{2}\right\}$

4. What is NOT in the domain of $f(x) = \dfrac{17}{|3x+4| - 2}$?

   A. $\left\{\dfrac{-8}{3}, -2\right\}$

   B. $\left\{\dfrac{-2}{3}, -4\right\}$

   C. $\left\{\dfrac{2}{3}, -2\right\}$

   D. $\left\{\dfrac{-4}{3}, -2\right\}$

   E. $\left\{\dfrac{-2}{3}, -2\right\}$

5. What is the domain of $f(x) = \sqrt{x+5} + \sqrt{3-x}$?

   A. $[-5, \infty)$
   B. $(-5, 3]$
   C. $[5, 5]$
   D. $(-5, 3)$
   E. $[-5, 3]$

6. If a and b are real, what value(s) are NOT in the domain of $y = \dfrac{x+a}{x - b^2}$?

   A. $\{b\}$
   B. $\{b, -b, -a\}$
   C. $\{b, -b\}$
   D. $\{-b, 0\}$
   E. $\{-a, -b\}$

7. What numbers are NOT in the domain of $f(x) = \dfrac{3}{5 - |2x|}$?

    A. $\dfrac{5}{2}$ and $\dfrac{-5}{2}$

    B. $\dfrac{5}{2}$ and $\dfrac{-2}{5}$

    C. $\dfrac{5}{2}$

    D. $\dfrac{5}{2}$ and -5

    E. 5 and -5

8. What is the domain of $\log(x^2 + 2x - 15)$?

    A. $-3 < x < 5$

    B. $x \leq -3$ or $x \geq 5$

    C. $x < -3$ or $x > 5$

    D. $-3 \leq x \leq 5$

    E. $x < -5$ or $x > 3$

9. Assuming a, b, and c are real, for what values is $\dfrac{(x + a)(x^2 - b)}{x^2 - c}$ undefined?

    A. $\pm\sqrt{c}$ and $-a$

    B. $\pm\sqrt{c}$ and $\pm\sqrt{b}$ and $-a$

    C. $\sqrt{c}$

    D. $\pm\sqrt{c}$

    E. It is defined everywhere

10. If $f(x) = \dfrac{x + 3}{(x + 1)(x + 6)}$, what numbers are NOT in the domain of $f(x - 4)$?

    A. -1 and -6

    B. -3, -1 and -6

    C. 1 and 6

    D. -2 and 3

    E. 2 and -3

11. What is the domain of $\sqrt{(x-5)^7}$?

    A. $[5, \infty)$

    B. $[125, \infty)$

    C. $(5, \infty)$

    D. $(-\infty, 5]$

    E. $[25, \infty)$

12. What is the domain of $\sqrt{x^3 - 8}$?

    A. $(-\infty, \infty)$

    B. $(2, \infty)$

    C. $[2, 4]$

    D. $[2, \infty)$

    E. $(-\infty, -2] \cup [2, \infty)$

Solutions

1. (C) $2 - 3x \geq 0 \Rightarrow \dfrac{2}{3} \geq x$ and $x + 4 > 0 \Rightarrow x > -4 \Rightarrow \left(-4, \dfrac{2}{3}\right]$

   Note it is a $>$ condition in the denominator because you can't divide by 0

2. (E) $25 - x^2 = 0 \Rightarrow x = \pm 5 \Rightarrow$ The expression is nonnegative for $x \geq -5$ or $x \leq 5$

3. (A) $|2x + 3| = 0 \Rightarrow 2x + 3 = 0 \Rightarrow x = \dfrac{-3}{2}$ (Note there is only one solution).

4. (E) $3x + 4 - 2 = 0 \Rightarrow -3x - 4 - 2 = 0 \Rightarrow 3x = -2 \Rightarrow x = \dfrac{-2}{3}$ and $3x = -6 \Rightarrow$ $x = -2$

5. (E) $x + 5 \geq 0 \Rightarrow x \geq -5$ and $3 - x \geq 0 \Rightarrow 3 \geq x \Rightarrow [-5, 3]$

6. (C) $x - b^2 = 0 \Rightarrow x = b^2 \Rightarrow x = \pm b$

7. (A) $5 - |2x| = 0 \Rightarrow |2x| = 5 \Rightarrow 2x = 5$ or $2x = -5 \Rightarrow \dfrac{5}{2}$ or $\dfrac{-5}{2}$

8. (E) $x^2 + 2x - 15 > 0 \Rightarrow (x + 5)(x - 3) > 0 \Rightarrow x < -5$ or $x > 3$

9. (D) $x^2 - c = 0 \Rightarrow x = \pm\sqrt{c}$

10. (D) $f(x - 4) = \dfrac{x - 1}{(x - 3)(x + 2)} \Rightarrow x - 3 = 0$ or $x + 2 = 0 \Rightarrow x = 3$ or -2

    So the domain is $(-\infty, -2) \cup (-2, 3) \cup (3, \infty)$

11. (A) $x - 5 \geq 0 \Rightarrow x \geq 5$

12. (D) $x^3 - 8 \geq 0 \Rightarrow x^3 \geq 8 \Rightarrow x \geq 2$

Chapter XXXVIII

Variation

These problems are solved by finding the constant k.

y is directly proportional to x and $y = 8$ when $x = 3$. What does $y =$ when x is 4?

$$y = kx \Rightarrow 8 = k \cdot 3 \Rightarrow k = \frac{8}{3} \Rightarrow y = \frac{8x}{3} \Rightarrow y = \frac{32}{3}$$

y is directly proportional to the cube of x and $y = 8$ when $x = 3$. What does $y =$ when x is 4?

$$y = kx^3 \Rightarrow 8 = k \cdot 3^3 \Rightarrow k = \frac{8}{27} \Rightarrow y = \frac{8x^3}{27} \Rightarrow y = 8 \cdot \frac{64}{27} = \frac{512}{27}$$

1. y is directly proportional to x and $y = 5$ when $x = 2$, what does y equal when $x = 5$?

    A. 10
    B. 12.5
    C. 15
    D. 17.5
    E. 12

2. y varies inversely as x. When $x = 2$, $y = 5$. When $x = 5$, what does $y =$?

    A. 1.8
    B. 1.5
    C. 2.5
    D. 2
    E. 1.7

3. y varies directly as the square of x. When $x = 2$, $y = 5$. When $x = 5$, what does $y =$?

    A. 33.25
    B. 32.25
    C. 34.25
    D. 31.25
    E. 30.25

4. y is inversely proportional to the square of x. If $y = 5$ when $x = 2$, what does y equal when x is 5?

A. $\dfrac{3}{125}$

B. $\dfrac{6}{125}$

C. $\dfrac{4}{5}$

D. $\dfrac{4}{25}$

E. $\dfrac{1}{25}$

5. What is an equation in which y varies directly with the square of x, inversely with the square root of v and inversely with the cube of w?

A. $y = k\dfrac{x^2 w^3}{\sqrt{v}}$

B. $y = k\dfrac{x^2}{v \cdot w^3}$

C. $y = k\dfrac{x^2}{\sqrt{v} \cdot w^2}$

D. $y = k\dfrac{x^2}{\sqrt{v} \cdot w^3}$

E. $y = k\dfrac{x^2}{\sqrt{v^3} \cdot w^3}$

Solutions

1. (B) $y = kx \Rightarrow 5 = k \cdot 2 \Rightarrow k = 2.5 \Rightarrow y = 2.5x \Rightarrow y = 2.5 \cdot 5 = 12.5$

2. (D) $y = \dfrac{k}{x} \Rightarrow 5 = \dfrac{k}{2} \Rightarrow k = 10 \Rightarrow y = \dfrac{10}{x} \Rightarrow y = \dfrac{10}{5} \Rightarrow y = 2$

3. (D) $y = kx^2 \Rightarrow 5 = k \cdot 2^2 \Rightarrow k = \dfrac{5}{4} \Rightarrow y = \dfrac{5x^2}{4} \Rightarrow y = \dfrac{5 \cdot 5^2}{4} = \dfrac{125}{4} = 31.25$

4. (C) $y = \dfrac{k}{x^2} \Rightarrow 5 = \dfrac{k}{4} \Rightarrow k = 20 \Rightarrow$ So $y = \dfrac{20}{x^2} \Rightarrow \dfrac{20}{25} = \dfrac{4}{5}$

5. (D) $y = k\dfrac{x^2}{\sqrt{v} \cdot w^3}$

Chapter XXXIX

Complex Fractions

With Numbers

1. What is $\dfrac{1}{1+\dfrac{1}{1+\dfrac{1}{3}}}$ simplified?

   A. $\dfrac{7}{4}$

   B. $\dfrac{4}{3}$

   C. $\dfrac{7}{11}$

   D. $\dfrac{4}{7}$

   E. $\dfrac{4}{9}$

2. What is $\dfrac{1}{1+\dfrac{1}{1+\dfrac{3}{8}}}$?

    A. $\dfrac{11}{19}$

    B. $\dfrac{8}{11}$

    C. $\dfrac{19}{11}$

    D. $\dfrac{11}{8}$

    E. $\dfrac{19}{30}$

Answer Key: $1D, 2A$

Solutions

1. (D) $\dfrac{1}{1+\dfrac{1}{\frac{4}{3}}} = \dfrac{1}{1+\dfrac{3}{4}} = \dfrac{1}{\frac{7}{4}} = \dfrac{4}{7}$

2. (A) $\dfrac{1}{1+\dfrac{1}{\frac{11}{8}}} = \dfrac{1}{1+\dfrac{8}{11}} = \dfrac{1}{\frac{19}{11}} = \dfrac{11}{19}$

With Variables

1. What is the numerator of $\dfrac{1}{\dfrac{1}{x}+\dfrac{1}{x+3}}$?

   A. $x^2 + 4x + 2$

   B. $x^2 + 4x + 5$

   C. $x^2 + 4x + 3$

   D. $x^2 + 3x$

   E. $x^2 + 4x + 1$

2. What is $\dfrac{c}{d} + \dfrac{d}{c}$ as one fraction?

   A. $\dfrac{c^2 + d^2}{c + d}$

   B. $\dfrac{c^2 + d^2}{cd}$

   C. $\dfrac{c + d}{cd}$

   D. $\dfrac{c^2 + d^2}{c^2 d^2}$

   E. $c^2 + d^2$

3. $\dfrac{1}{x + y} + \dfrac{1}{x - y} = \ ?$

   A. $\dfrac{x + 1}{x^2 - y^2}$

   B. $\dfrac{2x + 1}{x^2 - y^2}$

   C. $\dfrac{x}{x^2 - y^2}$

   D. $\dfrac{2x + y}{x^2 - y^2}$

   E. $\dfrac{2x}{x^2 - y^2}$

4. What is $\dfrac{2+\dfrac{1}{x}}{5+\dfrac{1}{x}}$?

   A. $\dfrac{3x+1}{5x+1}$

   B. $\dfrac{x+1}{5x+1}$

   C. $\dfrac{2x+1}{5x+1}$

   D. $\dfrac{2x+3}{5x+1}$

   E. $\dfrac{4x+3}{5x+1}$

5. If $f(x) = \dfrac{x+3}{x}$, what is $f\left(\dfrac{1}{x}\right)$?

   A. $\dfrac{1+3x}{x}$

   B. $\dfrac{1+4x}{x}$

   C. $1+4x$

   D. $1+3x$

   E. $2+3x$

6. What is the numerator of $\dfrac{\dfrac{1}{2}+\dfrac{x}{3}}{\dfrac{1}{4}+\dfrac{x}{5}}$ simplified?

   A. $20x+30$

   B. $2x+3$

   C. $4x+6$

   D. $20x+32$

   E. $20x+36$

7. What is $\dfrac{1}{1+\dfrac{1}{1+\dfrac{1}{x}}}$?

  A. $\dfrac{x+2}{2x+1}$

  B. $\dfrac{x+1}{2x+1}$

  C. $\dfrac{x+3}{2x+1}$

  D. $\dfrac{x+4}{2x+1}$

  E. $\dfrac{x+5}{2x+1}$

8. What is $\dfrac{\dfrac{1}{x}-\dfrac{1}{y}}{\dfrac{1}{x}+\dfrac{1}{y}}$?

  A. $\dfrac{x-y}{y+x}$

  B. $\dfrac{y}{y+x}$

  C. $\dfrac{x}{y+x}$

  D. $\dfrac{y-x}{y+x}$

  E. $\dfrac{3y-x}{y+x}$

Solutions

1. (D) $\dfrac{\dfrac{1}{x+3+x}}{x(x+3)} = \dfrac{x^2+3x}{2x+3}$

2. (B) $\dfrac{c^2+d^2}{cd}$

3. (E) $\dfrac{x-y+x+y}{(x+y)(x-y)} = \dfrac{2x}{x^2-y^2}$

4. (C) $\dfrac{\dfrac{2x+1}{x}}{\dfrac{5x+1}{x}} = \dfrac{2x+1}{5x+1}$

5. (D) $\dfrac{\dfrac{1}{x}+3}{\dfrac{1}{x}} = \dfrac{\dfrac{1+3x}{x}}{\dfrac{1}{x}} = 1+3x$

6. (A) $\dfrac{\dfrac{3+2x}{6}}{\dfrac{5+4x}{20}} = \dfrac{20(3+2x)}{6(4x+5)} = \dfrac{20x+30}{12x+15}$

7. (B) $\dfrac{1}{1+\dfrac{1}{\dfrac{x+1}{x}}} = \dfrac{1}{1+\dfrac{x}{x+1}} = \dfrac{1}{\dfrac{2x+1}{x+1}} = \dfrac{x+1}{2x+1}$

8. (D) $\dfrac{\dfrac{y-x}{xy}}{\dfrac{y+x}{xy}} = \dfrac{y-x}{y+x}$

253

Chapter XL

Fractions with Exponentials

These are very challenging problems, but they can be solved by finding the least common denominator. What is $\dfrac{1}{3^{27}} + \dfrac{5}{3^{29}}$? The least common denominator is 3^{29}, so $\dfrac{9}{3^{29}} + \dfrac{5}{3^{29}} = \dfrac{14}{3^{29}}$.

1. What fraction is equal to $\dfrac{1}{3^{20}} + \dfrac{1}{3^{21}}$?

    A. $\dfrac{2}{3^{21}}$

    B. $\dfrac{4}{3^{21}}$

    C. $\dfrac{1}{3^{21}}$

    D. $\dfrac{5}{3^{21}}$

    E. $\dfrac{8}{3^{21}}$

2. What is $\dfrac{1}{7^{20}} - \dfrac{1}{7^{21}}$?

A. $\dfrac{4}{7^{21}}$

B. $\dfrac{5}{7^{21}}$

C. $\dfrac{6}{7^{21}}$

D. $\dfrac{8}{7^{21}}$

E. $\dfrac{5}{7^{22}}$

3. What is the average of $\dfrac{1}{2^{30}}$ and $\dfrac{1}{2^{32}}$?

A. $\dfrac{5}{2^{32}}$

B. $\dfrac{3}{2^{32}}$

C. $\dfrac{5}{2^{31}}$

D. $\dfrac{7}{2^{33}}$

E. $\dfrac{5}{2^{33}}$

Answer Key: $1B, 2C, 3E$

Solutions

1. (B) $\dfrac{3}{3^{21}} + \dfrac{1}{3^{21}} = \dfrac{4}{3^{21}}$

2. (C) $\dfrac{7}{7^{21}} - \dfrac{1}{7^{21}} = \dfrac{6}{7^{21}}$

3. (E) $\dfrac{\dfrac{4}{2^{32}} + \dfrac{1}{2^{32}}}{2} = \dfrac{5}{2^{33}}$

Chapter XLI

Trigonometry

Numeric Value from Another

1. If $\tan x = \sqrt{2}, 0 < x < 90$, what is $\cos x$?

    A. $\dfrac{\sqrt{5}}{5}$

    B. $\dfrac{2}{5}$

    C. $\dfrac{4}{7}$

    D. $\dfrac{\sqrt{3}}{3}$

    E. $\dfrac{2\sqrt{3}}{3}$

2. If $\tan^2 x = 10$, what does $\sec^2 x = ?$

    A. 9

    B. 11

    C. $8 - \sqrt{10}$

    D. 3

    E. $\sqrt{11}$

3. If $\sin x = \dfrac{2}{3}$, what is $\sec^2 x - \tan^2 x$?

A. $\sin x$

B. $\cos x$

C. $\cos 2x$

D. $-\cos 2x$

E. 1

4. $0 < x < 90$ and $\tan x = \dfrac{5}{2}$. What is $\sin x + \cos x$?

A. $\dfrac{7}{\sqrt{29}}$

B. $\dfrac{2}{\sqrt{29}}$

C. $\dfrac{5}{\sqrt{29}}$

D. $\dfrac{-7}{\sqrt{29}}$

E. $\dfrac{-5}{\sqrt{29}}$

5. $\tan x = \dfrac{-12}{5}$. What is $\sin x \cos x$?

A. $\dfrac{60}{169}$

B. $\dfrac{-60}{169}$

C. $\dfrac{-5}{13}$

D. $\dfrac{5}{13}$

E. $\dfrac{12}{13}$

6. If $\sin x = \dfrac{3}{11}$, what is $\sec^2 x$?

   A. $\dfrac{121}{56}$

   B. $\dfrac{121}{100}$

   C. $\dfrac{121}{112}$

   D. $\dfrac{121}{116}$

   E. $\dfrac{11}{10}$

7. If $\sin x = \dfrac{\sqrt{11}}{5}$ and $90 < x < 180$, what is $\tan x$?

   A. $\dfrac{\sqrt{154}}{14}$

   B. $\dfrac{-\sqrt{151}}{14}$

   C. $\dfrac{\sqrt{151}}{14}$

   D. $\dfrac{-\sqrt{155}}{14}$

   E. $\dfrac{-\sqrt{154}}{14}$

8. If $\sin x = \dfrac{1}{5}$, what is $\tan^2 x$?

A. $\dfrac{1}{24}$

B. $\dfrac{-1}{24}$

C. $\dfrac{7}{24}$

D. $\dfrac{7}{25}$

E. $\dfrac{3}{24}$

9. If $\cos x = \dfrac{3}{4}$, what is $\cos 2x$?

A. $\dfrac{-1}{8}$

B. $\dfrac{1}{4}$

C. $\dfrac{-1}{4}$

D. $\dfrac{1}{8}$

E. $\dfrac{3}{16}$

Answer Key: $1D, 2B, 3E, 4A, 5B, 6C, 7E, 8A, 9D$

Solutions

1. (D) Set opposite $= \sqrt{2}$ and adjacent $= 1$, so,

   hypotenuse $= \sqrt{((\sqrt{2})^2 + 1^2} = \sqrt{3}$, $\cos = \dfrac{\text{adjacent}}{\text{hypotenuse}} = \dfrac{1}{\sqrt{3}} = \dfrac{\sqrt{3}}{3}$

2. (B) $\sec^2 x = \tan^2 x + 1$, $\sec^2 x = 11$. You can also find the answer algebraically or using $\tan^{-1}$ etc. with your calculator.

3. (E) $\sec^2 - \tan^2$ is always 1. That is a Pythagorean identity.

4. (A) $\sin x = \dfrac{5}{\sqrt{29}}$, $\cos x = \dfrac{2}{\sqrt{29}}$, $\dfrac{5}{\sqrt{29}} + \dfrac{2}{\sqrt{29}} = \dfrac{7}{\sqrt{29}}$

5. (B) $\sqrt{(-12x)^2 + (5x)^2} = 13$, $\sin x = \pm\dfrac{12}{13}$, $\cos x = \pm\dfrac{5}{13}$, $\sin x \cos x = \dfrac{-60}{169}$ (if $\sin x / \cos x$ is negative, so must $\sin x \cos x$ be)

6. (C) $\sin^2 x + \cos^2 x = 1$, $\dfrac{9}{121} + \cos^2 x = 1$, $\cos^2 x = \dfrac{112}{121}$, $\sec^2 x = \dfrac{121}{112}$

7. (E) $\cos^2 x + \sin^2 x = 1$, $\cos^2 x + \dfrac{11}{25} = 1$, $\cos^2 x = \dfrac{14}{25}$, $\cos x = \dfrac{-\sqrt{14}}{5}$,

   $\tan x = \dfrac{\dfrac{\sqrt{11}}{5}}{\dfrac{-\sqrt{14}}{5}} = \dfrac{-\sqrt{11}}{\sqrt{14}} = \dfrac{-\sqrt{154}}{14}$. You can also use $\cos\left(180 - \sin^{-1}\left(\dfrac{\sqrt{11}}{5}\right)\right)$ with your calculator

8. (A) $\cos^2 + \left(\dfrac{1}{5}\right)^2 = 1$, $\cos x = \pm\dfrac{\sqrt{24}}{5}$, $\tan x = \dfrac{1}{5} \pm \dfrac{\sqrt{24}}{5} = \pm\dfrac{1}{\sqrt{24}}$, so $\tan^2 x = \dfrac{1}{24}$. You could also take $\tan^2\left(\sin^{-1}\left(\dfrac{1}{5}\right)\right)$

9. (D) $\sin x = \pm\dfrac{\sqrt{7}}{4}$, $\cos 2x = \cos^2 x - \sin^2 x = \left(\dfrac{3}{4}\right)^2 - \left(\pm\dfrac{\sqrt{7}}{4}\right)^2 = \dfrac{9}{16} - \dfrac{7}{16} = \dfrac{1}{8}$. You can also use $\cos^{-1}$ with your calculator, double the value and take cos of that, or $\cos 2x = 2\cos^2 x - 1 = 2\left(\dfrac{3}{4}\right)^2 - 1 = 2 \cdot \dfrac{9}{16} - 1 = \dfrac{1}{8}$

Variable Value from Another

1. If $\tan x = \sqrt{a}$ and $0 < x < \dfrac{\pi}{2}$, what is $\cos x$?

    A. $\dfrac{1}{\sqrt{a-1}}$

    B. $\dfrac{1}{\sqrt{a^2+1}}$

    C. $\dfrac{1}{\sqrt{a+1}}$

    D. $\dfrac{1}{a+1}$

    E. $\dfrac{1}{a-1}$

2. If $\cos x = 3a$, what is $\tan x$?

    A. $\dfrac{1-9a^2}{3a}$

    B. $\dfrac{\sqrt{1-9a^2}}{3a}$

    C. $\dfrac{\sqrt{1-9a^2}}{9a^2}$

    D. $\dfrac{\sqrt{1-3a^2}}{3a}$

    E. $\dfrac{\sqrt{4-9a^2}}{3a}$

3. If $\sin x = a$, what does $\sin 2x = $?

    A. $\pm 4a\sqrt{1-4a^2}$

    B. $\pm 4a\sqrt{1-a^2}$

    C. $\pm 6a\sqrt{1-a^2}$

    D. $\pm a\sqrt{1-a^2}$

    E. $\pm 2a\sqrt{1-a^2}$

264

4. $\sin x = a$ and $0 < x < 90$. What is $\sec x \tan x$?

A. $\dfrac{a}{1 - a^2}$

B. $\dfrac{a^2}{1 - a^2}$

C. $\dfrac{a}{1 - a}$

D. $\dfrac{a}{\sqrt{1 - a^2}}$

E. $\dfrac{1}{1 - a^2}$

Answer Key: $1C, 2B, 3E, 4A$

Solutions

1. (C) $\sec^2 = 1 + \tan^2, \sec^2 x = 1 + (\sqrt{a})^2, \sec x = \sqrt{1+a}, \cos x = \dfrac{1}{\sqrt{a+1}}$

2. (B) $\cos^2 x + \sin^2 x = 1, 9a^2 + \sin^2 x = 1, \sin x = \sqrt{1 - 9a^2},$

   $\tan x = \dfrac{\sin x}{\cos x} = \dfrac{\sqrt{1 - 9a^2}}{3a}$

3. (E) $\cos x = \pm\sqrt{1 - a^2}, \sin 2x = 2\sin x \cos x = \pm 2a\sqrt{1 - a^2}$

4. (A) $\cos x = \sqrt{1 - a^2}$ so $\tan x = \dfrac{a}{\sqrt{1 - a^2}}$ and $\sec x = \dfrac{1}{\sqrt{1 - a^2}}$, so

   $\sec x \tan x = \dfrac{a}{1 - a^2}$

Law of Sines

The law of sines is $\dfrac{a}{\sin A} = \dfrac{b}{\sin B} = \dfrac{c}{\sin C}$. You can use it to solve a triangle given an angle and opposite side and one other piece of information. They may ask you to find an expression rather than the answer, so you may not have to memorize the formula or get the answer. There are cases with 2 triangles or no triangles, but to my knowledge those have not appeared on the exam.

1. In triangle $\triangle ABC$, angle $A = 2°$, angle $B = 70°$, $BC = 5$, what is AB?

   A. 56

   B. 76

   C. 96

   D. 116

   E. 136

2. The interior angles of a triangle are of the ratio of $2 : 3 : 4$. What is the ratio of the longest side to the shortest side?

   A. $1.33 : 1$

   B. $1.43 : 1$

   C. $1.53 : 1$

   D. $1.38 : 1$

   E. $1.48 : 1$

Solutions

1. (E) Angle $C = 108°$, $\dfrac{AB}{\sin 108°} = \dfrac{5}{\sin 2°}$, $AB \approx 136.3$

2. (C) The angles are $40°, 60°$, and $80°$. By the law of sines, $\dfrac{\sin 80°}{\sin 40°} \approx 1.53$

Law of Cosines

You use the law of cosines to solve a general triangle when the law of sines doesn't work, but you have 3 pieces of information. That is, if you have all 3 sides or 2 sides and an included angle. You can use the law of cosines either to solve for an angle or the missing side. The law of cosines is $c^2 = a^2 + b^2 - 2ab\cos C$. You will not have to memorize the formula. You will either be given the formula or just need to find the correct expression to solve a problem.

1. In triangle $\triangle ABC$, angle $A = 60°$, $AB = 4$ and $AC = 5$, what is BC?

   A. 4.6

   B. 4.5

   C. 4.4

   D. 4.3

   E. 4.2

2. If it is 11 miles from Chapel Hill to Durham, 31 miles from Chapel Hill to Raleigh and 37 miles from Durham to Raleigh, what expression gives the angle between the path from Chapel Hill to Durham and the path from Chapel Hill to Raleigh?

   A. $\arccos \dfrac{11^2 - 31^2 - 37^2}{2 \cdot 37 \cdot 31}$

   B. $\arccos \dfrac{37^2 - 31^2 - 11^2}{2 \cdot 11 \cdot 31}$

   C. $\arccos \dfrac{31^2 - 37^2 - 11^2}{2 \cdot 11 \cdot 37}$

   D. $\arccos \dfrac{37^2 - 31^2 + 11^2}{2 \cdot 11 \cdot 31}$

   E. $\arccos \dfrac{37^2 - 31^2 - 11^2}{11 \cdot 31}$

3. If the distance from Paris to Berlin is 878 kilometers, from Paris to Vienna is 1034 kilometers, and from Berlin to Vienna is 674 kilometers, what is the angle in to the nearest degree at Paris between the direct path to Berlin and the direct path to Vienna?

    A. 46°

    B. 44°

    C. 42°

    D. 40°

    E. 38°

4. For triangle $\triangle ABC$, the coordinates of A are $(1, 2)$, $B(4, 7)$ and $C(3, 5)$. What is angle C to the nearest degree?

    A. 173

    B. 91

    C. 93

    D. 97

    E. 103

Solutions

1. (A) We have 2 sides and an included angle, so use the law of cosines, $c^2 = a^2 + b^2 - 2ab \cos C$,
   $c^2 = 16 + 25 - 40 \cdot \dfrac{1}{2} = 21$, $c = \sqrt{21} \approx 4.58$

2. (B) By the law of cosines, $\arccos \dfrac{37^2 - 31^2 - 11^2}{2 \cdot 11 \cdot 31}$

3. (D) $674^2 = 1034^2 + 878^2 - 2 \cdot 1034 \cdot 878 \cos x$,
   $454276 = 1069196 + 770884 - 1815704 \cos x$,
   $0.7635 = \cos x, x \approx 40°$

4. (A) $AB = \sqrt{(4-1)^2 + (7-2)^2} = \sqrt{34}$,
   $BC = \sqrt{(7-5)^2 + (4-3)^2} = \sqrt{5}$,
   $AC = \sqrt{(5-2)^2 + (3-1)^2} = \sqrt{13}$,
   $(\sqrt{34})^2 = (\sqrt{5})^2 + (\sqrt{13})^2 - 2 \cdot \sqrt{5} \cdot \sqrt{13} \cdot \cos C$,
   $34 = 5 + 13 - 2\sqrt{65} \cos C, 16 = -2\sqrt{65} \cos C$,
   $\cos C = \dfrac{-8}{\sqrt{65}}, \cos^{-1}\left(\dfrac{-8}{\sqrt{65}}\right) \approx 173°$

Radians and Degrees

Radians to Degrees

To convert from radians to degrees, multiply by $\dfrac{180}{\pi}$, so
$$\frac{11\pi}{12} = \frac{11\pi}{12} \cdot \frac{180}{\pi} = 11 \cdot \frac{180}{12} = 165°.$$

1. $\dfrac{5\pi}{24}$ radians is how many degrees?

    A. 32.5

    B. 35

    C. 37.5

    D. 42.5

    E. 47.5

2. What is $\dfrac{-33\pi}{10}$ radians in degrees between 0 and 360?

    A. 63

    B. 126

    C. 202

    D. 234

    E. 252

3. What is $\dfrac{107\pi}{12}$ in degrees between 0 and 360?

    A. 15

    B. 145

    C. 165

    D. 195

    E. 345

4. What is $\dfrac{3a\pi}{b}$ radians in degrees?

A. $\dfrac{180a}{b}$

B. $\dfrac{360a}{b}$

C. $\dfrac{480a}{b}$

D. $\dfrac{540a}{b}$

E. $\dfrac{600a}{b}$

Answer Key: $1C, 2B, 3C, 4D$

Solutions

1. (C) $\dfrac{5\pi}{24} \cdot \dfrac{180}{\pi} = \dfrac{75}{2} = 37.5$

2. (B) $\dfrac{-33\pi}{10} + \dfrac{40\pi}{10} = \dfrac{7\pi}{10} \rightarrow \dfrac{7\pi}{10} \cdot \dfrac{180}{\pi} = 7 \cdot 18 = 126°$

3. (C) $\dfrac{107}{24} = 4$ remainder 11, so

   $\dfrac{107\pi}{12} - \dfrac{96\pi}{12} = \dfrac{11\pi}{12} \cdot \dfrac{180}{\pi} = 11 \cdot 15 = 165°$

4. (D) $\dfrac{3a\pi}{b} \cdot \dfrac{180}{\pi} = \dfrac{540a}{b}$

Degrees to Radians

To convert from degrees to radians, multiply by $\dfrac{\pi}{180}$, so
$126° = \dfrac{126\pi}{180}$ radians $= \dfrac{7\pi}{10}$ radians.

1. $102°$ is how many radians?

  A. $\dfrac{11\pi}{30}$

  B. $\dfrac{17\pi}{30}$

  C. $\dfrac{19\pi}{30}$

  D. $\dfrac{37\pi}{30}$

  E. $\dfrac{39\pi}{30}$

2. An angle has measure $23450°$. What angle in radians between 0 and 2π is it coterminal with?

  A. $\dfrac{5\pi}{9}$

  B. $\dfrac{23\pi}{18}$

  C. $\dfrac{13\pi}{18}$

  D. $\dfrac{31\pi}{15}$

  E. $\dfrac{5\pi}{18}$

3. What is $11111°$ in radians between 0 and 2π?

   A. $\dfrac{211\pi}{180}$

   B. $\dfrac{111\pi}{180}$

   C. $\dfrac{311\pi}{180}$

   D. $\dfrac{11\pi}{180}$

   E. $\dfrac{61\pi}{180}$

Answer Key: $1B, 2E, 3C$

Solutions

1. (B) $102 \cdot \dfrac{\pi}{180} = \dfrac{17\pi}{30}$

2. (E) $23450 \bmod 360 = 50, 50 \cdot \dfrac{\pi}{180} = \dfrac{5\pi}{18}$

3. (C) $11111 \bmod 360 = 311$. You can divide by 360 by hand and take the remainder or divide with your calculator and multiply the decimal part by 360; $311 \cdot \dfrac{\pi}{180} = \dfrac{311\pi}{180}$

Coterminal

1. An angle has measure 2345°. What angle between 0 and 360 is it coterminal with?

    A. 145

    B. 85

    C. 125

    D. 185

    E. 65

Answer Key: 1D

Solutions

1. (D) $\dfrac{2345}{360} = 6$ remainder 185

Trigonometric Equations

1. What are the solutions in degrees between 0 and 360 of $2\sin x = -1$?

    A. $\{330\}$

    B. $\{210\}$

    C. $\{30, 150\}$

    D. $\{30, 150, 210, 330\}$

    E. $\{210, 330\}$

2. What are all the value from 0 to 360 degrees where $4\sin^2 x = 3$?

    A. $\{60, 120\}$

    B. $\{60, 120, 240, 300\}$

    C. $\{240, 300\}$

    D. $\{60, 300\}$

    E. $\{120, 240\}$

3. What is the solution in degrees of $sin^2x + cos^2x = \dfrac{2}{3}$?

    A. No solution

    B. 0

    C. 50

    D. 70

    E. $(70, 110)$

4. What are the solutions between 0 and 360 of $2\cos^2 x + \sin^2 x = \dfrac{3}{2}$?

   A. $\{45, 135\}$

   B. $\{225, 315\}$

   C. $\{45, 135, 225, 315\}$

   D. $\{45, 225\}$

   E. $\{45\}$

5. What is the smallest positive x for which $\sin 3x = 1$?

   A. $\dfrac{\pi}{2}$

   B. $\dfrac{\pi}{3}$

   C. $\dfrac{\pi}{4}$

   D. $\dfrac{\pi}{6}$

   E. $\dfrac{\pi}{12}$

6. If $4\sin^2 x = 3$. What could $\sec x$ be?

   A. 2

   B. -6 or 6

   C. -2 or 2

   D. $-2\sqrt{2}$ or $2\sqrt{2}$

   E. $-\sqrt{5}$ or $\sqrt{5}$

Solutions

1. (E) $\sin x = \dfrac{-1}{2}, x = 210, 330$

2. (B) $\sin^2 x = \dfrac{3}{4}, \sin x = \pm\dfrac{\sqrt{3}}{2}$, $x = 60$,120, 240, 300

3. (A) $\sin^2 x + \cos^2 x = 1, 1 = \dfrac{2}{3}$, this is a contradiction, so no solutions

4. (C) $\cos^2 x + (\cos^2 x + \sin^2 x) = \dfrac{3}{2}, \cos^2 x = \dfrac{1}{2}, \cos x = \pm\dfrac{\sqrt{2}}{2}$,
   $x = 45, 135, 225, 315$

5. (D) $\sin^{-1}(1) = \dfrac{\pi}{2}, 3x = \dfrac{\pi}{2}, x = \dfrac{\pi}{6}$

6. (C) $\sin^2 x = \dfrac{3}{4}, \sin = \pm\dfrac{\sqrt{3}}{4}, \cos x = \pm\dfrac{1}{2}$ by $\sin^2 + \cos^2 = 1$ or the
   $30 - 60 - 90$ triangle, $\sec x = \dfrac{1}{\cos x} = \pm 2$

Range

The range goes up and down by the amplitude from the center line. In $y = a \sin x + b$, the range would be $b \pm a$.

1. What is the range of $y = a \cos(bx + c) + d$?

    A. $[d - a, d + a]$

    B. $(d - a, d + a)$

    C. $[d, d + a]$

    D. $[d - 2a, d + 2a]$

    E. $[d - a, d + a + 1]$

2. What is the range of $y = 4 \sin 3x - 2$?

    A. $[-4, 0]$

    B. $[-12, 8]$

    C. $[-6, -2]$

    D. $[-6, 2]$

    E. $[-2, 2]$

Answer Key: $1A, 2D$

Solutions

1. (A) $d \pm a$

2. (D) -2 ± 4

Period

The period of $y = \cos x, \sin x, \sec x,$ or $\csc x$ is 2π. The period of $y = \tan x$ or $\cot x$ is π. You can verify that tan has a shorter period by graphing or by the unit circle. For $y = \sin ax$, the period is $\dfrac{2\pi}{a}$; so the period of $y = \sin 4x$ is $\dfrac{2\pi}{4} = \dfrac{\pi}{2}$ and the period of $y = \sin \dfrac{x}{6}$ is $\dfrac{2\pi}{\frac{1}{6}} = 12\pi$. If you put a number greater than 1 in front of x, it increases the value you are taking sin of and speeds up the function.

1. If $y = \sin ax$ has a period of $\dfrac{5}{2}$, what could a be?

A. $\dfrac{8\pi}{5}$

B. $\dfrac{2\pi}{5}$

C. $\dfrac{6\pi}{5}$

D. $\dfrac{\pi}{5}$

E. $\dfrac{4\pi}{5}$

2. What is the period of $f(x) = a\sin(bx + c) + d$?

A. $\dfrac{\pi}{b}$

B. $\dfrac{2\pi}{b}$

C. $\dfrac{\pi}{2b}$

D. $\dfrac{1}{b}$

E. $\dfrac{4\pi}{b}$

3. What is the period of $y = \tan 8x$?

   A. 2π

   B. 8π

   C. $\dfrac{\pi}{4}$

   D. $\dfrac{\pi}{8}$

   E. $\dfrac{\pi}{16}$

4. If the period of $y = 3\cos(ax + 2)$ is 10π, what is a?

   A. $\dfrac{1}{5}$

   B. $\dfrac{1}{10}$

   C. $\dfrac{2}{5}$

   D. $\dfrac{1}{20}$

   E. $\dfrac{1}{5\pi}$

5. What is the period of $y = 4\sec(6x + 1) + 3$?

   A. $\dfrac{2\pi}{3}$

   B. $\dfrac{\pi}{6}$

   C. $\dfrac{\pi}{3}$

   D. $\dfrac{\pi}{9}$

   E. $\dfrac{\pi}{12}$

6. What is the smallest positive value for which $y = \sin \dfrac{x}{4}$ is a minimum?

    A. 3π

    B. 6π

    C. $\dfrac{3\pi}{2}$

    D. $\dfrac{\pi}{6}$

    E. $\dfrac{\pi}{12}$

7. What is the smallest positive value for which $y = 11 \sin 10x$ is a maximum?

    A. 5π

    B. $\dfrac{\pi}{2}$

    C. $\dfrac{\pi}{5}$

    D. $\dfrac{\pi}{10}$

    E. $\dfrac{\pi}{20}$

Solutions

1. (E) $\dfrac{2\pi}{\frac{5}{2}} = \dfrac{4\pi}{5}$

2. (B) $\dfrac{2\pi}{b}$

3. (D) $\dfrac{\pi}{8}$, for tan the basic period is π

4. (A) $\dfrac{2\pi}{a} = 10\pi, a = \dfrac{1}{5}$

5. (C) $\dfrac{2\pi}{6} = \dfrac{\pi}{3}$

6. (B) Period is $\dfrac{2\pi}{\frac{1}{4}} = 8\pi$, the minimum is at $8\pi\dfrac{\frac{3\pi}{2}}{2\pi} = 6\pi$

7. (E) Period is $\dfrac{2\pi}{10} = \dfrac{\pi}{5}$, maximum is $\dfrac{1}{4}$ period.

Triangle Area

The trigonometric formula for area of a triangle given sides and the included angle is $AB \cdot AC \cdot \dfrac{\sin A}{2}$. So if $AB = 5$, $AC = 8$, and $A = 30°$, area $= 5 \cdot 8 \cdot \dfrac{\frac{1}{2}}{2} = 10$.

1. If in triangle $\triangle ABC$, $\cos A = \dfrac{3}{4}$, $AB = 2$ and $AC = 5$, what is the area of the triangle?

   A. $\dfrac{5\sqrt{3}}{2}$

   B. $\dfrac{5\sqrt{5}}{4}$

   C. $\dfrac{5\sqrt{7}}{4}$

   D. $\dfrac{7\sqrt{5}}{4}$

   E. $\dfrac{3\sqrt{11}}{4}$

2. How much larger in square inches is a triangle with sides 2 inches and 3 inches and included angle $60°$ than a triangle with the same sides and included angle $30°$?

   A. 1.1

   B. 1.4

   C. 2.1

   D. 2.2

   E. 2.3

Answer Key: $1C, 2A$

Solutions

1. (C) $\sin A = \sqrt{1 - \left(\dfrac{3}{4}\right)^2} = \dfrac{\sqrt{7}}{4}$. Area $= \dfrac{2 \cdot 5 \cdot \dfrac{\sqrt{7}}{4}}{2} = \dfrac{5\sqrt{7}}{4}$

2. (A) $\dfrac{2 \cdot 3 \cdot \dfrac{\sqrt{3}}{2}}{2} - \dfrac{2 \cdot 3 \cdot \dfrac{1}{2}}{2} = \dfrac{3(\sqrt{3} - 1)}{2} \approx 1.1$

Trigonometric Expressions

1. $\dfrac{\sin^2 x}{\tan^3 x} = ?$

    A. $\cos^2 x \tan x$

    B. $\cos x \cot x$

    C. $\cos^2 x \cot x$

    D. $\cos x \cot^2 x$

    E. $\cos^2 x \cot^2 x$

2. What is $\dfrac{\sin^2 x + \cos^2 x}{\tan^2 x - \sec^2 x}$?

    A. -1

    B. 2

    C. $\sin x$

    D. 1

    E. $\cos x$

3. $\sec x \tan x \cos^2 x = ?$

    A. $\tan x$

    B. $2 \sin x$

    C. $\sin x \cos x$

    D. $\sin x$

    E. $\cos x$

4. What is $\dfrac{\sin 2x}{\cos x}$?

    A. $\tan x$

    B. $2 \sin x$

    C. $\cos x$

    D. $\sin 3x$

    E. $2 \tan x$

5. $10 \sin x \cos x =$?

    A. $5 \csc 2x$

    B. $5 \tan x$

    C. $5 \cos 2x$

    D. $10 \sin 2x$

    E. $5 \sin 2x$

6. $\dfrac{\tan^2 x}{\sec^2 x} =$?

    A. $\cos^2 x$

    B. $1 - \cos^2 x$

    C. $- \cos^2 x$

    D. $\sin x$

    E. $\sin^3 x$

7. What is $\dfrac{1 - \sin^2 x}{\cot^2 x}$?

    A. $\cos x$

    B. $\sin x$

    C. $\csc^2 x$

    D. $\tan^2 x$

    E. $\sin^2 x$

8. The expression $4 \sin^2 x - 4 \cos^2 x$ is equivalent to what?

    A. $4 \cos 2x$

    B. $- 2 \cos 2x$

    C. $- 4 \cos 2x$

    D. $4 \cos 8x$

    E. $2 \cos 2x$

Answer Key: 1C, 2A, 3D, 4B, 5E, 6B, 7E, 8C

Solutions

1. (C) $\dfrac{\sin^2 x}{\frac{\sin^3 x}{\cos^3 x}} = \dfrac{\cos^3 x}{\sin x} = \cos^2 x \cot x$

2. (A) By the Pythagorean identities, $\dfrac{1}{-1} = -1$

3. (D) $\dfrac{1}{\cos x} \cdot \dfrac{\sin x}{\cos x} \cdot \cos^2 x = \sin x$

4. (B) $\dfrac{2 \sin x \cos x}{\cos x} = 2 \sin x$

5. (E) $\sin 2x = 2 \sin x \cos x \Rightarrow$ So $10 \sin x \cos x = 5 \sin 2x$

6. (B) $\dfrac{\frac{\sin^2 x}{\cos^2 x}}{\frac{1}{\cos^2 x}} = \sin^2 x = 1 - \cos^2 x$

7. (E) $\dfrac{\cos^2 x}{\frac{\cos^2 x}{\sin^2 x}} = \sin^2 x$

8. (C) $-4 \left(\cos^2 x - \sin^2 x \right) = -4 \cos 2x$

Other Trigonometry

1. The vertex angle in an isosceles triangle is 50° and the side opposite the vertex has length 10. What is the area of the triangle?

   A. 61.1

   B. 59.1

   C. 65.1

   D. 63.1

   E. 57.1

2. Say you measure the angle to the top of a building as 45°. Approaching 200 ft closer to the building along a flat street, the angle increases to 60°. What is the height of the building in feet?

   A. 463

   B. 473

   C. 443

   D. 453

   E. 433

Solutions

1. (B) $\dfrac{5}{Altitude} = \sin 25° \Rightarrow Altitude = \dfrac{5}{\sin 25°} = 11.83 \Rightarrow Area = 11.83 \cdot \dfrac{10}{2} = 59.1$

2. (B) Let x be the distance to the building when you get closer and let h be the height of the building.

   Then, $\tan 60° = \dfrac{h}{x} \Rightarrow \tan 45° = \dfrac{h}{x + 200}$ and $h = x\sqrt{3} \Rightarrow 1 = \dfrac{h}{x + 200} \Rightarrow x + 200 = h$

   $\Rightarrow x + 200 = x\sqrt{3} \Rightarrow 200 = x\left(\sqrt{3} - 1\right) \Rightarrow \dfrac{200}{\sqrt{3} - 1} = x \approx 273.2 \Rightarrow h = 273.2 \cdot \sqrt{3} \approx 473.2$

Chapter XLII

Logarithms

Finding Logarithms

1. What is $\log_a b \cdot \log_b a$?

    A. a^b

    B. $a + b$

    C. ab

    D. 1

    E. 2

2. What is $\log_4 8^{\frac{7}{5}}$?

    A. $\dfrac{11}{5}$

    B. $\dfrac{21}{20}$

    C. 2

    D. $\dfrac{21}{10}$

    E. $\dfrac{21}{5}$

3. What is $\log_2 93,000,000$ to the nearest hundredth?

    A. 25.9

    B. 26.3

    C. 26.5

    D. 26.1

    E. 26.7

4. What is $\log_5 32$?

    A. 2.15

    B. 2.05

    C. 1.95

    D. 2.2

    E. 2.25

5. What is $\log_3 2 + \log_2 3$ to the nearest tenth?

    A. 2.2

    B. 2.1

    C. 2.0

    D. 1.9

    E. 2.3

6. What is $\log_8 32$?

    A. $\dfrac{5}{3}$

    B. $\dfrac{5}{2}$

    C. $\dfrac{10}{3}$

    D. $\dfrac{5}{4}$

    E. $\dfrac{3}{5}$

7. What is $\log_2 48 - \log_2 6$?

    A. 4

    B. 3

    C. $3\log 8$

    D. $3\log 6$

    E. $\log_2 16$

8. What is $\log \dfrac{\sqrt[5]{10^7}}{10^{10}}$?

    A. -9.3

    B. -8.6

    C. $-.7$

    D. -3

    E. -7.9

9. What is $\log_2 \left(\sqrt[5]{8} \cdot \sqrt[3]{16} \right)$?

    A. $\dfrac{32}{15}$

    B. 2

    C. $\dfrac{31}{15}$

    D. $\dfrac{9}{5}$

    E. $\dfrac{29}{15}$

10. What is $\log_2 8^{\frac{11}{5}}$?

    A. $\dfrac{13}{2}$

    B. $\dfrac{22}{5}$

    C. $\dfrac{99}{10}$

    D. 6

    E. $\dfrac{33}{5}$

11. What is $\log_4 \left(\dfrac{1}{2} \right)^{\frac{7}{5}}$?

    A. $\dfrac{-7}{10}$

    B. $\dfrac{7}{5}$

    C. $\dfrac{-7}{5}$

    D. $\dfrac{7}{10}$

    E. $\dfrac{7}{20}$

12. What is $\log \dfrac{100^7}{1000}$?

    A. 17

    B. 12.5

    C. 4

    D. 11

    E. 5.5

Answer Key: 1D, 2D, 3C, 4A, 5A, 6A, 7B, 8B, 9E, 10E, 11A, 12D

Solutions

1. (D) $\dfrac{\ln b}{\ln a} \cdot \dfrac{\ln a}{\ln b} = 1$

2. (D) $\log_{2^2}(2^3)^{\frac{7}{5}} = \dfrac{1}{2}\log_2 2^{\frac{21}{5}} = \dfrac{1}{2}\cdot\dfrac{21}{5} = \dfrac{21}{10}$

3. (C) $\dfrac{\log 93,000,000}{\log 2} = 26.47$

   You can also use $\dfrac{\ln 93,000,000}{\ln 2}$

4. (A) $\dfrac{\ln 32}{\ln 5} = 2.15$

5. (A) $\dfrac{\ln 2}{\ln 3} + \dfrac{\ln 3}{\ln 2} \approx 2.2$

6. (A) $(2^3)^x = 2^5 \Rightarrow$ Taking the log based 2 of both sides, $3x = 5 \Rightarrow x = \dfrac{5}{3}$

7. (B) $\log_2 \dfrac{48}{6} = \log_2 8 = 3$

8. (B) $\log 10^{\frac{7}{5}} - \log 10^{10} = 1.4 - 10 = -8.6$

9. (E) $\log_2\left((2^3)^{\frac{1}{5}}\cdot(2^4)^{\frac{1}{3}}\right) = \log_2\left(2^{\frac{3}{5}}\cdot 2^{\frac{4}{3}}\right) = \log_2 2^{\frac{29}{15}} = \dfrac{29}{15}$

10. (E) $\log_2 2^{3\frac{11}{5}} = \log_2 2^{\frac{33}{5}} = \dfrac{33}{5}$

11. (A) $\log_{2^2}(2^{-1})^{\frac{7}{5}} = \log_{2^2} 2^{\frac{-7}{5}} = \dfrac{1}{2}\log_2 2^{\frac{-7}{5}} = \dfrac{1}{2}\cdot\left(\dfrac{-7}{5}\right) = \dfrac{-7}{10}$

12. (D) $\log\dfrac{(10^2)^7}{10^3} = \log\dfrac{10^{14}}{10^3} = \log 10^{11} = 11$

Logarithms with Variable Expressions

1. $\log_a \dfrac{a^4}{a^{15}} = ?$

   A. a^{11}

   B. -19

   C. -11

   D. -60

   E. a^{-11}

2. $\log_a \sqrt[15]{a^4} = ?$

   A. $\dfrac{4}{5}$

   B. $\dfrac{4}{45}$

   C. $\dfrac{2}{15}$

   D. $\dfrac{2}{5}$

   E. $\dfrac{4}{15}$

3. What is $\log a^b = ?$

   A. ab^2

   B. $b \log a$

   C. $\log a + \log b$

   D. $a \log b$

   E. ab

4. What is $\log_2 \dfrac{8^{3x+3}}{4^{x+5}}$?

   A. $7x \; - \; 2$

   B. $5x \; - \; 2$

   C. $5x + 2$

   D. $7x \; - \; 1$

   E. $7x + 2$

5. What is $\log_a \dfrac{a^5}{\left(\sqrt{a}\right)^3}$?

    A. $\dfrac{7}{2}$

    B. $\dfrac{5}{2}$

    C. $\dfrac{11}{2}$

    D. $\dfrac{9}{2}$

    E. $\dfrac{13}{2}$

6. $a = 100^{2b+5c}$. What is $\log a$?

    A. $4b + 10c$

    B. $4b + 12c$

    C. $4b + 15c$

    D. $2b + 5c$

    E. $2b + 10c$

7. What is $\log_a \dfrac{b^c}{d}$ in terms of natural logarithms?

    A. $c \ln b - \ln d$

    B. $\dfrac{c \ln b + \ln d}{\ln a}$

    C. $c \ln b - \ln d$

    D. $\dfrac{\ln b - \ln d}{\ln a}$

    E. $\dfrac{c \ln b - \ln d}{\ln a}$

8. What is $\log_a \left(5b^3\right)$ in natural logarithms?

    A. $(\ln 5 + 3 \ln b) \cdot \ln a$

    B. $\ln 5 + 3 \ln b$

    C. $\dfrac{\ln 5 + \ln b}{\ln a}$

    D. $\dfrac{3 \ln b}{\ln a}$

    E. $\dfrac{\ln 5 + 3 \ln b}{\ln a}$

9. What is $\log \dfrac{100^a}{1000^b}$?

    A. $2a + 3b$

    B. $a + b$

    C. $3a - 2b$

    D. $a - 3b$

    E. $2a - 3b$

10. If $\log 2 = a$ and $\log 3 = b$, which is equal to 288?

    A. 6^{5a+2b}

    B. 10^{5a+2b}

    C. e^{5a+2b}

    D. 10^{5a+3b}

    E. $10^{5a - 3b}$

Answer Key: 1C, 2E, 3B, 4D, 5A, 6A, 7E, 8E, 9E, 10B

Solutions

1. (C) $\log_a a^{-11} = -11$

2. (E) $\log_a a^{\frac{4}{15}} = \dfrac{4}{15}$

3. (B) By the laws of logarithms.

4. (D) $\log_2 \dfrac{2^{9x+9}}{2^{2x+10}} = \log_2 2^{7x-1} = 7x - 1$

5. (A) $\log_a \dfrac{a^5}{a^{\frac{3}{2}}} = \log_a a^{\frac{7}{2}} = \dfrac{7}{2}$

6. (A) $\log \left(10^2\right)^{2b+5c} = \log 10^{4b+10c} = 4b + 10c$

7. (E) By the laws of logarithms and change of base formula, $\dfrac{c\ln b - \ln d}{\ln a}$

8. (E) By the change of base formula and the laws of logarithms, $\dfrac{\ln 5 + 3\ln b}{\ln a}$

9. (E) $a\log 100 - b\log 1000 = 2a - 3b$

10. (B) $288 = 2^5 \cdot 3^2 \Rightarrow \log 288 = 5a + 2b \Rightarrow$ Taking both sides 10 to the power, $288 = 10^{5a+2b}$

Finding What Logarithm is of

The basic problem here is fairly straightforward.

$$\log_3 x = 4 \Rightarrow x = 3^4 = 81$$

1. $\log_2 x = -5$. What is x?

    A. $\dfrac{-5}{2}$

    B. $\dfrac{1}{16}$

    C. $\dfrac{1}{32}$

    D. 32

    E. $\dfrac{2}{5}$

2. If $\log x = \dfrac{5}{2}$, what is x?

    A. 100

    B. $100\sqrt{10}$

    C. 1000

    D. $1000\sqrt{10}$

    E. 250

3. $\log_2 x = \dfrac{11}{2}$. What is x?

    A. 32

    B. 48

    C. $16\sqrt{2}$

    D. 64

    E. $32\sqrt{2}$

4. $\log_{32} x = \dfrac{-8}{5}$. What is x?

    A. $\dfrac{1}{256}$

    B. 256

    C. 128

    D. $\dfrac{1}{512}$

    E. $\dfrac{1}{128}$

5. If $\log_2 x = 5a - 2b$, what is x?

    A. $\dfrac{32^a}{4^b}$

    B. $\dfrac{64^a}{4^b}$

    C. $\dfrac{16^a}{4^b}$

    D. $\dfrac{8^a}{4^b}$

    E. $\dfrac{32^a}{8^b}$

6. If $\log x = 3a$, what is x?

    A. 100^{2+a}

    B. $100 \cdot 10^a$

    C. $1000 \cdot 10^a$

    D. 1000^a

    E. 10000^a

Solutions

1. (C) In exponential form, $x = 2^{-5} = \dfrac{1}{2^5} = \dfrac{1}{32}$

2. (B) $x = 10^{\frac{5}{2}} = 10^2 \cdot 10^{\frac{1}{2}} = 100\sqrt{10}$

3. (E) $2^{\frac{11}{2}} = 2^5 \cdot 2^{\frac{1}{2}} = 32\sqrt{2}$

4. (A) $32^{\frac{-8}{5}} = (2^5)^{\frac{-8}{5}} = 2^{-8} = \dfrac{1}{2^8} = \dfrac{1}{256}$

5. (A) $x = 2^{5a - 2b} = \dfrac{2^{5a}}{2^{2b}} = \dfrac{32^a}{4^b}$

6. (C) $x = 10^{3a} = 10^3 \cdot 10^a = 1000 \cdot 10^a$

Finding Bases

$\log_a 32 = \dfrac{5}{4}$. What is a?

You may be able to figure out intuitive that $16^{\frac{5}{4}} = 32$.

You can also do

$$(2^x)^{\frac{5}{4}} = 2^5 \Rightarrow \frac{5x}{4} = 5 \Rightarrow x = 4 \Rightarrow \text{ So } 2^4 = 16$$

It is not the best way, but you can do

$$a^{\frac{5}{4}} = 32 \Rightarrow \frac{5}{4} \cdot \ln a = \ln 32 \Rightarrow \ln a = \frac{4}{5} \ln 32 \Rightarrow \ln a \approx 2.77 \Rightarrow e^{2.77} \approx 16$$

If 32 wasn't a power of 2, then logs would be the best approach. You can also use log based 10 with your calculator rather than ln.

1. If $\log_a 8 = \dfrac{3}{5}$, what is a?

    A. 32

    B. $\dfrac{1}{16}$

    C. 128

    D. 16

    E. $\dfrac{1}{32}$

2. $\log_a 243 = \dfrac{5}{3}$. What is a?

    A. $27\sqrt{3}$

    B. 27

    C. 81

    D. 9

    E. $6561\sqrt{3}$

3. $\log_a \dfrac{1}{4} = \dfrac{-2}{3}$. What is a?

    A. $2\sqrt{2}$

    B. 4

    C. 10

    D. 12

    E. 8

4. $\log_a \dfrac{1}{32} = \dfrac{5}{2}$. What is a?

    A. $\dfrac{1}{2}$

    B. $\dfrac{1}{16}$

    C. $\dfrac{1}{8}$

    D. $\dfrac{1}{4}$

    E. $\dfrac{3}{8}$

5. If $\log_a 50 = 3$, what is a?

    A. 3.48

    B. 3.68

    C. 3.88

    D. 3.28

    E. 3.08

Solutions

1. (A) $a = 8^{\frac{5}{3}} = 32$ or $x^{\frac{3}{5}} = 8 \Rightarrow (2^a)^{\frac{3}{5}} = 2^3 \Rightarrow \dfrac{3a}{5} = 3 \Rightarrow a = 5 \Rightarrow 2^5 = 32$

   Or $\dfrac{\ln 8}{\ln a} = \dfrac{3}{5} \Rightarrow \ln a = \dfrac{5}{3} \cdot \ln 8 = 3.466 \Rightarrow e^{3.466} \approx 32$

2. (B) $(3^x)^{\frac{5}{3}} = 3^5 \Rightarrow \dfrac{5x}{3} = 5 \Rightarrow x = 3 \Rightarrow 3^3 = 27$

3. (E) $(2^x)^{\frac{-2}{3}} = 2^{-2} \Rightarrow \dfrac{-2x}{3} = -2 \Rightarrow x = 3 \Rightarrow 2^3 = 8$

4. (D) $(2^x)^{\frac{5}{2}} = \dfrac{1}{32} \Rightarrow \dfrac{5x}{2} = -5 \Rightarrow x = -2 \Rightarrow 2^{-2} = \dfrac{1}{4}$

5. (B) $\dfrac{\ln 50}{\ln a} = 3$ (by the change of base formula) $\Rightarrow \ln a = \dfrac{\ln 50}{3} \approx 1.304 \Rightarrow e^{1.304} \approx 3.68$

Logs Set Equal to a Value

1. If $\log_7 2 = a$ and $\log_7 3 = b$, which is equal to 4.5?

   A. 7^{3b-a}

   B. 7^{b+a}

   C. 7^{b-a}

   D. 7^{2b+a}

   E. 7^{2b-a}

2. If $\log 2 = a$ and $\log 5 = b$, what is $\log 6.25$?

   A. $2a - 2b$

   B. $2a + 2b$

   C. $2a - b$

   D. $2b - 2a$

   E. $a - b$

Solutions

1. (E) $\log_7 4.5 = \log_7 \dfrac{3^2}{2} = 2\log_7 3 - \log_7 2 = 2b - a \Rightarrow 4.5 = 7^{2b-a}$

2. (D) $\log 6.25 = \log \dfrac{25}{4} = \log \dfrac{5^2}{2^2} = 2\log 5 - 2\log 2 = 2b - 2a$

Logarithmic Equations

1. $\log_2 48 - \log_2 6 = \log_5 x?$

   A. $25\sqrt{5}$

   B. 375

   C. 625

   D. 125

   E. 25

2. What is the exact value of the x coordinate of the intersection of $y = \ln(2x + 5) + 7$ and $y = 10$?

   A. $\dfrac{e^4 - 5}{2}$

   B. $\dfrac{e^3 - 5}{3}$

   C. $\dfrac{e^3 - 5}{4}$

   D. $\dfrac{e - 5}{2}$

   E. $\dfrac{e^3 - 5}{2}$

3. What is the x coordinate of the intersection of $y = \log(x + 4) + 2$ and $y = 5$?

   A. 996

   B. 1004

   C. 1996

   D. 296

   E. 96

4. $\log_4(x^2 + x - 4) = 2$. What is x?

   A. 4

   B. -5

   C. 2 or -5

   D. 5 or -4

   E. 4 or -5

5. $\log(x^2 + 3x) = 1$. What is x?

    A. -5 or 2

    B. -5 or 4

    C. -5

    D. -5 or 1

    E. 2

Answer Key: 1D, 2E, 3A, 4E, 5A

Solutions

1. (D) $\log_2 \dfrac{48}{6} = \log_5 x \Rightarrow \log_2 8 = \log_5 x \Rightarrow 3 = \log_5 x \Rightarrow x = 125$

2. (E) $10 = \ln(2x+5) + 7 \Rightarrow 3 = \ln(2x+5) \Rightarrow e^3 = 2x+5 \Rightarrow \dfrac{e^3 - 5}{2} = x$

3. (A) $\log(x+4) + 2 = 5 \Rightarrow \log(x+4) = 3 \Rightarrow x+4 = 10^3 \Rightarrow x+4 = 1000 \Rightarrow x = 996$

4. (E) Taking both sides 4 to the power, $x^2 + x - 4 = 4^2 \Rightarrow x^2 + x - 4 = 16 \Rightarrow x^2 + x - 20 = 0$

   $\Rightarrow x = 4$ or -5. Both answers check.

5. (A) $x^2 + 3x = 10 \Rightarrow x^2 + 3x - 10 = 0 \Rightarrow (x+5)(x-2) = 0 \Rightarrow -5$ or 2

Finding Value from Logarithm

1. If $\log a = 3 + b$, what is 10^a?

   A. $1000b$

   B. $1000\sqrt{b}$

   C. $1000ab$

   D. $100b$

   E. $1000 \cdot 10^b$

2. If $\log a = 4 + \log 4.3$, what is 10^a?

   A. 430,000

   B. 21,500

   C. 43,000

   D. 4,300

   E. 2,150

Solutions

1. (E) $10^{3+b} = 10^3 \cdot 10^b = 1000 \cdot 10^b$

2. (C) $10^a = 10^{4+\log 4.3} = 10^4 \cdot 10^{\log 4.3} = 10,000 \cdot 4.3 = 43,000$

Chapter XLIII

Matrices

1. What is the matrix product $\begin{pmatrix} 1 & 2 \\ 3 & 4 \end{pmatrix} \cdot \begin{pmatrix} a \\ b \end{pmatrix}$?

    A. $\begin{pmatrix} a + 2b \\ 3 + 4b \end{pmatrix}$

    B. $\begin{pmatrix} 1 + 2b \\ 3 + 4b \end{pmatrix}$

    C. $\begin{pmatrix} a + 2b \\ 3a + 4b \end{pmatrix}$

    D. $\begin{pmatrix} a + 3b & 2a + 4b \end{pmatrix}$

    E. $\begin{pmatrix} 1 & 2b \\ 3a & 4b \end{pmatrix}$

2. If the determinant of $\begin{vmatrix} x^2 & 5 \\ 11 & x \end{vmatrix} = 0$, what is x to the nearest tenth?

    A. 3.6

    B. 3.8

    C. 3.4

    D. 3.5

    E. 3.7

3. If the determinant of $\begin{vmatrix} a & 2 \\ b & 5 \end{vmatrix} = 4$ and $a = 2b$, what is a?

    A. 0

    B. 1

    C. 2

    D. 3

    E. 4

4. What is the matrix product $(1) \cdot (4 \quad 5 \quad 6)$?

    A. $\begin{pmatrix} 4 & 5 & 6 \\ 8 & 10 & 12 \\ 12 & 15 & 18 \end{pmatrix}$

    B. (15)

    C. $\begin{pmatrix} 1 \\ 2 \\ 3 \end{pmatrix}$

    D. $\begin{pmatrix} 4 \\ 5 \\ 6 \end{pmatrix}$

    E. $(4 \quad 5 \quad 6)$

5. What is the matrix product $(1 \quad 2 \quad 3) \cdot \begin{pmatrix} 4 \\ 5 \\ 6 \end{pmatrix}$?

    A. $\begin{pmatrix} 4 \\ 10 \\ 18 \end{pmatrix}$

    B. (12)

    C. $(4 \quad 10 \quad 18)$

    D. (32)

    E. $\begin{pmatrix} 4 & 5 & 6 \\ 8 & 10 & 12 \\ 2 & 15 & 18 \end{pmatrix}$

6. What is the product of the matrices $\begin{pmatrix} 1 & 2 \\ 3 & 4 \end{pmatrix}$ and $\begin{pmatrix} 4 & 2 \\ a & b \end{pmatrix}$?

    A. $\begin{pmatrix} 4+a & 4+2b \\ 12+3a & 8+4b \end{pmatrix}$

    B. $\begin{pmatrix} 4+2a & 2+2b \\ 12+4a & 6+4b \end{pmatrix}$

    C. $\begin{pmatrix} 4+2a & 2+2b \end{pmatrix}$

    D. $\begin{pmatrix} 4+2a \\ 12+4a \end{pmatrix}$

    E. $\begin{pmatrix} 10+5a & 6+3b \\ 28+7a & 20+5b \end{pmatrix}$

7. If $\begin{vmatrix} x & 3 \\ x & x \end{vmatrix} = 10$, what does $x =$?

    A. 2

    B. 2 or -5

    C. 2 or -3

    D. 2 or -6

    E. -2 or 5

Solutions

1. (C) By matrix multiplication, $\begin{pmatrix} a + 2b \\ 3a + 4b \end{pmatrix}$

2. (B) $x^3 - 55 = 0 \Rightarrow x = \sqrt[3]{55}$

3. (B) $5a - 2b = 4 \Rightarrow a = 2b \Rightarrow 8b = 4 \Rightarrow b = \dfrac{1}{2} \Rightarrow a = 1$

4. (E) These are each 1 element multiplications.

5. (D) $\left(1 \cdot 4 + 2 \cdot 5 + 3 \cdot 6 \right) = \left(32 \right)$

6. (B) By matrix multiplication, $\begin{pmatrix} 1 \cdot 4 + 2 \cdot a & 1 \cdot 2 + 2 \cdot b \\ 3 \cdot 4 + 4 \cdot a & 3 \cdot 2 + 4 \cdot b \end{pmatrix}$

7. (E) $x^2 - 3x = 10 \Rightarrow x^2 - 3x - 10 = 0 \Rightarrow x = -2 \text{ or } 5$

Chapter XLIV

Complex Numbers

Complex Powers

You just foil everything out and replace i^2 with -1.

1. What is $(3 + 5i)^2$?

    A. $30i + 41$

    B. $30i - 20$

    C. $32i - 16$

    D. $30i - 16$

    E. $32i + 41$

2. What is $(\sqrt{5} + i\sqrt{2})^2$?

    A. $3 \pm 2i\sqrt{10}$

    B. $3 + 2i\sqrt{10}$

    C. $6 + 2i\sqrt{10}$

    D. $3 + 4i\sqrt{5}$

    E. $3 + i\sqrt{20}$

3. What is $(5 + 2i)^{-2}$?

    A. $\dfrac{21 - 20i}{841}$

    B. $21 - 20i$

    C. $21 + 20i$

    D. $\dfrac{21 - 20i}{441}$

    E. $\dfrac{21 - 20i}{400}$

4. What is $(2 + 3i)^3$?

    A. $10i - 46$

    B. $10i - 44$

    C. $9i - 46$

    D. $10i - 50$

    E. $-5 + 12i$

5. What is $(2 + i)^4$?

    A. $3 + 4i$

    B. $24i + 7$

    C. $7 - 24i$

    D. $7 - 17i$

    E. $24i - 7$

6. What is $(1 + i)^4$?

    A. 4

    B. 1

    C. -4

    D. $16 + 16i$

    E. $2 - 4i$

Answer Key: 1D, 2B, 3A, 4C, 5E, 6C

Solutions

1. (D) $(3 + 5i)(3 + 5i) = 9 + 15i + 15i + 25i^2 = 30i - 16$

2. (B) $5 + 2i\sqrt{10} + i^2 \times 2 = 3 + 2i\sqrt{10}$

3. (A) $\dfrac{1}{(5 + 2i)^2} = \dfrac{1}{21 + 20i} = \dfrac{21 - 20i}{(21 + 20i)(21 - 20i)} = \dfrac{21 - 20i}{441 + 400} = \dfrac{21 - 20i}{841}$

4. (C) $(2 + 3i)^2 = 4 + 12i + 9i^2 = (-5 + 12i)(2 + 3i) = -10 + 24i - 15i + 36i^2$
   $= -10 + 9i - 36 = 9i - 46$

5. (E) $(2 + i)^2 = 4 + 4i + i^2 = 3 + 4i \implies (3 + 4i)^2 = 9 + 24i + 16i^2 = 24i - 7$

6. (C) $(1 + i)^2 = 1 + 2i + i^2 = 2i \implies (2i)^2 = 4i^2 = -4$
   It is also possible to use trigonometric form $(\sqrt{2}, 45 \text{ degrees})$ taking the the 4th power, $(\sqrt{2}^4, 45 \times 4) = (4, 180 \; degrees) = 4\cos(180 \text{ degrees}) + i\sin(180 \text{ degrees}) = -4$

High Complex Powers

$i^2 = -1$, $i^3 = -i$, $i^4 = 1$, $i^5 = 1$. So i powers repeat every 4. In fact that makes sense, as i is a fourth root of 1. So $i^{337} = i^1 = i$, $337 \mod 4 = 1$. You can determine what something is mod 4 by dividing by hand and taking the remainder or dividing by the calculator and multiplying the decimal part by 4. You might be able to get the remainder directly from some calculators.

1. If k is a positive integer, what is i^{176k+3}?

    A. i

    B. $-i$

    C. 1

    D. -1

    E. 0

2. What is i^{20k-1} where k is a positive integer?

    A. $-i$

    B. i

    C. 1

    D. -1

    E. 0

3. What is $i^{9 \times 10 \times 11}$?

    A. i

    B. $-i$

    C. -1

    D. 1

    E. 0

4. What is $i^{4k-2} + i^{12k-3}$ where k is a positive integer?

    A. $i + 1$

    B. i

    C. $i - 1$

    D. $-i$

    E. $2 + i$

5. What is i^{-11}?

    A. -1

    B. $-i$

    C. i

    D. 1

    E. 0

6. What is $(3i^{97} + 2i^{96})^2$?

    A. $2 + 3i$

    B. $5 + 12i$

    C. $-5 + 12i$

    D. $-5 + 14i$

    E. $5 + 14i$

7. What is $(i^{88} + i^{89} - i^{91})^2$?

    A. $2i$

    B. $1 + i$

    C. $4i + 3$

    D. $4i + 5$

    E. $4i - 3$

Solutions

1. (B) $i^{176k+3} = i^3 = -i$

2. (A) $i^{20k-1} = i^3 = -i$

3. (C) i^{990}, $990 \div 4$ has remainder 2, so $i^2 = -1$

4. (C) $i^{4k-2} + i^{12k-3} = i^2 + i = i - 1$

5. (C) $i^{-11} = \dfrac{1}{i^{11}}$

   $i^{11} = i^3 = -i \implies \dfrac{1}{-i} = \dfrac{i}{-i} \times i = \dfrac{i}{-i^2} = i$ or $i^{-i} \times i^{12} = i^1 = i$ ($i^{12} = 1$, as does i to any multiple of 4).

6. (C) $(2 + 3i)^2 = 4 + 6i + 6i + 9i^2 = -5 + 12i$

7. (E) $(1 + i - (-i))^2 = (1 + 2i)^2 = 1 + 2i + 2i + 4i^2 = 4i - 3$

Complex Division

To divide complex numbers, you multiply the numerator and denominator by the conjugate of the denominator, which rationalizes the denominator.

$$\frac{2+3i}{5+2i} = \frac{(2+3i)(5-2i)}{(5+2i)(5-2i)} = \frac{10-4i+15i-6i^2}{25-10i+10i-4i^2} = \frac{16-11i}{29}$$

The problems cover various more complicated cases which could appear on the exam.

1. What is $\dfrac{i}{\sqrt{3}-i}$?

   A. $\dfrac{i\sqrt{3}+1}{4}$

   B. $\dfrac{i\sqrt{3}-1}{2}$

   C. $\dfrac{i\sqrt{3}-6}{4}$

   D. $\dfrac{i\sqrt{3}-1}{4}$

   E. $\dfrac{i\sqrt{3}-1}{8}$

2. What is $\dfrac{1}{5+i\sqrt{7}}$ with a rational denominator?

   A. $\dfrac{5-i\sqrt{7}}{16}$

   B. $\dfrac{5-i\sqrt{7}}{32}$

   C. $\dfrac{5-i\sqrt{7}}{30}$

   D. $\dfrac{5-2i\sqrt{7}}{16}$

   E. $\dfrac{5-2i\sqrt{7}}{30}$

3. What is $\dfrac{1}{a + bi}$?

    A. $\dfrac{a + bi}{a^2 + b^2}$

    B. $\dfrac{a - bi}{a^2 + b^2}$

    C. $\dfrac{a - bi}{a + b}$

    D. $\dfrac{-a - bi}{a^2 + b^2}$

    E. $\dfrac{a - b}{a^2 + b^2}$

4. If $x \times (2 + i)^2 = 1$, what is x?

    A. $\dfrac{3 + 4i}{25}$

    B. $\dfrac{3 + 5i}{25}$

    C. $\dfrac{3 - 4i}{7}$

    D. $\dfrac{3 + 4i}{7}$

    E. $\dfrac{3 - 4i}{25}$

5. What is $\dfrac{1}{x^2 + i}$ with a rational denominator?

    A. $\dfrac{x^2 - i}{x^4 + 1}$

    B. $\dfrac{x^2 - 1}{x^4 + 1}$

    C. $\dfrac{ix^2 - 1}{x^4 + 1}$

    D. $\dfrac{ix^2 - i}{x^4 + 1}$

    E. $\dfrac{-x^2 - i}{x^4 + 1}$

Solutions

1. (D) $i\dfrac{\sqrt{3}+i}{(\sqrt{3}+i)(\sqrt{3}-i)} = \dfrac{i\sqrt{3}-1}{4}$

2. (B) $1 \times \dfrac{5-i\sqrt{7}}{(5-i\sqrt{7})(5+i\sqrt{7})} = \dfrac{5-i\sqrt{7}}{32}$

3. (B) Multiplying by the conjugate, $1 \times \dfrac{a-bi}{(a+bi)(a-bi)} = \dfrac{a-bi}{a^2+abi-abi-bi^2}$
   $= \dfrac{a-bi}{a^2+b^2}$

4. (E) $x(3+4i)=1 \implies x = \dfrac{1}{3+4i} = \dfrac{3-4i}{25}$

5. (A) $\dfrac{x^2-i}{(x^2+i)(x^2-i)} = \dfrac{x^2-i}{x^4+1}$

Complex Roots

You could be given a quadratic equation and need to find to complex solutions with the quadratic formula or by completing the square. You can also be given a solution and need to find the equation. You should be aware that if given a complex solution, the other solution is its conjugate. For example, if $2-i$ is a solution, the other solution is $2+i$, so $(x-2+i)(x-2-i) = x^2 - 2x + ix - 2x + 4 - 2i - ix + 2i - i^2 = x^2 - 4x + 5$. The imaginary terms will always drop out with the conjugates.

1. What are the solutions of $x^2 + 6x + 11 = 0$?

   A. $-2 \pm i\sqrt{2}$

   B. $-5 \pm i\sqrt{2}$

   C. $-2 \pm 2i\sqrt{2}$

   D. $-5 \pm 2i\sqrt{2}$

   E. $-3 \pm i\sqrt{2}$

2. What quadratic equation has solution $8 - 5i$?

   A. $x^2 - 16x + 85 = 0$

   B. $x^2 - 16x + 87 = 0$

   C. $x^2 - 16x + 91 = 0$

   D. $x^2 - 16x + 89 = 0$

   E. $x^2 - 16x + 93 = 0$

3. What quadratic equation has a solution $5 + i\sqrt{3}$?

   A. $x^2 - 10x + 22$

   B. $x^2 + 10x + 22$

   C. $x^2 - 10x + 28$

   D. $x^2 + 10x + 28$

   E. $x^2 - 10x + 34$

4. What are the solutions of $5^{x^2+3} = 25$?

   A. $3i$ and $-3i$

   B. $2i$ and $-2i$

   C. i and $-i$

   D. $1+i$ and $1-i$

   E. $4+i$ and $4-i$

Solutions

1. (E) $\dfrac{-6 \pm \sqrt{36 - 44}}{2} = \dfrac{-6 \pm 2i\sqrt{2}}{2} = -3 \pm i\sqrt{2}$

2. (D) $(x - 8 + 5i)(x - 8 - 5i) = x^2 - 16x + 89$

3. (C) The other root is the conjugate, $5 - i\sqrt{3}$, so $(x - 5 - i\sqrt{3})(x - 5 + i\sqrt{3})$
$= x^2 - 10x + 25 - 3i^2 = x^2 - 10x + 28$

4. (C) $5^{x^2+3} = 5^2 \implies x^2 + 3 = 2 \implies x^2 = -1 \implies x = \pm i$

Higher Polynomials

Finding Equation

You take x - each solution and multiply them. If you are asked to find a 4th degree equation with roots $2+i$ and $3+i$, you know the other roots are the conjugates, $2-i$ and $3-i$. So $(x-2-i)(x-2+i)(x-3-i)(x-3+i) = (x^2 - 4x + 5)(x^2 - 6x + 10)$
$= x^4 - 6x^3 + 10x^2 - 4x^3 + 24x^2 - 40x + 5x^2 - 30x + 50 = x^4 - 10x^3 + 39x^2 - 70x + 50.$

1. What is the x term of a 3rd degree equation with integer coefficients and solutions $\dfrac{2}{5}$ and $3i$?

   A. 2

   B. 45

   C. -45

   D. 18

   E. -30

2. What is the x term of a 4th degree equation with real coefficients with solutions $2+\sqrt{2}$ and $3+i$?

   A. 36

   B. -56

   C. -36

   D. -48

   E. -52

Solutions

1. (B) $(x + 3i)(x - 3i) = x^2 + 9$. $(5x - 2)(x^2 + 9) = 5x^3 + 45x - 2x^2 - 18 = 0$

2. (E) $(x - 2 - \sqrt{2})(x - 2 + \sqrt{2})(x - 3 - i)(x - 3 + i) = (x^2 - 4x + 2)(x^2 - 6x + 10)$
   $= x^4 - 6x^3 + 10x^2 - 4x^3 + 24x^2 - 40x + 2x^2 - 12x + 20 = x^4 - 10x^3 + 36x^2 - 52x + 20$

Finding Roots

Factor the expression and when you are left with a quadratic, use the quadratic formula or completing the square to find complex solutions.

1. What are the solutions of $x^3 + 25x = 0$ over complex numbers?

    A. $\{0, 5i, -5i\}$

    B. $\{0, 5i\}$

    C. $\{5i, -5i\}$

    D. $\{0, -5i\}$

    E. $\{0, 1 + 2i, 1 - 2i\}$

2. What are the complex solutions of $8x^3 - 27 = 0$?

    A. $\dfrac{3 \pm \sqrt{3}i}{4}$

    B. $\dfrac{3}{2}$

    C. $\dfrac{-3 - \sqrt{3}i}{4}$

    D. $\dfrac{-3 + \sqrt{3}i}{4}$

    E. $\dfrac{3}{2}i$

3. What are the solutions of $x^4 + 29x^2 + 100 = 0$?

    A. $\{2i, -2i, 5, -5\}$

    B. $\{2i, -2i, 5i, -5i\}$

    C. $\{2, -2, 5, -5\}$

    D. $\{-4, -2\}$

    E. $\{i, -i, 10i, -10i\}$

4. What are the solutions of $x^3 + 9x^2 + x + 9 = 0$?

    A. $\{-1, 3i, -3i\}$

    B. $\{1, 3i, -3i\}$

    C. $\{-9, i, -i\}$

    D. $\{9, i, -i\}$

    E. $\{-9, 1 + i, 1 - i\}$

Answer Key: 1A, 2A, 3B, 4C

Solutions

1. (A) $x(x^2 + 25) = 0 \implies x = 0$ or $x^2 + 25 = 0 \implies x^2 = -25 \implies x = \pm 5i$

2. (A) $(2x - 3)(4x^2 + 6x + 9) = 0$ by the cubic factoring formula or by finding one solution and dividing. $\dfrac{-6 \pm \sqrt{36 - 144}}{8} = \dfrac{-6 \pm 6\sqrt{3}i}{8} = \dfrac{-3 \pm 3\sqrt{3}i}{4}$

3. (B) $(x^2 + 25)(x^2 + 4) = 0 \implies x^2 + 25 = 0 \implies x^2 = -25 \implies x = \pm 5i$, $x^2 + 4 = 0 \implies x^2 = -4 \implies x = \pm 2i$
   $2i, -2i, 5i, -5i$

4. (C) Factoring by grouping $x^2(x + 9) + 1(x + 9) = (x^2 + 1)(x + 9) \implies x = -9$ or $x^2 = -1 \implies x = \pm i$

   You can also find the real root by graphic with your calculator. Synthetic division is possible, but probably more time consuming than needed.

Factored Form

1. What is the factored form of a polynomial with roots $\dfrac{1}{5}, -\dfrac{3}{7}, \dfrac{8}{3}$, and $5i$?

    A. $(x^2 - 25)(3x - 8)(5x - 1)(7x + 3)$

    B. $(x^2 - 25)(3x + 8)(5x - 1)(7x + 3)$

    C. $(x^2 + 25)(3x - 8)(5x - 1)(7x + 3)$

    D. $(x^2 + 25)(3x - 8)(5x - 2)(7x + 3)$

    E. $(x^2 + 25)(3x + 8)(5x - 2)(7x + 3)$

Solutions

1. (C) $(x - 5i)(x + 5i) = x^2 + 25$. Multiply the other terms to get integer coefficients.
   $(x^2 + 25)(3x - 8)(5x - 1)(7x + 3)$

Square Roots of Negatives

In these problems, convert the expression into a negative number and do complex arithmetic.

1. What is $\sqrt{-50} + \sqrt{-18}$?

    A. $4i.\sqrt{2}$

    B. $8i.\sqrt{2}$

    C. $8.\sqrt{2}$

    D. $16i.\sqrt{2}$

    E. $12i.\sqrt{2}$

2. Using complex arithmetic, what is $\sqrt{-50} \times \sqrt{-18}$?

    A. -24

    B. -30

    C. -25

    D. -32

    E. -36

3. In complex arithmetic, what is $(\sqrt{-75} - \sqrt{-12})^2$?

    A. 27

    B. 18

    C. -27

    D. -18

    E. -36

Answer Key: 1B, 2B, 3C

Solutions

1. (B) $5\sqrt{2}i + 3\sqrt{2}i = 8\sqrt{2}i$

2. (B) $5\sqrt{2}i \times 3\sqrt{2}i = 15 \times 2i^2 = -30$

3. (C) $(5i\sqrt{3} - 2i\sqrt{3})^2 = (3i\sqrt{3})^2 = 27i^2 = -27$

Complex Plane

You can graph complex numbers with the real part the x coordinate and the imaginary part the y coordinate. Some honors precalculus classes go into ways to convert that to polar form and use trigonometry to find roots of complex numbers. However, for this test you should just need to know the distance between numbers on the complex plane. The distance between $a + bi$ and $c + di$ is $\sqrt{(a - c)^2 + (b - d)^2}$, by the distance formula.

1. What is the distance between $-3 - 7i$ and $2 - i$ in the complex plane?

    A. $\sqrt{51}$

    B. $\sqrt{47}$

    C. $\sqrt{61}$

    D. $\sqrt{53}$

    E. 7

2. What is the distance in the complex plane between $2 + i$ and $(2 + i)^2$?

    A. 3

    B. 4

    C. $\sqrt{11}$

    D. $\sqrt{10}$

    E. $2\sqrt{3}$

Answer Key: 1C, 2D

Solutions

1. (C) $\sqrt{(2-(-3))^2 + (-7-(-1))^2} = \sqrt{25+36} = \sqrt{61}$

2. (D) $(2+i)^2 = 3+4i \implies \sqrt{(3-2)^2 + (4-1)^2} = \sqrt{10}$

Chapter XLV

Circles Using Analytic Geometry

Finding Area of Circle

The area of a circle is πr^2, so with the circle in the form $x^2 + y^2 = r^2$, we multiply r^2 by π to get the area.

1. What is the area of the circle $(x - 3)^2 + (y + 5)^2 = 11$?

   A. 11

   B. 11π

   C. 22π

   D. 33π

   E. 121π

2. What is the area of the circle $x^2 + y^2 = a$?

   A. $a^2\pi$

   B. $\sqrt{a}\pi$

   C. $a\pi$

   D. $2a\pi$

   E. $\dfrac{a\pi}{2}$

3. What is the area of $x^2 + y^2 = 25\pi$?

    A. $25\pi^2$

    B. 25π

    C. $15\pi^2$

    D. 625π

    E. $5\pi^2$

4. Two endpoints of a diameter of a circle are $(-3, 8)$ and $(7, 2)$. What is the area of the circle?

    A. 33π

    B. 34π

    C. 35π

    D. 36π

    E. 37π

5. What is the area of the circle $x^2 + y^2 + 4x + 10y = 0$?

    A. 6π

    B. 25π

    C. 29π

    D. 31π

    E. 32π

Answer Key: $1B, 2C, 3A, 4B, 5C$

Solutions

1. (B) $r = \sqrt{11}, A = \pi r^2 = \pi(\sqrt{11})^2 = 11\pi$

2. (C) Radius $= \sqrt{a}$. Area$= \pi r^2 = \pi(\sqrt{a})^2 = a\pi$

3. (A) $r = 5\sqrt{\pi}, A = \pi r^2 = \pi(5\sqrt{\pi})^2 = 25\pi^2$

4. (B) The distance between the points is $\sqrt{(2-8)^2 + (7-(-3))^2} = \sqrt{36+100} = \sqrt{136} = 2\sqrt{34}$. So the radius is $\sqrt{34}$. Then the area of the circle is $\pi r^2 = \pi(\sqrt{34})^2 = 34\pi$

5. (C) $x^2 + 4x + 4 + y^2 + 10y + 25 = 29, (x+2)^2 + (y+5)^2 = 29$. The radius is $\sqrt{29}$. The area $= \pi r^2 = 29\pi$

Finding Equation of Circle

The formula for a equation of a circle is $(x - a)^2 + (y - b)^2 = r^2$, where the center is (a, b) and the radius is r. You should be able to find the equation from the center and radius and vice versa.

1. What is the equation of a circle with center $(\sqrt{2}, \sqrt{3})$ and radius $\sqrt{5}$?

    A. $((x - \sqrt{2})^2 + (y - \sqrt{3})^2 = 5$

    B. $(x - \sqrt{2})^2 + (y - \sqrt{3})^2 = \sqrt{5}$

    C. $((x - \sqrt{2})^2 + (y - \sqrt{3})^2 = 25$

    D. $(x - 2)^2 + (y - 3)^2 = 5$

    E. $(x - 2)^2 + (y - 3)^2 = 25$

2. What is the equation of a circle with center $(11, 3)$ and area 12π?

    A. $(x - 11)^2 + (y - 3)^2 = 144$

    B. $(x - 11)^2 + (y - 3)^2 = 12\pi$

    C. $(x - 11)^2 + (y - 3)^2 = 24$

    D. $(x - 11)^2 + (y - 3)^2 = 36$

    E. $(x - 11)^2 + (y - 3)^2 = 12$

Solutions

1. (A) Plugging into standard form for a circle, $(x - \sqrt{2})^2 + (y - \sqrt{3})^2 = 5$

2. (E) $\pi r^2 = 12\pi, r = \sqrt{12}$ so $r^2 = 12, (x - 11)^2 + (y - 3)^2 = 12$

Other Circle

To find the x intercept, you set $y = 0$ and solve for x and vice versa. To find a tangent line to a circle , you find the slope at the point of tangency, as the negative reciprocal of the slope of the line from the center to the point. Then find the equation of the slope of the line using the point and slope.

1. What is the positive y-coordinate of a point on $x^2 + y^2 = 25$ that has an x-coordinate of -2?

A. $\sqrt{23}$

B. 4

C. $\dfrac{9}{2}$

D. $\sqrt{21}$

E. $2\sqrt{5}$

2. What are the x-intercepts of $(x + 2)^2 + (y + 3)^2 = 49$?

A. $-2 \pm 2\sqrt{11}$

B. $-2 \pm 2\sqrt{10}$

C. $-2 \pm 2\sqrt{13}$

D. $-2 \pm 2\sqrt{15}$

E. $-2 \pm 2\sqrt{14}$

3. What is the equation of the tangent to the circle $(x - 2)^2 + (y + 1)^2 = 26$ at $(3, 4)$?

A. $y = \dfrac{-x}{5} + \dfrac{17}{5}$

B. $y = \dfrac{-x}{5} + \dfrac{19}{5}$

C. $y = \dfrac{-x}{5} + \dfrac{29}{5}$

D. $y = \dfrac{-x}{5} + \dfrac{23}{5}$

E. $y = \dfrac{-x}{50 + \dfrac{21}{5}}$

Answer Key: $1D, 2B, 3D$

Solutions

1. (D) $(-2)^2 + y^2 = 25, y^2 = 21, y = \pm\sqrt{21}$

2. (B) $(x+2)^2 + 3^2 = 49, (x+2)^2 = 40, x = -2 \pm 2\sqrt{10}$

3. (D) The center is $(2, -1)$. The slope from the center to the point is $\dfrac{4 - (-1)}{3 - 2} = 5$. The slope of the tangent line is its negative reciprocal, $\dfrac{-1}{5}$. The equation of the tangent line is
$y - 4 = \dfrac{-1}{5}(x - 3), y - 4 = \dfrac{-x}{5} + \dfrac{3}{5}, y = \dfrac{-x}{5} + \dfrac{23}{5}$. You can also find the slope of the tangent line with calculus
$2(x - 2) + 2(y + 1)\dfrac{dy}{dx} = 0, \dfrac{dy}{dx} = \dfrac{2 - x}{y + 1} = \dfrac{2 - 3}{4 + 1} = \dfrac{-1}{5}$.

Chapter XLVI

Conic Sections

What is it?

Where $a > 0$, $b > 0$, $ax^2 + by^2 = c$ is an ellipse, $ax^2 - by^2 = c$ is a hyperbola, and $ax^2 + by = c$ is a parabola.

1. $x^2 + 6x + 3y + 11 = 0$ is a?

    A. Circle

    B. Ellipse

    C. Parabola

    D. Hyperbola

    E. Line

2. $\dfrac{x+3}{y+4} = \dfrac{y+1}{x-5}$ is a?

    A. Circle

    B. Ellipse

    C. Parabola

    D. Hyperbola

    E. Line

3. The graph of $y^2 = 2x^2 + 3x + 5$ is a?

    A. Circle

    B. Ellipse

    C. Parabola

    D. Hyperbola

    E. Line

4. The graph of $y^2 = -2x^2 + 3x + 5$ is a?

    A. Circle

    B. Ellipse

    C. Parabola

    D. Hyperbola

    E. Line

Solutions

1. (C) It is in the form $y = x^2$, so parabola.

2. (D) Cross multiplying, $(x+3)(x-5) = (y+1)(y+4)$. This is in the form $x^2 - y^2$, so hyperbola.

3. (D) In the form $2x^2 - y^2$, so hyperbola.

4. (B) In the form $2x^2 + y^2$, so ellipse.

Ellipses

If an ellipse has vertices $(0,5)$ and $(0,-5)$ and covertices $(3,0)$ and $(-3,0)$, the equation of the ellipse is $\dfrac{x^2}{9} + \dfrac{y^2}{25} = 1$. To find it foci, use $c^2 = a^2 - b^2$, $c^2 = 25 - 9$, $c = 4$. So the foci are along the major axis at $(0,4)$ and $(0,-4)$.

1. What is the equation of an ellipse with vertices $(11,0)$ and $(-11,0)$ and covertices $(0, \sqrt{89})$, $(0, -\sqrt{89})$?

    A. $\dfrac{x^2}{121} + \dfrac{y^2}{89} = 1$

    B. $\dfrac{x^2}{210} + \dfrac{y^2}{89} = 1$

    C. $\dfrac{x^2}{211} + \dfrac{y^2}{210} = 1$

    D. $\dfrac{x^2}{32} + \dfrac{y^2}{89} = 1$

    E. $\dfrac{x^2}{89} + \dfrac{y^2}{32} = 1$

2. What is the distance between the foci of the ellipse $\dfrac{(x+2)^2}{4} + \dfrac{(y-5)^2}{25} = 1$

    A. 10

    B. $\sqrt{21}$

    C. $2\sqrt{21}$

    D. $\sqrt{29}$

    E. $2\sqrt{29}$

3. $\dfrac{x^2}{152^2} + \dfrac{y^2}{148^2} = 1$ approximates the orbit of the earth in millions of kilometers from the sun. How many kilometers to the nearest million kilometer are the foci of the orbit apart from each other?

    A. 34

    B. 43

    C. 58

    D. 69

    E. 74

Answer Key: $1A, 2C, 3D$

Solutions

1. (A) Plugging into the general equation of an ellipse, $\dfrac{x^2}{121} + \dfrac{y^2}{89} = 1$

2. (C) $c^2 = a^2 - b^2, c^2 = 25 - 4, c = \sqrt{21}, 2c = 2\sqrt{21}$

3. (D) $c^2 = a^2 - b^2, c^2 - 152^2 - 148^2 = 1200, c = 20\sqrt{3} \approx 34.6, 2c \approx 69$

Other Conic Section Problems

1. A parabola may intersect a circle at most how many points?

   A. 1

   B. 2

   C. 3

   D. 4

   E. Infinitely many

2. What is the equation of an upward facing parabola with vertex $(2, 1)$ which goes through $(5, 7)$?

   A. $y - 1 = (x - 2)^2$

   B. $y - 1 = \dfrac{2}{3}(x - 2)^2$

   C. $y - 1 = \dfrac{3}{2}(x - 2)^2$

   D. $y - 1 = \dfrac{3}{4}(x - 2)^2$

   E. $y - 1 = \dfrac{7}{10}(x - 2)^2$

Solutions

1. (D) 4

2. (B) $y - 1 = a(x-2)^2, 7 - 1 = a(5-2)^2, 6 = a3^2, 6 = a9, a = \dfrac{2}{3}$

Chapter XLVII

Sequences and Series

Arithmetic Series

1. If the sum of all the integers from 1 to x is 105, what is x?

    A. 12

    B. 13

    C. 14

    D. 15

    E. 21

2. The 7th and 8th terms of an arithmetic series are 11 and 15 respectively. What is the sum of the of the first 20 terms of the series?

    A. 400

    B. 472

    C. 488

    D. 492

    E. 500

3. What is the sum of the first 1000 positive integers?

   A. 500.5

   B. 500, 000

   C. 501, 000

   D. 500, 500

   E. 1, 001, 000

4. The sum of 3 consecutive integers is a. What is the first of those integers in terms of a?

   A. $\dfrac{a-3}{3}$

   B. $\dfrac{a-2}{3}$

   C. $\dfrac{a-1}{3}$

   D. $\dfrac{a-4}{3}$

   E. $\dfrac{a+2}{3}$

5. What is the sum of the odd numbers from 1 to 199?

   A. 10, 100

   B. 10, 000

   C. 9990

   D. 5000

   E. 10, 200

6. What is the sum of the numbers from 101 to 300 inclusive?

    A. 40000

    B. 40100

    C. 41000

    D. 42000

    E. 43100

7. The first term in an arithmetic series is 11 and the common difference is 3. What is the sum of the first 40 elements in the series?

    A. 2720

    B. 2740

    C. 2760

    D. 2780

    E. 2800

8. The 10th term in an arithmetic sequence is 25 and the 13th term is 30. What is the sum of the first 5 terms of the sequence?

    A. 66

    B. 67

    C. $\dfrac{200}{3}$

    D. $\dfrac{202}{3}$

    E. $\dfrac{203}{3}$

Answer Key: $1C, 2E, 3D, 4A, 5B, 6B, 7D, 8C$

Solutions

1. (C) $\dfrac{x(x+1)}{2} = 105, x^2 + x - 210 = 0, (x+15)(x-14) = 0, x = 14$ or -15. We only use the positive solution. There are various other ways to solve the quadratic. You could also add the numbers starting at 1 until you get 105 or plug in the answers.

2. (E) Common difference $= 4$, 1st term $= 11 - 6 \cdot 4 = -13$,
   20th term $= 15 + 4 \cdot 12 = 63$, Sum $= (-13 + 63) \cdot \dfrac{20}{2} = 500$

3. (D) Taking the average of the first and last times the number of elements,
   $\dfrac{n(n+1)}{2} = \dfrac{1000 \cdot 1001}{2} = 500,500$

4. (A) $x + x + 1 + x + 2 = a, 3x + 3 = a, x = \dfrac{a-3}{3}$

5. (B) $\dfrac{(1+199) \cdot 100}{2} = 10,000$

6. (B) Number of elements $\cdot$ average of first and last elements $= \dfrac{200 \cdot (101 + 300)}{2} = 40100$

7. (D) $a_{40} = 11 + 39 \cdot 3 = 128$, Sum $= \dfrac{11 + 128}{2} \cdot 40 = 139 \cdot 20 = 2780$

8. (C) Common difference $= \dfrac{30 - 25}{13 - 10} = \dfrac{5}{3}$. $a_1 = 25 - 9 \cdot \dfrac{5}{3} = 25 - \dfrac{45}{3} = \dfrac{30}{3}$,
   $a_5 = \dfrac{30}{3} + 4 \cdot \dfrac{5}{3} = \dfrac{50}{3}$. Sum of 1st 5 terms $= \left(\dfrac{30}{3} + \dfrac{50}{3}\right) \cdot \dfrac{5}{2} = \dfrac{400}{6} = \dfrac{200}{3}$

Arithmetic Sequences

1. The first term in an arithmetic sequence is $\frac{2}{9}$ and the 7th term is $\frac{4}{3}$. What is the 11th term in the sequence?

   A. $\frac{14}{9}$

   B. $\frac{56}{27}$

   C. $\frac{224}{81}$

   D. $\frac{5}{2}$

   E. $\frac{8}{3}$

2. The 2nd and 5th terms in an arithmetic sequence are 5 and 38 respectively. What is the 100th term?

   A. 1068

   B. 1083

   C. 1108

   D. 1141

   E. 1121

3. What is an equivalent explicit sequence to $a_1 = 17$, $a_n = a_{n-1} + 11$?

   A. $a_n = 6 + 11n$

   B. $a_n = -7 + 11n$

   C. $a_n = 17 + 11n$

   D. $a_n = 11n$

   E. $a_n = 8 + 9n$

4. If the 11th term in an arithmetic sequence is $\dfrac{4}{3}$ and 17th term is $\dfrac{13}{6}$, what is the 30th term?

A. 4

B. $\dfrac{153}{36}$

C. $\dfrac{149}{36}$

D. $\dfrac{147}{36}$

E. $\dfrac{143}{36}$

Answer Key: $1B, 2B, 3A, 4E$

Solutions

1. (B) Common difference $= \dfrac{\dfrac{4}{3} - \dfrac{2}{9}}{7 - 1} = \dfrac{\dfrac{10}{9}}{6} = \dfrac{5}{27}$.

   11th term $= \dfrac{4}{3} + 4\left(\dfrac{5}{27}\right) = \dfrac{4}{3} + \dfrac{20}{27} = \dfrac{36 + 20}{27} = \dfrac{56}{27}$

2. (B) Common difference $= \dfrac{38 - 5}{5 - 2} = 11$.

   $a_{100} = 38 + 95 \cdot 11 = 38 + 1045 = 1083$

3. (A) $a_n = 6 + 11n$

4. (E) Common difference $= \dfrac{\dfrac{13}{6} - \dfrac{4}{3}}{17 - 11} = \dfrac{\dfrac{5}{6}}{6} = \dfrac{5}{36}$.

   $a_{30} = \dfrac{13}{6} + 13 \cdot \dfrac{5}{36} = \dfrac{13}{6} + \dfrac{65}{36} = \dfrac{78 + 65}{36} = \dfrac{143}{36}$

Geometric Series

You should be able to do sum of infinite series problems, such as those below. The formula sum $= \dfrac{a}{1-r}$, where a is the first element and r is the common ratio will probably be given. $|r| < 1$ for the series to converge.

1. What is the sum of the series $5 + 2 + \dfrac{4}{5} + \dfrac{8}{25} + ...$?

    A. $\dfrac{25}{3}$

    B. $\dfrac{25}{7}$

    C. $\dfrac{25}{4}$

    D. $\dfrac{26}{3}$

    E. 8

2. What is the sum of the series $5 - 2 + \dfrac{4}{5} - \dfrac{8}{25} + ...$?

    A. $\dfrac{25}{3}$

    B. $\dfrac{25}{7}$

    C. $\dfrac{26}{7}$

    D. 6

    E. 8

3. The sum of a geometric series is 64 and the common ratio is $\frac{3}{4}$. What is the third element in the series?

A. $\dfrac{27}{4}$

B. $\dfrac{37}{4}$

C. 12

D. 9

E. 16

Answer Key: $1A, 2B, 3D$

Solutions

1. (A) $\dfrac{a}{1-r} = \dfrac{5}{1-\dfrac{2}{5}} = \dfrac{5}{\dfrac{3}{5}} = \dfrac{25}{3}$

2. (B) $\dfrac{1}{1-r} = \dfrac{5}{1-\dfrac{-2}{5}} = \dfrac{5}{\dfrac{7}{5}} = \dfrac{25}{7}$

3. (D) $\dfrac{a}{1-\dfrac{3}{4}} = 64, a_1 = 16, a_3 = 16 \cdot \left(\dfrac{3}{4}\right)^2 = 16 \cdot \dfrac{9}{16} = 9$

Geometric Sequences

Likely problems involve find the common ratio and then another term. If the 1st term is 8 and the 4th term is 27, what is the 6th term. The common ratio is $\left(\dfrac{27}{8}\right)^{\frac{1}{3}} = \dfrac{3}{2}$. The 6th term $= 4^{th}$ term (common ratio)$^2 = 27\left(\dfrac{3}{2}\right)^2 = \dfrac{243}{4}$.

1. The first 3 terms in a geometric sequence are 4, 6, and 9. What is the 6th term?

    A. 12

    B. 15

    C. 16

    D. $\dfrac{81}{4}$

    E. $\dfrac{243}{8}$

2. What is the 8th term in the geometric sequence $27, -18, 12, -8, ...$?

    A. $\dfrac{64}{27}$

    B. $\dfrac{256}{243}$

    C. $\dfrac{128}{81}$

    D. $\dfrac{-128}{81}$

    E. $\dfrac{-256}{243}$

3. The 1st and 3rd terms of a geometric sequence are 2 and 6 respectively. What is the 8th term?

    A. 54

    B. $54\sqrt{3}$

    C. $54\sqrt[3]{3}$

    D. $27\sqrt{3}$

    E. 162

4. The 1st term in a geometric sequence is 128 and 4th term is 250. What is the 6th term?

    A. 313

    B. 380

    C. 391

    D. 400

    E. 411

5. What is an equivalent explicit sequence to $a_1 = 5, a_n = 3a_{n-1}$?

    A. $a_n = 5 \cdot 3^{n-1}$

    B. $a_n = 3 \cdot 5^n$

    C. $a_n = 3 \cdot 5^{n-2}$

    D. $a_n = 5^n$

    E. $a_n = 15^n$

Answer Key: $1E, 2D, 3B, 4C, 5A$

Solutions

1. (E) Common ratio $= \dfrac{3}{2}, 9 \cdot \left(\dfrac{3}{2}\right)^3 = 9 \cdot \dfrac{27}{8} = \dfrac{243}{8}$

2. (D) Common ratio $= \dfrac{-2}{3}, a_8 = -8 \cdot \left(\dfrac{-2}{3}\right)^4 = -8 \cdot \dfrac{16}{81} = \dfrac{-128}{81}$

3. (B) $\sqrt{\dfrac{6}{2}} = \sqrt{3}$ is common ratio. So $a_8 = 6 \cdot (\sqrt{3})^5 = 6 \cdot 9\sqrt{3} = 54\sqrt{3}$

4. (C) Common divisor $= \sqrt[3]{\dfrac{250}{128}} = \sqrt[3]{\dfrac{125}{64}} = \dfrac{5}{4}$,

   6th term $= 250 \cdot \left(\dfrac{5}{4}\right)^2 = 250 \cdot \dfrac{25}{16} = 390.625$

5. (A) $5 \cdot 3^{n-1}$. We start with 5 and multiply by 3 each time

Chapter XLVIII

Parametric Equations

The only problems likely are to get the equation in terms of x and y, which means eliminating t as shown.

1. $x = 3t + 5$, $y = 2t - 3$. What is y in terms of x?

    A. $y = \dfrac{2x}{3} - \dfrac{10}{3}$

    B. $y = \dfrac{2x}{3} - \dfrac{11}{3}$

    C. $y = \dfrac{2x}{3} - \dfrac{13}{3}$

    D. $y = \dfrac{2x}{3} - \dfrac{19}{3}$

    E. $y = \dfrac{2x}{3} - \dfrac{16}{3}$

Answer Key: $1D$

Solutions

1. (D) $t = \dfrac{x-5}{3}, y = \dfrac{2(x-5)}{3} - 3, y = \dfrac{2x}{3} - \dfrac{19}{3}$

Chapter XLIX

Permutations and Combinations

You use combinations when order does not matter and permutations when order does matter. For example if you needed to pick a committee of 3 from 10 peoples, that is combinations $_{10}C_3 = \dfrac{10!}{7! \cdot 3!} = 120$ ways. If you need to pick a President, Vice President and Treasurer from 10 people, that is $_{10}P_3 = \dfrac{10!}{7!} = 720$ ways. There are 6 ways of arranging the 3 people, so 6 times as many permutations as combinations.

Permutations

Permutations involve selecting items where order matters. The formula is $_nP_k = \dfrac{n!}{(n-k)!}$. Permutations are used in probability in selecting without replacement problems. This section also discusses the order n items can be arranged, which is $n!$. The number of distinct ways $aaabbcd$ can be arranged is the total number of letter factorial divided by the number of the repeats, $\dfrac{7!}{3! \cdot 2!} = 420$.

1. In how many distinct ways can 7 people stand in line?

   A. 720

   B. 40, 320

   C. 4000

   D. 2880

   E. 5040

2. There are 60 questions with 5 different answers on the math ACT. How many possible combinations of answers are there?

    A. 60^5

    B. 5^{60}

    C. $\dfrac{60!}{55!}$

    D. $\dfrac{60!}{5!}$

    E. $\dfrac{60!}{55! \cdot 5!}$

3. Of 20 people on a committee, how many ways can you pick a President, Vice President, and Treasurer?

    A. 1140

    B. 2280

    C. 6840

    D. 4560

    E. 3420

4. How many 3 digit orderings with no letter repeated can be made from the letters a-h?

    A. 336

    B. 448

    C. 256

    D. 216

    E. 224

5. How many distinct permutations of *aabbccc* are there?

    A. 35

    B. 70

    C. 105

    D. 210

    E. 420

6. How many distinct permutations of *aaaabbbccc* are there?

    A. 1400

    B. 4200

    C. 6300

    D. 8400

    E. 12600

7. What are the number of distinct permutations of the letters in MISSISSIPPI?

    A. 3465

    B. 17325

    C. 32400

    D. 34650

    E. 36000

Answer Key: $1E, 2B, 3C, 4A, 5D, 6B, 7D$

Solutions

1. (E) $7! = 5040$

2. (B) 5^{60}

3. (C) $_{20}P_3 - \dfrac{20!}{17!} = 20 \cdot 19 \cdot 18 = 6840$

4. (A) $_8P_3 = 8 \cdot 7 \cdot 6 = 336$

5. (D) $\dfrac{7!}{2! \cdot 2! \cdot 3!} = 210$

6. (B) $\dfrac{10!}{4! \cdot 3! \cdot 3!} = 4200$

7. (D) $\dfrac{11!}{4! \cdot 4! \cdot 2!} = 34650$

Combinations

The combinations formula is $_nC_k = \dfrac{n!}{k!(n-k)!}$. You use combinations when order does not matter. It is likely problems involving combinations will be $_nC_2$, such as matching people problems or diagonals of polygons problems.

1. What is $\dfrac{10!}{7! \cdot 3!}$

    A. 120

    B. 126

    C. 210

    D. 240

    E. 720

2. What is $\dfrac{8!}{4! \cdot 4! \cdot 2^8}$

    A. $\dfrac{33}{128}$

    B. $\dfrac{1}{4}$

    C. $\dfrac{1}{3}$

    D. $\dfrac{35}{128}$

    E. $\dfrac{5}{16}$

3. In a round robin tournament, each player plays each other twice. If there are 12 players, how many games are there?

    A. 66

    B. 108

    C. 132

    D. 144

    E. 126

4. How many diagonals does a 10-sided polygon have?

    A. 25

    B. 28

    C. 35

    D. 45

    E. 90

5. You can pick 2 of 5 appetizers and 2 of 8 entrees. How many possible dinners are there?

    A. 240

    B. 560

    C. 140

    D. 126

    E. 280

Solutions

1. (A) $\dfrac{10 \cdot 9 \cdot 8}{3 \cdot 2 \cdot 1} = 120$.

2. (D) This is the probability of 4 heads flipping 8 coins.

3. (C) $_{12}C_2 \cdot 2 = 66 \cdot 2 = 132$

4. (C) $_{10}C_2 - 10 = 45 - 10 = 35$. You subtract 10 for the 10 sides of the polygon, which are not diagonals.

5. (E) $_8C_2 \cdot {}_5C_2 = \dfrac{8 \cdot 7}{2} \cdot \dfrac{5 \cdot 4}{2} = 28 \cdot 10 = 280$

Codes

If a code is 4 digits that can repeat, there are $10^4 = 10,000$ possible codes. If the digits cannot repeat, there are $_{10}P_4 = 10 \cdot 9 \cdot 8 \cdot 7 = 5040$ possible codes.

1. A code consists of 2 letters followed by 2 digits and letters and digits CAN be repeated. How many possible codes are there?

    A. $63,600$

    B. $64,600$

    C. $65,600$

    D. $66,600$

    E. $67,600$

2. A code consists of 2 letters followed by 2 digits and letters and digits CANNOT be repeated. How many possible codes are there?

    A. $58,500$

    B. $59,000$

    C. $59,500$

    D. $60,000$

    E. $61,000$

3. A code consists of 4 of 26 letters that cannot repeat, followed by 3 numbers 0-9 that cannot repeat. What is an expression for the number of possible codes?

    A. $10^4 \cdot 26^4$

    B. $\dfrac{26! \cdot 10!}{22! \cdot 7!}$

    C. $\dfrac{26! \cdot 10!}{(22! \cdot 6! \cdot 4!)^2}$

    D. $\dfrac{26! \cdot 10!}{22! \cdot 6! \cdot 4!}$

    E. $\dfrac{10^4 \cdot 26^4}{4}!^2$

4. How many more codes can you make from 3 digits 0-9 that can repeat than from 3 digits that can't repeat?

  A. 560

  B. 420

  C. 350

  D. 280

  E. 210

Solutions

1. (E) $10^2 \cdot 26^2 = 67,600$

2. (A) $10 \cdot 9 \cdot 26 \cdot 25 = 58,500$

3. (B) $\dfrac{26! \cdot 10!}{22! \cdot 7!}$. Since it can repeat use permutations, $_{26}P_3 \cdot {}_{20}P_3$

4. (D) $10^3 - 10 \cdot 9 \cdot 8 = 1000 - 720 = 280$

Chapter L

Probability

This is may be the longest chapter in the book. Probability problems are not a large portion of the problems on the test, but they are a large portion of the difficult problems. Some of the problems in this guide are not standard problems in a high school textbook, but may be similar to those that have appeared on the exam. It is possible probability problems not similar to those in this guide may appear on future exams.

Without Replacement

In without replacement problems, the numerator and denominator are reduced by one each time.

For example, you have 7 red marbles and 7 green marbles and draw 3 marbles without replacement, what is the probability they will all be red?

$$\frac{7}{14} \cdot \frac{6}{13} \cdot \frac{5}{12} = \frac{5}{52}$$

1. If you draw 2 cards from a standard deck, what the probability that they are both aces.

   A. $\dfrac{1}{200}$

   B. $\dfrac{1}{26}$

   C. $\dfrac{1}{256}$

   D. $\dfrac{1}{221}$

   E. $\dfrac{1}{169}$

2. Say there are 7 red and 3 blue marbles and we take 2 marbles without replacement. What is the probability both marbles will be the same color?

    A. $\dfrac{23}{30}$

    B. $\dfrac{8}{15}$

    C. $\dfrac{7}{15}$

    D. $\dfrac{3}{5}$

    E. $\dfrac{2}{3}$

3. If there are 5 red and 4 blue marbles, and we draw 3 marbles without replacement, what is the probability that they are all red?

    A. $\dfrac{11}{84}$

    B. $\dfrac{9}{84}$

    C. $\dfrac{5}{42}$

    D. $\dfrac{1}{14}$

    E. $\dfrac{1}{6}$

4. If you draw 5 cards from a standard deck, what is the probability they are of the same suit?

    A. $\dfrac{33}{16660}$

    B. $\dfrac{77}{16660}$

    C. $\dfrac{21}{16660}$

    D. $\dfrac{51}{16660}$

    E. $\dfrac{27}{16660}$

5. Four balls, numbered 1 to 4 are placed in a bin. Two balls are drawn without replacement. What is the probability that the sum of the numbers drawn is 5?

   A. $\dfrac{1}{4}$

   B. $\dfrac{10}{31}$

   C. $\dfrac{3}{10}$

   D. $\dfrac{3}{8}$

   E. $\dfrac{1}{3}$

6. Seven balls, numbered 1 to 7 are placed in a bin. Two balls are drawn without replacement. What is the probability that the sum of the numbers drawn is 6?

   A. $\dfrac{2}{21}$

   B. $\dfrac{5}{42}$

   C. $\dfrac{3}{42}$

   D. $\dfrac{1}{11}$

   E. $\dfrac{1}{21}$

Solutions

1. (D) $\dfrac{4}{52} \cdot \dfrac{3}{51} = \dfrac{1}{221}$

2. (B) $\dfrac{7}{10} \cdot \dfrac{6}{9} + \dfrac{3}{10} \cdot \dfrac{2}{9} = \dfrac{42 + 6}{90} = \dfrac{48}{90} = \dfrac{8}{15}$

3. (C) $\dfrac{5}{9} \cdot \dfrac{4}{8} \cdot \dfrac{3}{7} = \dfrac{5}{42}$

4. (A) $\dfrac{{}_{12}P_4}{{}_{51}P_4} = \dfrac{12}{51} \cdot \dfrac{11}{50} \cdot \dfrac{10}{49} \cdot \dfrac{9}{48} = \dfrac{11 \cdot 9}{4 \cdot 5 \cdot 49 \cdot 51} = \dfrac{33}{4 \cdot 5 \cdot 49 \cdot 17} = \dfrac{33}{16660}$

5. (E) 1-4, 2-3, 3-2, 4-1 out of $4 \cdot 3 = 12$ possibilities $\Rightarrow$ So $\dfrac{4}{12} = \dfrac{1}{3}$

6. (A) 1-5, 2-4, 4-2, 5-1. 3-3 is not possible, since there is not replacement. There are $7 \cdot 6 = 42$ possibilities $\Rightarrow$ So $\dfrac{4}{42} = \dfrac{2}{21}$

Multiple Events

Many Times

If it is the probability of at least 1, you take 1 – probability of 0. So if a product is defective .05 of the time, the probability of at least 1 defective item in a group of 10 is

$$1 - .95^{10} = .401$$

The probability that if you flip 8 coins you get exactly 4 heads is

$$\frac{{}_8C_4}{2^8} = \frac{70}{256} = \frac{35}{128}$$

1. If 7 fair coins are tossed simultaneously, what is the probability they all land on heads?

    A. $\dfrac{1}{64}$

    B. $\dfrac{1}{128}$

    C. $\dfrac{1}{256}$

    D. $\dfrac{5}{512}$

    E. $\dfrac{3}{256}$

2. Say you randomly guessed all problems on the math ACT. The probability that you got all of them right is 1.15×10^a. What is a?

    A. -34

    B. -22

    C. -36

    D. -42

    E. -32

3. Say you toss a fair coin 10 times, what is the probability that it ends up either all 10 heads or all 10 tails?

    A. $\dfrac{1}{256}$

    B. $\dfrac{3}{1024}$

    C. $\dfrac{1}{1024}$

    D. $\dfrac{5}{2048}$

    E. $\dfrac{1}{512}$

391

4. Say you randomly guessed randomly 5 problems on the math ACT, what is the probability that you got all of them wrong?

    A. $\dfrac{3}{8}$

    B. $\dfrac{1}{3}$

    C. $\dfrac{256}{625}$

    D. $\dfrac{1024}{3125}$

    E. $\dfrac{216}{625}$

5. If you randomly guessed on 10 math ACT problems, what is the probability that you got at least 1 of them right?

    A. .89

    B. .87

    C. .88

    D. .9

    E. .91

6. If you tossed 7 fair coins, what is the probability of 3 heads?

    A. $\dfrac{1}{3}$

    B. $\dfrac{1}{4}$

    C. $\dfrac{33}{128}$

    D. $\dfrac{35}{128}$

    E. $\dfrac{5}{16}$

Answer Key: 1B, 2D, 3E, 4D, 5A, 6D

Solutions

1. (B) $\left(\dfrac{1}{2}\right)^7 = \dfrac{1}{128}$

2. (D) $\left(\dfrac{1}{5}\right)^{60} = 1.15 \times 10^{-42}$

3. (E) $2 \cdot \left(\dfrac{1}{2}\right)^{10} = 2 \cdot \dfrac{1}{1024} = \dfrac{1}{512}$

4. (D) $\left(\dfrac{4}{5}\right)^5$

5. (A) $1 - \left(\dfrac{4}{5}\right)^{10} = 1 - .107 \approx .89$

6. (D) $\dfrac{{}_7C_3}{2^7} = \dfrac{35}{128}$

2 to 4 Times

1. The probability the Tigers win the first game is .8. The probability they win the 2nd game is .6. What is the probability they win one and lose one if the event are independent?

   A. .40

   B. .50

   C. .25

   D. .56

   E. .44

2. A fair coin is tossed 4 times. What is the probability of exactly 2 heads?

   A. $\dfrac{1}{2}$

   B. $\dfrac{5}{16}$

   C. $\dfrac{1}{4}$

   D. $\dfrac{3}{8}$

   E. $\dfrac{11}{32}$

3. The probability the Tigers win each game is .7 and the games are independent events. What is the probability they win all 3 games?

   A. .25

   B. .3

   C. .512

   D. .343

   E. .125

4. Say you roll two dice. What is the probability the sum is 9?

   A. $\dfrac{1}{9}$

   B. $\dfrac{5}{36}$

   C. $\dfrac{1}{6}$

   D. $\dfrac{1}{12}$

   E. $\dfrac{1}{4}$

5. Say you randomly guessed 2 problems on the math ACT, what is the probability that you got exactly 1 right?

    A. $\dfrac{6}{25}$

    B. $\dfrac{1}{3}$

    C. $\dfrac{2}{5}$

    D. $\dfrac{8}{25}$

    E. $\dfrac{1}{4}$

6. Say you randomly guessed 3 problems on the math ACT, what is the probability you got at least 1 right?

    A. $\dfrac{64}{125}$

    B. $\dfrac{2}{5}$

    C. $\dfrac{12}{25}$

    D. $\dfrac{1}{2}$

    E. $\dfrac{61}{125}$

7. Say the probability the Tigers win each game is 60% and they are independent events. What is the probability the Tigers win at least one game of a 4 game series?

    A. 90%

    B. 88%

    C. 97%

    D. 95%

    E. 93%

8. The Giants have a 60% chance of winning each game. If the games are independent events, what is the chance the Giants lose both games?

    A. 25%

    B. 18%

    C. 16%

    D. 36%

    E. 20%

Answer Key: 1E, 2D, 3D, 4A, 5D, 6E, 7C, 8C

Solutions

1. (E) $.8 \cdot .4 + .2 \cdot .6 = .44$

2. (D) $\dfrac{_4C_2}{2^4} = \dfrac{6}{16} = \dfrac{3}{8} \Rightarrow$ You can also use a probability tree or Pascal's triangle.

3. (D) $.7^3 = .343$

4. (A) 3-6, 4-5, 5-4, 6-3 $\Rightarrow$ 4 possibilities out of 36 $\Rightarrow \dfrac{4}{36} = \dfrac{1}{9}$

5. (D) $2 \cdot \dfrac{1}{5} \cdot \dfrac{4}{5} = \dfrac{8}{25}$ or $1 - \left(\dfrac{1}{5}\right)^2 - \left(\dfrac{4}{5}\right)^2 = 1 - \dfrac{1}{25} - \dfrac{16}{25} = \dfrac{8}{25}$

6. (E) $1 - \left(\dfrac{4}{5}\right)^3 = 1 - \dfrac{64}{125} = \dfrac{61}{125}$

7. (C) $1 - .4^4 = 1 - .0256 = .974$

8. (C) $.4 \cdot .4 = .16$

Dice Problems

1. If you roll a standard die and flip a coin, what is the probability of heads or a 6?

    A. $\dfrac{5}{12}$

    B. $\dfrac{13}{24}$

    C. $\dfrac{7}{12}$

    D. $\dfrac{2}{3}$

    E. $\dfrac{1}{2}$

2. If you roll 2 6-sided dice, what is the probability that the sum will be 8 or greater?

    A. $\dfrac{7}{18}$

    B. $\dfrac{5}{12}$

    C. $\dfrac{4}{9}$

    D. $\dfrac{1}{3}$

    E. $\dfrac{1}{2}$

3. If we roll two 8-sided dice with sides numbered 1 to 8, what is the probability that the sum of the two dice is 10?

    A. $\dfrac{5}{64}$

    B. $\dfrac{1}{8}$

    C. $\dfrac{6}{49}$

    D. $\dfrac{7}{64}$

    E. $\dfrac{3}{32}$

Solutions

1. (C) $1 - \dfrac{1}{2} \cdot \dfrac{5}{6} = 1 - \dfrac{5}{12} = \dfrac{7}{12}$

2. (B) 2-6, 3-5, 3-6, 4-4, 4-5, 4-6, 5-3, 5-4, 5-5, 5-6, 6-2, 6-3, 6-4, 6-5, 6-6 = 15 possibilities out of 36

    $\Rightarrow$ So $\dfrac{15}{36} = \dfrac{5}{12}$

3. (D) 2-8, 3-7, 4-6, 5-5, 6-4, 7-3, 8-2 $\Rightarrow$ 7 possibilities out of 64 possible combinations.

Product Odd or Positive

For the product of 2 or 3 numbers to be odd, they all have to be odd. For the product to be positive, it needs to be *negative · negative* or *positive · positive*.

1. Say we randomly select 3 numbers which can repeat from $\{1, 2, 3, 4, 5\}$. What is the probability that the product of the numbers is odd?

   A. $\dfrac{1}{8}$

   B. $\dfrac{27}{125}$

   C. $\dfrac{1}{4}$

   D. $\dfrac{1}{10}$

   E. $\dfrac{1}{5}$

2. Say we randomly select 2 different numbers from $\{1, 2, 3, 4, 5\}$. What is the probability that the product of the numbers is odd?

   A. $\dfrac{1}{2}$

   B. $\dfrac{3}{5}$

   C. $\dfrac{3}{10}$

   D. $\dfrac{1}{4}$

   E. $\dfrac{9}{25}$

3. Say we randomly select one number from $\{1, 2, 3, 4, 5\}$ and another number from $\{6, 7, 8, 9, 10\}$. What is the probability that the product of the numbers is odd?

   A. $\dfrac{2}{9}$

   B. $\dfrac{1}{3}$

   C. $\dfrac{17}{75}$

   D. $\dfrac{6}{25}$

   E. $\dfrac{1}{4}$

4. Say we take an integer at random from 1 to 5 and another integer at random from 11-17. What is the probability that the product of the two integers is odd?

   A. $\dfrac{13}{35}$

   B. $\dfrac{1}{3}$

   C. $\dfrac{12}{35}$

   D. $\dfrac{1}{4}$

   E. $\dfrac{11}{35}$

5. Suppose a is randomly selected for $\{-2, -1, 0, 1, 2\}$ and b is randomly selected from $\{-3, -2, -1, 0, 1, 2, 3\}$. What is the probability that $ab > 0$?

   A. $\dfrac{1}{2}$

   B. $\dfrac{13}{35}$

   C. $\dfrac{12}{35}$

   D. $\dfrac{2}{5}$

   E. $\dfrac{11}{35}$

Answer Key: 1B, 2C, 3D, 4C, 5C

Solutions

1. (B) $\left(\dfrac{3}{5}\right)^3 = \dfrac{27}{125}$

2. (C) For the product to be odd, they both have to be odd, so $\dfrac{3}{5} \cdot \dfrac{1}{2} = \dfrac{3}{10}$

3. (D) $\dfrac{3}{5} \cdot \dfrac{2}{5} = \dfrac{6}{25}$

4. (C) $\dfrac{3}{5} \cdot \dfrac{4}{7} = \dfrac{12}{35}$

5. (C) $negative \cdot negative = 2 \cdot 3 = 6$ and $positive \cdot positive = 2 \cdot 3 = 6 \Rightarrow \dfrac{6+6}{35} = \dfrac{12}{35}$

In Same Group or Next to Each Other

These problems are challenging and not emphasized in standard text books.

If asked if Alice and Lisa will be in the same group of 5 out of 10 people, put Alice in one group, then there are 9 places for Lisa, 4 of which are in Alice's group, so $\frac{4}{9}$.

1. Bob and Kevin will be among 10 people seated at a circular table. What is the probability that they will be seated next to each other?

   A. $\frac{2}{9}$

   B. $\frac{4}{9}$

   C. $\frac{1}{3}$

   D. $\frac{1}{4}$

   E. $\frac{1}{5}$

2. 6 people are randomly split into groups of 3. if Alvin and Bob are among the 6, what is the probability they will be in the same group?

   A. $\frac{2}{5}$

   B. $\frac{4}{9}$

   C. $\frac{3}{7}$

   D. $\frac{1}{3}$

   E. $\frac{1}{2}$

3. Jane and July are among 8 players in a tennis tournament. What is the probability that they will be paired together in the first round?

   A. $\frac{1}{5}$

   B. $\frac{3}{14}$

   C. $\frac{1}{4}$

   D. $\frac{1}{7}$

   E. $\frac{3}{16}$

Answer Key: 1A, 2A, 3D

Solutions

1. (A) If Bob is in a certain seat, there are 2 seats next to him out of a total of 9 other seats.

2. (A) If Alvin is in one group, there are 2 places for Bob in the same group and 3 places in the other group, so $\dfrac{2}{5}$

3. (D) There are 7 people Jane can be paired with, one of whom is July.

Draw One Card

The probability of one event or another is the sum of the probabilities of each minus the probability of both, so you do not double count.

So the probability of drawing an ace or a spade is

$$\frac{13}{52} + \frac{4}{52} - \frac{1}{52} = \frac{16}{52} = \frac{4}{13}$$

1. Say you draw a card from a standard deck, what is the probability that it is an spade and a face card?

    A. $\frac{11}{26}$

    B. $\frac{1}{52}$

    C. $\frac{3}{52}$

    D. $\frac{1}{13}$

    E. $\frac{5}{52}$

2. Say you draw a card from a standard deck, what is the probability that it is an spade or a face card?

    A. $\frac{25}{52}$

    B. $\frac{5}{13}$

    C. $\frac{23}{52}$

    D. $\frac{11}{26}$

    E. $\frac{6}{13}$

Answer Key: 1C, 2D

Solutions

1. (C) $\dfrac{1}{4} \cdot \dfrac{3}{13} = \dfrac{3}{52}$

2. (D) 13 spades + 12 face cards – 3 both = 22 $\Rightarrow \dfrac{22}{52} = \dfrac{11}{26}$

Chapter LI

Composition of Functions

With Value

The easiest way is to plug the value in at the beginning.
For example, if given $f(x) = \sqrt{x+1}$, what is $f(f(f(5)))$?

$$f(5) = \sqrt{6} = 2.449 \Rightarrow f(2.449) = \sqrt{3.449} = 1.857 \Rightarrow f(1.857) = \sqrt{2.857} = 1.690$$

Finding $f(f(f(x)))$ algebraically would be difficult.

1. $f(x) = x + \dfrac{1}{x}$. What is $f(f(2))$?

   A. $\dfrac{10}{29}$

   B. $\dfrac{5}{2}$

   C. $\dfrac{29}{10}$

   D. $\dfrac{31}{10}$

   E. 3

2. If $f(x) = x^2 - 4$, what is $f(f(f(3)))$?

   A. 417

   B. 447

   C. 427

   D. 407

   E. 437

3. $f(x) = x^3 - 3$. what is $f(f(2))$?

   A. 128
   B. 125
   C. 122
   D. 72
   E. 5

4. If $f(x) = 3x - 1$ for $x < 3$ and $x - 2$ for $x \geq 3$, what is $f(f(f(3)))$?

   A. 3
   B. 14
   C. 2
   D. 4
   E. 5

Solutions

1. (C) $2 + \dfrac{1}{2} = \dfrac{5}{2} \Rightarrow \dfrac{5}{2} + \dfrac{2}{5} = \dfrac{29}{10}$

2. (E) $3^2 - 2 = 5 \Rightarrow 5^2 - 4 = 21 \Rightarrow 21^2 - 4 = 441 - 4 = 437$

3. (C) $2^3 - 3 = 5 \Rightarrow 5^3 - 2 = 122 \Rightarrow$ Finding $f(f(x))$ is possible but too much work.

4. (E) $f(3) = 1 \Rightarrow f(1) = 2 \Rightarrow f(2) = 5$

Complications

There can be some challenging problems.

$f(x) = 2x + 5$ and $g(x) = ax - 2$. Find a for which $f(g(x)) = g(f(x))$.

Plug into each equation, set them equal, and solve for a.

$$2(ax - 2) + 5 = a(2x + 5) - 2 \Rightarrow 2ax - 4 + 5 = 2ax + 5a - 2 \Rightarrow 3 = 5a \Rightarrow a = \frac{3}{5}$$

1. $f(x) = 3x + 2$ and $g(x) = 5x + a$. What is a for which $f(g(x)) = g(f(x))$?

   A. 2

   B. 5

   C. 8

   D. 4

   E. 3

2. $f(x) = 2x + 5$ and $g(x) = ax + 3$. What is a so that $f(g(x)) = g(f(x))$?

   A. $\dfrac{5}{3}$

   B. $\dfrac{11}{5}$

   C. $\dfrac{8}{5}$

   D. 2

   E. $\dfrac{4}{5}$

3. If $f(x) = x^2$ and $g(f(x)) = \dfrac{1 + x^2}{x^2}$, what is $f(g(x))$?

   A. $\left(\dfrac{1 + x}{x}\right)^3$

   B. $\left(\dfrac{1 + x}{1 - x}\right)^2$

   C. $\dfrac{1 + x}{1 - x}$

   D. $\left(\dfrac{1 + x}{x}\right)^2$

   E. $\dfrac{1 + x}{x}$

4. If $f(x) = x + 4$ and $g(f(x)) = 3x + 7$, what is $f(g(x))$?

    A. $3x - 5$

    B. $3x - 1$

    C. $x - 1$

    D. $3x + 2$

    E. $x - 5$

Solutions

1. (D) $3(5x + a) + 2 = 5(3x + 2) + a \Rightarrow 15x + 3a + 2 = 15x + 10 + a \Rightarrow 2a = 8 \Rightarrow a = 4$

2. (C) $2(ax + 3) + 5 = a(2x + 5) + 3 \Rightarrow 2ax + 11 = 2ax + 5a + 3 \Rightarrow 11 = 5a + 3 \Rightarrow a = \dfrac{8}{5}$

3. (D) $g(x) = \dfrac{1 + x}{x} \Rightarrow f(g(x)) = \left(\dfrac{1 + x}{x}\right)^2$

4. (B) Let $g(x) = ax + b \Rightarrow a(x+4)+b = 3x+7 \Rightarrow ax+4a+b = 3x+7 \Rightarrow ax = 3x \Rightarrow a = 3$

   $\Rightarrow 4a + b = 7 \Rightarrow 4 \cdot 3 + b = 7 \Rightarrow b = -5$

   So $g(x) = 3x - 5 \Rightarrow f(g(x)) = (3x - 5) + 4 = 3x - 1$

$f(f(x))$

To find $f(f(x))$, plug in $f(x)$ for x.
  For example $f(x) = 3x + 2$, what is $f(f(x))$?

$$3(3x + 2) + 2 = 9x + 8$$

1. $f(x) = x^4$. What is $f(f(x))$?

   A. x^{16}

   B. $4x^8$

   C. x^8

   D. x^{256}

   E. $4x^{16}$

2. $f(x) = 4x + 7$. What is $f(f(x))$?

   A. $12x + 28$

   B. $16x + 49$

   C. $16x + 28$

   D. $8x + 21$

   E. $16x + 35$

3. $f(x) = x^2 + 3$. What is $f(f(x))$?

   A. $x^4 + 6x^2 + 16$

   B. $x^4 + 6x^2 + 9$

   C. $x^4 + 6x^2 + 18$

   D. $x^4 + 6x^2 + 12$

   E. $x^4 + 6x^2 + 15$

4. If $f(x) = \dfrac{-1}{x^5}$, what is $f(f(x))$?

   A. x^{25}

   B. $\dfrac{-1}{x^{25}}$

   C. x^{10}

   D. $\dfrac{1}{x^{10}}$

   E. $\dfrac{1}{x^{25}}$

5. $f(x) = \dfrac{x}{1+x}$. What is $f(f(x))$?

A. $\dfrac{2x}{2x+1}$

B. $\dfrac{x}{3x+1}$

C. $\dfrac{x}{3x-1}$

D. $\dfrac{x}{3x+2}$

E. $\dfrac{x}{2x+1}$

Solutions

1. (A) $\left(x^4\right)^4 = x^{16}$

2. (E) $4(4x + 7) + 7 = 16x + 35$

3. (D) $\left(x^2 + 3\right)^2 + 3 = x^4 + 6x^2 + 9 + 3 = x^4 + 6x^2 + 12$

4. (A) $\dfrac{-1}{\left(\dfrac{-1}{x^5}\right)^5} = \dfrac{-1}{\dfrac{-1}{x^{25}}} = x^{25}$

5. (E) $\dfrac{\dfrac{x}{1+x}}{1 + \dfrac{x}{1+x}} = \dfrac{\dfrac{x}{1+x}}{\dfrac{1+x+x}{1+x}} = \dfrac{x}{2x+1}$

Other

1. $f(x) = x^2 + 3x + 2$. What is $f(x^5)$?

    A. $x^7 + 3x^6 + 2$

    B. $4x^{10} + 6x^5 + 2$

    C. $x^7 + 3x^5 + 2$

    D. $4x^{10} + 3x^5 + 2$

    E. $x^{10} + 3x^5 + 2$

2. $f(x) = x^2 + 3x + 2$. What is $f(3x^2)$?

    A. $9x^4 + 27x^2 + 2$

    B. $9x^4 + 9x^2 + 2$

    C. $3x^4 + 9x^2 + 2$

    D. $27x^4 + 27x^2 + 2$

    E. $9x^4 + 9x^2 + 2x$

3. $f(x) = \dfrac{x}{1+x}$ and $g(x) = \dfrac{3}{x+4}$. What is $f(g(x))$ simplified?

    A. $\dfrac{3}{x+8}$

    B. $\dfrac{3}{x+6}$

    C. $\dfrac{3}{x+9}$

    D. $\dfrac{3}{x+7}$

    E. $\dfrac{3}{x+5}$

4. $f(x) = \dfrac{x}{1+x}$ and $g(x) = \dfrac{3}{x+4}$. What is $g(f(x))$ simplified?

    A. $\dfrac{3x+3}{5x+4}$

    B. $\dfrac{6x}{x+4}$

    C. $\dfrac{3x}{x+4}$

    D. $\dfrac{4x}{x+4}$

    E. $\dfrac{5x}{x+4}$

Solutions

1. (E) $\left(x^5\right)^2 + 3x^5 + 2 = x^{10} + 3x^5 + 2$

2. (B) $\left(3x^2\right)^2 + 3 \cdot 3x^2 + 2 = 9x^4 + 9x^2 + 2$

3. (D) $\dfrac{\dfrac{3}{x+4}}{1 + \dfrac{3}{x+4}} = \dfrac{\dfrac{3}{x+4}}{\dfrac{x+4+3}{x+4}} = \dfrac{3}{x+7}$

4. (A) $\dfrac{3}{\dfrac{x}{1+x} + 4} = \dfrac{3}{\dfrac{x+4x+4}{1+x}} = \dfrac{3}{\dfrac{5x+4}{1+x}} = \dfrac{3x+3}{5x+4}$

Chapter LII

Inverse Functions

To find the inverse of a function, switch the x and y and then solve for y.

First Degree

The basic problem is find the inverse of $y = 3x + 2, x = 3y + 2, x - 2 = 3y,$
$$\frac{x - 2}{3} = y$$

1. If $f(x) = 11x - 5$, what is $f^{-1}(x)$?

    A. $\dfrac{x + 1}{11}$

    B. $\dfrac{x + 2}{11}$

    C. $\dfrac{x + 3}{11}$

    D. $\dfrac{x + 4}{11}$

    E. $\dfrac{x + 5}{11}$

2. $f(x) = \dfrac{3x + 2}{5x - 8}$. What is $f^{-1}(x)$

    A. $y = \dfrac{8x + 3}{5x + 3}$

    B. $y = \dfrac{8x + 2}{5x - 4}$

    C. $y = \dfrac{8x - 2}{8x - 3}$

    D. $y = \dfrac{8x + 2}{5x - 3}$

    E. $y = \dfrac{8x + 2}{8x - 3}$

3. If $f(x) = ax + b$, what is $f^{-1}(x)$?

    A. $y = \dfrac{x - a}{b}$

    B. $y = \dfrac{x - b}{a}$

    C. $y = \dfrac{b - x}{a}$

    D. $y = \dfrac{x + b}{a}$

    E. $y = \dfrac{x - b}{ab}$

Solutions

1. (E) $x = 11y - 5, x + 5 = 11y, \dfrac{x+5}{11} = y$

2. (D) $x = \dfrac{3y+2}{5y-8}, 5xy - 8x = 3y + 2, 5xy - 3y = 8x + 2, y = \dfrac{8x+2}{5x-3}$

3. (B) $ay + b = x, ay = x - b, y = \dfrac{x-b}{a}$

Not First Degree

You switch x and y and solve for x as before. I mostly used odd powers in the exercises to avoid issues with restricted domains, which should not be on the test. The following is a really complicated example. $f(x) = \log(4x^3 + 11) + 5$, what is $f^{-1}(x)$?

$x = \log(4y^3 + 11) + 5$, $x - 5 = \log(4y^3 + 11)$, $10^{x-5} = 4y^3 + 11$, $\dfrac{10^{x-5} - 11}{4} = y^3$, $\sqrt[3]{\dfrac{10^{x-5} - 11}{4}} = y$

1. $f(x) = \sqrt[3]{3x + 8}$. What is $f^{-1}(x)$?

A. $\dfrac{x^3 - 8}{4} = y$

B. $\dfrac{x^3 - 3}{8} = y$

C. $\dfrac{x^3 + 8}{3} = y$

D. $\dfrac{x^3 - 8}{3} = y$

E. $\dfrac{x^3 + 8}{6} = y$

2. $f(x) = x^5 + 4$. What is $f^{-1}(x)$?

A. $\sqrt[5]{x + 4}$

B. $\sqrt[5]{x - 4}$

C. $\sqrt[5]{x - 16}$

D. $-\sqrt[5]{x - 4}$

E. $\sqrt[5]{x - 2}$

3. $f(x) = \log(3x - 11)$. What is $f^{-1}(x)$?

   A. $\dfrac{e^x + 11}{3} = y$

   B. $\dfrac{e^x - 11}{3} = y$

   C. $\dfrac{10^x + 11}{3} = y$

   D. $\dfrac{10^x - 11}{3} = y$

   E. $\dfrac{10^x + 11}{9} = y$

4. $f(x) = 2^{5x+4}$. What is $f^{-1}(100)$?

   A. 0.53

   B. 0.63

   C. 0.73

   D. 0.83

   E. 0.93

5. $f(x) = 5^{2x-1}$. What is $f^{-1}(x)$?

   A. $\dfrac{\log_5 x + 1}{2}$

   B. $\dfrac{\log_5 x}{2} + 1$

   C. $\dfrac{\log_5 x - 1}{2}$

   D. $\dfrac{\log_5 x}{2} - 1$

   E. $\dfrac{\log_5 x + 3}{2}$

6. If $f(x) = \sqrt[3]{x^5 + 8}$, what is $f^{-1}(x)$?

A. $\sqrt[5]{x^3 + 8} = y$

B. $\sqrt[5]{x^3 - 8} = y$

C. $\sqrt[3]{x^5 - 8} = y$

D. $\sqrt[3]{x^5 + 8} = y$

E. $(x^3 - 8)^5 = y$

Answer Key: $1D, 2B, 3C, 4A, 5A, 6B$

Solutions

1. (D) $x = \sqrt[3]{3y+8}, x^3 = 3y+8, x^3 - 8 = 3y, \dfrac{x^3-8}{3} = y$

2. (B) $x = y^5 + 4, x - 4 = y^5, \sqrt[5]{x-4} = y$

3. (C) $x = \log(3y-11), 10^x = 3y-11, \dfrac{10^x + 11}{3} = y$

4. (A) When taking f^{-1} of a value, plug that value in for y in the original equation.
   $100 = 2^{5x+4}, \dfrac{\ln 100}{\ln 2} = 5x+4, 6.644 = 5x + 4, 2.644 = 5x,$
   $x \approx 0.53.$ Or $x = 2^{5y+4}, \log_2 x = 5y+4, \dfrac{\log_2 x - 4}{5} = y, \dfrac{6.44-4}{5} = y,$
   $y \approx 0.53$

5. (A) $x = 5^{2y-1}, \log_5 x = 2y - 1, \dfrac{\log_5 x + 1}{2} = y$

6. (B) $x = \sqrt[3]{y^5 + 8}, x^3 = y^5 + 8, x^3 - 8 = y^5, \sqrt[5]{x^3 - 8} = y$

Chapter LIII

Exponential Equations

Word Problems

For depreciation, $A = P(1-r)^t$. For simple interest $A = P(1+r)^t$. For compound interest $A = P\left(1 - \dfrac{r}{n}\right)^{nt}$. For continuous interest $A = Pe^{rt}$. You may be given the formula or asked to find and expression with the formula, rather than the answer.

1. What is an expression for $\$10,000$ at 8% interest compounded quarterly for 20 years?

    A. $10,000(1 + 0.08)^{20}$

    B. $10,000\left(1 + \dfrac{0.08}{4}\right)^{80}$

    C. $10,000 \cdot e^{1.6}$

    D. $10,000\left(1 + \dfrac{0.08}{12}\right)^{240}$

    E. $10,000\left(1 + \dfrac{0.08}{4}\right)^{20}$

2. What is an expression for $10,000 at 8% interest compounded continuously for 20 years?

    A. $10,000(1.08)^{20}$

    B. $10,000 \cdot e^{0.8}$

    C. $10,000(1.02)^{80}$

    D. $10,000 \cdot e^{2.4}$

    E. $10,000 \cdot e^{1.6}$

3. You buy a car for $40,000 that depreciates at 12% per year. What will it be worth after 10 years?

    A. $11,140$

    B. $10,140$

    C. $9,140$

    D. $8,140$

    E. $7,140$

4. You buy a car for $50,000 that depreciates 25% the first year and 10% per year after that. What will it be worth after 5 years?

    A. $23,600$

    B. $24,600$

    C. $25,600$

    D. $26,600$

    E. $27,600$

5. If you invested $1000 at 6% interest for 10 years, how much more would you make if it was compounded quarterly than if it was compounded annually?

    A. $23

    B. $36

    C. $44

    D. $74

    E. $108

6. If you invested $1000 at 6% interest for 10 years, how much more would you make if it was compounded continuously than if it was compounded monthly?

    A. $2.72

    B. $2.92

    C. $3.42

    D. $4.12

    E. $5.44

7. Say you deposited $1,000 at 6% interest compounded annually for 100 years. How much would it be worth in thousands of dollars?

    A. 219

    B. 227

    C. 282

    D. 327

    E. 339

Answer Key: $1B, 2E, 3A, 4B, 5A, 6A, 7E$

Solutions

1. (B) Plug into the compound interest formula $A = P\left(1 + \dfrac{r}{n}\right)^{nt}$

2. (E) The formula for continuous interest is $A = Pe^{rt}$.
   $Pe^{rt} = 10,000 \cdot e^{rt} = 10,000 \cdot e^{0.08 \cdot 20} = 10,000 \cdot e^{1.6}$

3. (A) $40000 \cdot 0.88^{10} = 11,140$

4. (B) $50,000 \cdot 0.75 \cdot 0.9^4 = 24603.75$

5. (A) $1000 \cdot 1.015^{40} - 1000 \cdot 1.06^{10} = 1,814.02 - 1,790.85 = \$23.17$

6. (A) $1000 \cdot e^{0.06 \cdot 10} - 1000 \cdot 1.005^{120} = 1922.12 - 1819.40 = \$2.72$

7. (E) $1,000 \cdot 1.06^{100} = 339,302$

Numeric Equations

1. If $2^{\frac{3x+4}{x+8}} = 32$, what is x?

    A. -12

    B. -15

    C. -16

    D. -18

    E. -20

2. $8^x = \dfrac{1}{32^{x+2}}$. What is x?

    A. $\dfrac{13}{5}$

    B. $\dfrac{-13}{5}$

    C. $\dfrac{-12}{5}$

    D. $\dfrac{-5}{4}$

    E. -3

3. What is the exact value of the x coordinate of the intersection of $y = e^{x+5}$ and $y = 100$.

    A. $\ln 10 - 5$

    B. $\ln 100 + 5$

    C. $\ln 100 - 5$

    D. $\ln 100 - 8$

    E. $\ln 100 - 12$

4. $(\sqrt{2})^c = \dfrac{1}{128^d}$. What is the ratio $c : d$?

    A. -14

    B. 14

    C. -7

    D. -21

    E. -28

5. If $(4\sqrt{2})^a = 128^b$, what is $\dfrac{a}{b}$?

    A. $\dfrac{7}{5}$

    B. $\dfrac{7}{10}$

    C. $\dfrac{16}{5}$

    D. $\dfrac{12}{5}$

    E. $\dfrac{14}{5}$

Answer Key: $1D, 2D, 3C, 4A, 5E$

Solutions

1. (D) Taking the $\log_2$ of both sides, $\dfrac{3x+4}{x+8} = 5, 3x+4 = 5x+40,$
   $-36 = 2x, x = -18$

2. (D) $(2^3)^x = (2^{-5})^{x+2}, 2^{3x} = 2^{-5x-10}, 3x = -5x - 10, 8x = -10, x = \dfrac{-5}{4}$

3. (C) $100 = e^{x+5}, \ln 100 = x+5, \ln 100 - 5 = x$

4. (A) $2^{\frac{c}{2}} = 2^{-7d}, \dfrac{c}{2} = -7d, \dfrac{c}{d} = -14$

5. (E) $(2^{\frac{5}{2}})^a = (2^7)^b, 2^{\frac{5a}{2}} = 2^{7b}$, taking the $\log_2$ of both sides, $\dfrac{5a}{2} = 7b, \dfrac{a}{b} = \dfrac{7}{\frac{5}{2}} = \dfrac{14}{5}$. It

   is possible to solve these problems by taking the log or ln of both sides with your
   calculator, but that is not the best approach.

Chapter LIV

Reflections, Translations, and Rotations

Reflections

The might have you reflect an equation about the y-axis, which means change all the x terms to $-x$, which means negate the odd powered terms. I haven't seen any problems involving reflecting about a line other than the axis.

1. What is the graph of $y = x^2 + 3x + 2$ reflected about the y-axis?

   A. $y = -x^2 + 3x - 2$

   B. $y = -x^2 - 3x - 2$

   C. $y = x^2 - 3x + 5$

   D. $y = x^2 - 3x + 2$

   E. $y = x^2 - 3x + 12$

2. What is $y = e^{x+3} + 4$ reflected about the y-axis?

   A. $y = e^{x+3} - 4$

   B. $y = e^{x-3} + 4$

   C. $y = -e^{3-x} - 4$

   D. $y = -e^{x+3} - 4$

   E. $y = e^{3-x} + 4$

3. What is $y = x^3 + 3x^2 + 3x + 1$ reflected about the y-axis?

    A. $y = -x^3 + 3x^2 - 3x + 1$

    B. $y = -x^3 - 3x^2 - 3x + 1$

    C. $y = x^3 + 3x^2 - 3x + 1$

    D. $y = -x^3 - 3x^2 - 3x - 1$

    E. $y = x^3 + 3x^2 + 3x + 1$

4. What is $y = x^2$ moved down 3 and left 5 and then reflected about the y-axis?

    A. $y = (x + 5)^2 - 3$

    B. $y = (x - 5)^2 - 3$

    C. $y = (x - 3)^2 - 5$

    D. $y = (x - 5)^2 - 8$

    E. $y = (x - 5)^2 - 1$

Answer Key: $1D, 2E, 3A, 4B$

Solutions

1. (D) Replace x with $-x$, $y = (-x)^2 + 3(-x) + 2 = y = x^2 - 3x + 2$.

2. (E) Replace x with $-x$, $e^{3-x} + 4$

3. (A) Replace x with $-x$, $y = -x^3 + 3x^2 - 3x + 1$

4. (B) $y + 3 = (x + 5)^2$, doing the shifts. To reflect about the x-axis replace x with $-x$, $y + 3 = (5 - x)^2$, $y = (x - 5)^2 - 3$

Translations

If you shift left 3, you substitute $x + 3$ for x, and right 3, $x - 3$ for x. It works the same way for $y, y - a$ if up a etc.

1. What is $y = x^2 + 5x + 6$ shifted up 4 and right 3?

    A. $y = x^2 + x + 4$

    B. $y = x^2 - 2x + 4$

    C. $y = x^2 - x + 4$

    D. $y = x^2 - 3x + 4$

    E. $y = x^2 - 5x + 4$

2. If you move $y = \sqrt{x}$ 5 left and 12 down, what is the new equation?

    A. $y = \sqrt{x + 5} - 10$

    B. $y = \sqrt{x + 5} + 12$

    C. $y = \sqrt{x + 5} - 17$

    D. $y = \sqrt{x + 5} - 12$

    E. $y = \sqrt{x + 5} + 10$

3. $g(x) = f(x + 4) + 7$ is $f(x)$ shifted how?

    A. 4 left and 7 down

    B. 4 right and 7 down

    C. 14 left and 7 up

    D. 14 left and 7 down

    E. 4 left and 7 up

4. What transformations of $y = x^3$ results in $y = (x-3)^2 - 8$?

A. 3 left and 8 down

B. 3 right and 8 down

C. 27 right and 8 down

D. 27 left and 8 down

E. 3 right and 8 up

5. If the circle $(x-3)^2 + (y+4)^2 = 17$ is moved up 3 and right 5 and the radius is tripled. What is the equation of the new circle?

A. $(x-8)^2 + (y+1)^2 = 153$

B. $(x-8)^2 + (y+1)^2 = 51$

C. $(x-8)^2 + (y+7)^2 = 459$

D. $(x+8)^2 + (y+7)^2 = 153$

E. $(x+8)^2 + (y-7)^2 = 153$

Solutions

1. (C) $y - 4 = (x - 3)^2 + 5(x - 3) + 6$,
   $y = x^2 - 6x + 9 + 5x - 15 + 6 + 4 = x^2 - x + 4$

2. (D) $y = \sqrt{x + 5} - 12$

3. (E) 4 left and 7 up. Adding to the x term means shifting left.

4. (B) 3 right and 8 down.

5. (A) If the radius is tripled r^2 is multiplied by 9, so 153. Performing the shifts, $(x - 8)^2 + (y + 1)^2 = 153$

Rotations

Rotation problems have appeared on the exam. These require uncommon formulas or reasoning what the formula should be. Rotating 90° clockwise: $(a, b) \rightarrow (b, -a)$, rotating 90° counterclockwise: $(a, b) \rightarrow (-b, a)$, rotating 180°: $(a, b) \rightarrow (-a, -b)$. If you are really going for a perfect score, you can memorize these formulas, but it is better to reason what the rotations should be, perhaps by drawing a diagram on the question booklet. I am assuming they will not ask about rotating equations, which would be more difficult.

1. What is the coordinates of $(2, 5)$ after it is rotated 180° about the origin?

 A. $(-2, 5)$

 B. $(2, -5)$

 C. $(5, 2)$

 D. $(-5, -2)$

 E. $(-2, -5)$

2. What is the coordinates of $(2, 5)$ after it is rotated 90° clockwise about the origin?

 A. $(-2, 5)$

 B. $(2, -5)$

 C. $(5, 2)$

 D. $(5, -2)$

 E. $(-5, -2)$

3. What is the coordinates of $(2, 5)$ after it is rotated 90° counterclockwise about the origin?

 A. $(-2, 5)$

 B. $(2, -5)$

 C. $(5, 2)$

 D. $(-5, -2)$

 E. $(-5, 2)$

Solutions

1. (E) $(a, b) \rightarrow (-a, -b)(-2, -5)$

2. (D) $(a, b) \rightarrow (b, -a), (5, -2)$. If you don't know the formula, you can figure it out by drawing a sketch.

3. (E) $(a, b) \rightarrow (-b, a)(-5, 2)$

Chapter LV

Asymptotes and Limits

Asymptotes

To find vertical asymptotes of a rational equation, set the denominator $= 0$. To find horizontal asymptotes, if the degree of the numerator and denominator are the same, take the ratio of the coefficients of the highest order terms. If the degree of the denominator is higher than that of the numerator, the horizontal asymptote is $y = 0$. If the degree of the numerator is 1 higher than that of the denominator, there is a slant asymptote, which is a line that can be obtained by dividing the numerator by the denominator.

1. What are the vertical and horizontal asymptotes of $y = \dfrac{5x^2 + 2}{4x^2 - 9}$?

A. $\left(y = \dfrac{5}{4}, x = \dfrac{3}{2}, x = \dfrac{-3}{2} \right)$

B. $\left(y = \dfrac{5}{2}, x = \dfrac{3}{2}, x = \dfrac{-3}{2} \right)$

C. $\left(y = \dfrac{5}{8}, x = \dfrac{3}{2}, x = \dfrac{-3}{2} \right)$

D. $\left(y = \dfrac{5}{2}, x = \dfrac{3}{2} \right)$

E. $\left(y = \dfrac{5}{4}, x = \dfrac{3}{2} \right)$

2. What is the slant asymptote of $y = \dfrac{3x^2 + 2x + 7}{x + 4}$?

    A. $y = 3x - 6$

    B. $y = 3x - 8$

    C. $y = 3x - 10$

    D. $y = 4x - 10$

    E. $y = 4x - 6$

3. What is the intersection point of the asymptotes of $y = \dfrac{x^2}{x + 2}$?

    A. $(-2, -1)$

    B. $(-2, -2)$

    C. $(-2, -3)$

    D. $(-2, -4)$

    E. $(-2, -5)$

4. $y = \dfrac{51x + 52}{53x + 54}$. What is the intersection point of the asymptotes?

    A. $\left(\dfrac{54}{53}, \dfrac{51}{53}\right)$

    B. $\left(\dfrac{54}{53}, \dfrac{51}{54}\right)$

    C. $\left(\dfrac{-54}{53}, \dfrac{26}{27}\right)$

    D. $\left(\dfrac{-54}{53}, 1\right)$

    E. $\left(\dfrac{-54}{53}, \dfrac{51}{53}\right)$

5. What is the intersection point of the asymptotes of $y = \dfrac{3x^3 + 2x^2 + x + 4}{(2x+5)(x^2+3)}$?

A. $\left(\dfrac{-5}{2}, \dfrac{5}{2}\right)$

B. $\left(\dfrac{5}{2}, \dfrac{3}{2}\right)$

C. $\left(\dfrac{-5}{2}, \dfrac{3}{2}\right)$

D. $\left(\dfrac{2}{5}, \dfrac{3}{2}\right)$

E. $\left(\dfrac{5}{2}, \dfrac{-3}{2}\right)$

6. What is the intersection of the asymptotes of $y = \dfrac{ax+b}{cx+d}$?

A. $\left(\dfrac{-d}{c}, \dfrac{a}{c}\right)$

B. $\left(\dfrac{d}{c}, \dfrac{a}{c}\right)$

C. $\left(\dfrac{-d}{c}, \dfrac{a}{b}\right)$

D. $\left(\dfrac{-d}{c}, \dfrac{c}{d}\right)$

E. $\left(\dfrac{-d}{c}, \dfrac{b}{c}\right)$

Answer Key: $1A, 2C, 3D, 4E, 5C, 6A$

Solutions

1. (A) $y = \dfrac{5x^2}{4x^2} = \dfrac{5}{4}, 4x^2 - 9 = 0, x^2 = \dfrac{9}{4}, x = \pm\dfrac{3}{2}$

2. (A) Slant asymptote is the quotient on the polynomials division.

$$
\begin{array}{r}
3x \quad -10 \\
\hline
x+4 \,\big)\, 3x^2 \quad +2x \quad +7 \\
\underline{3x^2 \quad +12x} \\
0 \quad -10x \quad +7 \\
\underline{-10x \quad -40} \\
0 \quad +47
\end{array}
$$

Then, dividend is $3x^2 + 2x + 7$, divisor is $x + 4$, quotient is $3x - 10$ and remainder $+47 \Rightarrow$ Slant asymptote is $3x - 10$.

3. (B) First do long division (or synthetic divison) to find the slant asymptote, since the degree of the numerator is one higher than the degree of the denominator.

$$
\begin{array}{r}
x \quad -2 \\
\hline
x+2 \,\big)\, x^2 \\
\underline{x^2 \quad +2x} \\
0 \quad -2x \\
\underline{-2x \quad -4} \\
0 \quad +4
\end{array}
$$

So we need the intersection points of $y = x - 2$ and $x = -2 \Rightarrow (-2, -4)$

4. (E) $y = \dfrac{51}{53}, 53x + 54 = 0, x = \dfrac{-54}{53}$

5. (C) The horizontal asymptote is the ratio of highest order terms, $y = \dfrac{3}{2}$, vertical asymptote when denominator is $0, 2x + 5 = 0, x = \dfrac{-5}{2}$

6. (A) Ratio of highest order terms $= \dfrac{a}{c}$, denominator $= 0, cx + d = 0, x = \dfrac{-d}{c}$

Limits

1. As x increases without bound, $\dfrac{3x + 2}{5x^2 - 2}$ approaches what?

   A. 1

   B. 0

   C. $\dfrac{2}{5}$

   D. $\dfrac{3}{5}$

   E. $\dfrac{\sqrt{10}}{5}$

2. As x increases without bound, $\dfrac{3x + 2}{5x - 2}$ approaches what?

   A. 1

   B. 0

   C. 3

   D. $\dfrac{3}{5}$

   E. $\dfrac{2}{5}$

Answer Key: $1B, 2D$

Solutions

1. (B) If the denominator is of higher degree than the numerator,it approaches 0. You can show this by dividing everything by x^2 or by L'Hopital's rule

2. (D) You take the ratio of the highest order terms. You can also divide everything by x and get $\dfrac{3 + \dfrac{2}{x}}{5 - \dfrac{2}{x}}$. As x goes to infinity, this becomes $\dfrac{3}{5}$. You can also use L'Hopital's rule, taking the derivative of the top and bottom and getting $\dfrac{3}{5}$. You can also graph the expression with your calculator or plug in a large value for x.

Chapter LVI

Preparation for Differentiation

They probably will at most ask for $f(x + h) - f(x)$, and maybe just $f(x + h)$, not the full limit from calculus.

1. What is $(x + a)^3 - x^3$?

   A. $x^2a + xa^2 + a^3$

   B. $x^3 + 3x^2a + 3xa^2 + a^3$

   C. $3x^2a + 3xa^2 + a^3$

   D. $3x^2 + 3xa + a^2$

   E. $3x^2$

2. $f(x) = x^2 + 3x + 2$. What is $f(x + h) - f(x)$?

   A. $2x + 3$

   B. $2x + h + 3$

   C. $2hx + h^2 + 5h$

   D. $2hx + 2h^2 + 3h$

   E. $2hx + h^2 + 3h$

3. $f(x) = \dfrac{1}{x}$, what is $f(x+h) - f(x)$?

A. $\dfrac{1}{x^2}$

B. $\dfrac{-h}{(x+h)x}$

C. $\dfrac{h}{(x+h)x}$

D. $\dfrac{-1}{(x+h)x}$

E. $\dfrac{2h}{(x+h)x}$

Answer Key: $1C, 2E, 3B$

Solutions

1. (C) $x^3 + 3x^2a + 3xa^2 + a^3 - x^3 = 3x^2a + 3xa^2 + a^3$

2. (E) $(x+h)^2 + 3(x+h) + 2 - (x^2 + 3x + 2) = x^2 + 2hx + h^2 + 3x + 3h + 2 - x^2 - 3x - 2 = 2hx + h^2 + 3h$

3. (B) $\dfrac{1}{x+h} - \dfrac{1}{x} = \dfrac{x - x - h}{(x+h)x} = \dfrac{-h}{(x+h)x}$

Chapter LVII

Coefficients

To find the coefficient in a binomial expansion, you can use the binomial theorem. They may give a question where you can multiply it out.

1. What is the coefficient of the x^3 term in $(x+1)^6$?

   A. 18

   B. 20

   C. 24

   D. 30

   E. 32

2. What is the coefficient of the x^2 term in $(2x+3)^5$?

   A. 270

   B. 540

   C. 1080

   D. 1440

   E. 1620

Answer Key: $1B, 2C$

Solutions

1. (B) By the binomial theorem, $_6C_3 \cdot x^3 \cdot 1^3 = 20x^3$. You could also multiply it out.

2. (C) $_5C_3 \cdot (2x)^2 \cdot 3^3 = 10 \cdot 4x^2 \cdot 27 = 1080x^2$

Chapter LVIII

Other Problems

1. A parabola with y-intercept $(0, 20)$ and vertex $(-4, 2)$ has equation $y - 2 = a(x + 4)^2$. What is a ?

   A. 1

   B. 2

   C. $\dfrac{9}{8}$

   D. $\dfrac{5}{4}$

   E. $\dfrac{3}{2}$

2. If $a = b + \dfrac{2}{3}$, what does $(a - b)^5$ equal?

   A. $\dfrac{8}{27}$

   B. $\dfrac{32}{243}$

   C. $\dfrac{-32}{243}$

   D. $\dfrac{32}{81}$

   E. $\dfrac{64}{243}$

3. If $(x+y)^2 = 20$ and $xy = 3$, what is $(x-y)^2$?

    A. 4

    B. 5

    C. 6

    D. 8

    E. 12

4. If $-3 \leq x \leq 2$ and $-4 < y < 7$, what is the maximum value of $|y - 3x|$?

    A. 5

    B. 10

    C. 14

    D. 16

    E. 20

5. If $-3 \leq x \leq 2$ and $-4 < y < 7$, what is the maximum value of $|y - 5x|$?

    A. 22

    B. 27

    C. 21

    D. 14

    E. 11

Solutions

1. (C) $y - 2 = a(x+4)^2$. Substituting $20 - 2 = a(0+4)^2 \rightarrow 18 = 16a \rightarrow a = \dfrac{9}{8}$

2. (B) $a - b = \dfrac{2}{3}$, $(a-b)^2 = \dfrac{32}{243}$

3. (D) $(x-y)^2 = x^2 - 2xy + y^2 = (x+y)^2 - 4xy = 20 - 3 \cdot 4 = 8$

4. (D) Consider all the extremes, $|7 - 3(-3)| = |16| = 16$,
   $|7 - 3 \cdot 2| = |1| = 1, |-4 - 3 \cdot (-3)| = |5| = 5, |(-4) - 3 \cdot 2| = |-10| = 10$

5. (A) Consider all the extremes, $|7 - 5(-3)| = |22| = 22$,
   $|7 - 5 \cdot 2| = |-3| = 3, |-4 - 5 \cdot (-3)| = |11| = 11, |(-4) - 5 \cdot 2| = |-14| = 14$. So the maximum is 22.

Made in the USA
Middletown, DE
01 March 2021

34614243R00256